TO RUSSIA AND RETURN

TO *R*USSIA AND RETURN

An Annotated Bibliography of Travelers'
English-Language Accounts of Russia from
the Ninth Century to the Present

COMPILED BY
HARRY W. NERHOOD

OHIO STATE UNIVERSITY PRESS

FOR AWNIE

To Russia and Return is a guidebook to travelers' accounts. Its purpose is to bring together in one place the pertinent information on all available reports of journeys to Russia that have been published in the English language. Reflecting as they do the conditions prevailing at the time of the visit, as seen through the eyes of the traveler, these accounts supply detail that can give depth and dimension to the flat surface of historical fact.

The traveler, as we see him here, is usually a non-Russian who journeys to Russia once or many times and remains for any length of time, be it four days or forty years; occasionally, he is born in Russia to non-Russian parents; and rarely, but with distinction, he is a Russian who left his homeland in his youth.

The Russia to which the traveler journeys alters in size and character with time and circumstance, from the land of the "Beormas" referred to by Ohthere in the year 890 to the Soviet Union stretching from the Baltic Sea to the Pacific Ocean visited by Mihajlo Mihajlov in 1964. Between these outer boundaries of time and space are the various degrees of elevation in the economic, social, political, and religious life of the people as observed by the travelers. The name "Russia" is used freely before and after 1917.

Each account, be it of one page or one thousand, is by the traveler or in his own words as quoted by an editor, compiler, or joint author; therefore, books about the travelers do not qualify for inclusion here. It is the traveler and his experience that is the life blood of this bibliography.

A desideratum was that each account actually be examined before its inclusion, and for the most part this requirement has been met. The several known about but not examined are designated by an asterisk.

My thanks go to President Paul S. Smith of Whittier College, who made funds available for research at the Library of Congress in 1963. Thanks are extended for the many courtesies by libraries and staffs of the following: the Bonnie Bell Wardman Library of

Whittier College (Dr. Benjamin G. Whitten, librarian); the Whittier Public Library (Miss Margaret Fulmer, librarian; Mrs. Lillian Flanders, reference librarian); the Honnold Library; the Henry E. Huntingdon Library and Art Gallery; the Los Angeles Public Library; the Doheny Library of the University of Southern California; the Hoover Institution on War, Revolution, and Peace; the library of Stanford University; the Library of Congress; the British Museum; and the Research Library of the University of California at Los Angeles.

Special appreciation goes to my secretaries: Miss Maxine Kane, who assisted in the initial research, and Miss Carol Wunder, excellent typist and gentle critic.

Finally, sincerest thanks to my wife, who has edited, to my great profit, so much of my life.

H. W. N.

CONTENTS

INTRODUCTION

I cannot forecast to you the action of Russia. It is a
riddle wrapped in a mystery inside an enigma.
WINSTON CHURCHILL

Puzzles have always fascinated men. So intrigued have they been with the "riddle . . . mystery . . . enigma" of Russia that for eleven centuries, one after another, male and female, Jew and gentile, singly and in groups, colored and white, rabbi and bishop, young and old, intellectual and merchant, Hindu and Moslem—even the blind—have traveled from all points of the compass to Muscovy, to czarist Russia, and to the Soviet Union.

A sampling of the travelers yields politicians and statesmen of national and international reputation such as John Quincy Adams, Herbert Hoover, Edouard Herriott, Milovan Djilas, and Richard Nixon; world-famous philosophers Bentham, Keynes, and Tagore; nation-makers and world-shakers like Napoleon, Chiang Kai-shek, and Churchill; social reformers Jane Addams, John Reed, and Clarence Pickett; literary figures John Lothrop Motley, Alexandre Dumas, Lewis Carroll, and Mark Twain; entertainers Bob Hope and Jack Paar; soldiers, sailors, explorers, cartoonists, scientists, and, of course, one notorious police spy and lover, Casanova.

Moses sent twelve men into Canaan to spy out the land. Forty days later the twelve returned, ten with the pessimistic report, "They are stronger than we"; and two, Joshua and Caleb, with news of "an exceeding good land." An analysis of travelers' accounts of Russia yields about the same averages: 16 per cent for and 84 per cent against. These averages change somewhat dramatically in the Soviet Union's favor between 1927 and 1937, less so between 1958 and 1964. Generally speaking, however, travelers to Russia have been overly critical, perhaps because they have often come from areas that were more advanced in personal freedoms and in the creature comforts.

Lee Meriwether (see no. 357), Missouri author and lawyer, journeying through imperial Russia in 1885–86, concluded that "to know a country one must fraternize with its people, must live with them, sympathize with them, win their confidence." Two additional elements may be added: one, to better fraternize one should know the language of the people; and two, one should live with them long enough to set aside hindrances to mutual understanding.

It is true that most of our travelers did not know the language; altogether, about 25 per cent have been Russian-speaking. How long one must live with another people before mutual understanding and friendship develop is a question not easily answered. Five years would seem to be sufficient time in which to develop some rapport, especially if the language barrier does not exist. Approximately 9 per cent of our travelers since the sixteenth century remained in Russia five years or longer, and of these, 73 of a total of 131 spoke Russian.

Travelers have long been accused of drawing conclusions after too short a journey covering too little territory. Travelers to Russia are in double jeopardy here. A nation covering half a continent, with scores of national minorities, dozens of languages, and an immense variety of customs is not understood after three days in Moscow, two in Leningrad, a week on the Russian "Riviera," and a stopover in Tashkent on the way to India. Among our travelers are some of these, and their opinions have value in spite of their limitations. However, dozens of the accounts are the result of long journeys over years of time, and must be given due respect.

Fyodr Tyutchev appears to express a truism common to the understanding of all nations when he observes:

> *Not with the mind is Russia comprehended*
> *The common yardstick will deceive*
> *In gauging her: so singular her nature—*
> *In Russia you must just believe.*

The annotated bibliography, comprising the main part of this book consists of 1,422 numbered entries, chronologically arranged, each of which provides basic bibliographic data on a traveler's account and a brief analysis of its contents. Entries marked with an asterisk usually do not have an annotation. Only books and, rarely, pamphlets of twenty-five or more pages are included.

Every attempt has been made to provide accurate dates for the time the traveler actually spent in Russia. Occasionally I have been forced to use the seasons to determine placement of a work rather than the exact dates.

Following each number, which serves to locate a particular account and its parts throughout the book, is the traveler's name, if he is the author of the account, or the name of his biographer, editor, or compiler. The title is from the title page of the account and is in full, thus adding data to the annotation following. After the title is listed the editor, compiler, or translator, along with the usual bibliographic data: place of publication, publisher, date of publication, volume (vol.), pages (pp.), illustrations (illus.), maps, portrait of the traveler (port.), appendix (app.), bibliography (biblio.), and index. Only the pages dealing with the traveler's experiences *in Russia* are noted.

The analytical annotation is the author's attempt to provide the reader with some insight into the nature of a particular traveler. In addition to the name (and title, if indicated) provided in the bibliographic data, the traveler's nationality, occupation, knowledge of Russian, purpose of his journey, general attitude toward Russia before and after his journey, where he went and how long he stayed, are usually included, as well as any peculiarities noted. Words, phrases, and sentences within quotation marks are always those of the traveler. Value judgments of the accounts are those of the author unless otherwise stated.

Following the annotated bibliography are entries 1,423 through 1,473, the chief bibliographic sources from which this book grew.

The Index is a dictionary catalogue of travelers, their accounts, authors, joint authors, editors, compilers, and translators, followed by the entry number that locates the information in the annotated bibliography. It is in the Index that all accounts by the same author are listed together. Also, at this point, all the contributions of a single individual—traveler, author, joint author, editor, compiler, translator—are treated as equal and arranged alphabetically.

ANNOTATED BIBLIOGRAPHY

֎

1. Ohthere (Oether). "Voyages of Ohthere to the White Sea and the Baltic in the ninth century." In Kerr, *Voyages and Travels,* I, 8–12. (See no. 1447.)

Earliest-known traveler to "Russia," in 890, speaks of the "Beormas" who had indeed "well peopled their country, for which reason he did not venture to enter upon it. . . . " (Kerr: Biarmians or Permians—among the numerous names attributed to Russians [I, 9, note 6].)

2. Benjamin of Tudela. *Early travels in Palestine.* Thomas Wright, editor. London, Henry G. Bohn, 1893. pp. 63–126.

Learned Rabbi of Tudela (Navarre) journeys to Bagdad, 1160–73. Benjamin believes Russia to be part of Bohemia, and his cursory references emphasize the vastness of the country and the severity of its climate.

3. John de Plano Carpini. *The journey of Friar John of Pian de Carpine to the court of Kayuk Khan, 1245–1247, as narrated by himself.* Translated and edited by William Woodville Rockhill. London, Hakluyt Society, 1900. pp. 1–38.

Italian Minorite sent by Innocent IV to visit the Khan of Mongolia, passing through Bohemia, Poland, the Ukraine (Kiev), and to the East, comments on the climate and scenery. He fails to distinguish between Bohemians and Russians, but sees the difference between Russians and Tartars.

4. De Sancto Quintino, (Friar) Simon. "Relations of Vincentius Beluacencis, the most of which he received from Friar Simon de Sancto Quintino, one of the foure friars sent by Pope Innocent the Fourth to the Tartars." In Purchas, *Hayklutus posthumus,* XI, 168–72. (See no. 1462.)

Friar Simon describes Tartar life in 1246–47, with some emphasis on the relationships between the leader and his men.

5.   William of Rubruck. *The journey of William of Rubruck to the eastern parts of the world, 1253–1255, as narrated by himself.* Translated and edited by William Woodville Rockhill. London, Hakluyt Society, 1900. pp. 40–282.

Friar William describes the Tartars and their way of life soon after they had destroyed the Kievan state.

6.   Polo, Marco. "The travels of Marco Polo." In Astley, *Voyages and travels,* IV, 580–619. (See no. 1426.) Marco Polo's journey may be found in many versions.

Between 1271 and 1286, Marco Polo and his merchant uncles journey from Venice to Cathay by land and return by land and sea. Marco describes dog-sledges, white bears, and reindeer-riding Tunguses in the land of the Tartars, the "Region of Darkness," and "Of the province of Russia"—his account probably augmented from other travelers' tales.

7.   Montecroix, Ricold de. "Travels." In Murray, *Discoveries and travels,* I, 198–200. (See no. 1457.)

Brief contact with the Tartars made by Italian friar in 1296.

8.   Pegoletti, Francesco Balducci. "Guide for the route from Tana to Kathay, with merchandize, and back again." In Kerr, *Voyages and travels,* I, 435–37. (See no. 1447.)

Italian trader outlines route to the Far East in 1355 and mentions the use of paper money.

9.   Schildtberger, John. "Voyages of John Schildtberger in Tartary, in 1394." In Kerr, *Voyages and travels,* I, 456–60. (See no. 1447.)

German mercenary in Turkish and Tartar armies between 1394–1427 refers to conquest of Ibissibur or Issibur (Siberia).

10. González de Clavijo, Ruy. *Embassy to Tamerlane, 1403–1406*. E. Denison Ross and Eileen Power, editors. Translated from the Spanish by Guy le Strange. London, George Routledge, 1928. pp. 200–320. map.

Sent by Henry III of Castile to congratulate Timur, the envoy from Spain describes the court of Timur and the Tartar armies around Samarkand.

11. Barbaro, Giosofat. *Travels to Tana and Persia*. Lord Stanley of Alderley, editor. Translated from the Italian by William Thomas. London, Hakluyt Society, 1873. pp. 1–36.

Merchant of Venice describes Tartar customs around Moscow, Tiflis, and the Black Sea in 1436.

12. Contarini, Ambrosio. *The travels of the Magnificent M. Ambrosio Contarini*. Lord Stanley of Alderley, editor. Translated from the Italian by Mr. Roy. London, Hakluyt Society, 1873. pp. 111–23, 143–66.

On the journey to his post in April, 1473, the Venetian ambassador describes Moscow and observes about Kiev: "The country about Kiow abounds in grain and cattle. The inhabitants of this place occupy the whole day in their affairs until three oclock, employing all the rest, till night, in drinking and quarrels, the natural consequence of drunkenness."

13. Herberstein, Sigismund von. *Notes upon Russia: Being a translation of the earliest account of that country, entitled Rerum Moscoviticarum Commentarii*. Translated and edited by R. H. Major. New York, Dutton, 1907. I, 1–99. II, 1–256. map. port. index.

Russian-speaking Austrian ambassador to the court of Basil II in 1517 and between 1526 and 1533 objectively and exhaustively describes Muscovy and its people. His conclusions, neither condemning nor commending, are surprisingly like the subjective observations of Turberville in 1568–69 (see no. 30).

14.   Willoughby, Hugh. "Voyage for the discovery of regions, domains, islands, and places unknown." In Pinkerton, *Voyages and travels,* I, 1–15. (See no. 1461.)

Commander of three vessels voyages around northwest Europe to Muscovy. His pilot major, Richard Chancellor (see no. 15), and others reach their destination, but Captain Willoughby and sixty-two companions die of scurvy. Their bodies are found by the Russians in 1554.

15.   Chancellor, Richard. "The booke of the great and mighty Emperor of Russia, and Duke of Moscovia, and of the dominions, orders and commodities thereunto belonging: drawn by Richard Chancelour." In Hakluyt, *Principal navigations,* I, 254–66. (See no. 1440.)

Pilot major of British expedition sent by London Muscovy Company to search for northeast passage to Asia describes journey overland from the White Sea to Moscow in 1553, where he and his companions were well received by Ivan IV. This voyage marked the beginning of Anglo-Russian commercial and diplomatic relations.

16.   Burrough, William. "A dedicatorie Epistle unto the Queenes most excellent Majestie, written by Master William Burrough late Comptroller of her Highnesse navie, and annexed unto his exact and notable mappe of Russia, briefly containing (amongst other matters) his great travailes, observations, and experiments both by sea and land, especially in those northeastern parts." In Hakluyt, *Principal navigations,* II, 168–70. (See no. 1440.)

Observations by a trading agent of the Muscovy Company in Moscow, 1553–75.

17.   Milton, John. *Moscovia: or, Relations of Moscovia, as far as hath been discovered by English voyages; Gathered from the writings of several Eye-witnesses: And of other less-known countries lying eastward of Russia as far as Cathay, lately discovered at several times by Russians.* In Robert

Ralston Cawley. *Milton's Literary craftmanship. A study of A Brief History of Muscovia with an edition of the text.* Princeton, New Jersey, Princton University Press, 1941. pp. 49–105.

John Milton never journeyed to Russia, but this literary account creates the atmosphere of the sixteenth century by its dependence on the writings of the British voyager-traders, beginning with Chancellor. For a twentieth-century effort similar to this, but written in a humorous vein, see Atkinson and Searle, no. 1376.

18. Hasse, John. "The coines, weights, and measures used in Russia, written by John Hasse, in the year 1554." In Hakluyt, *Principal navigations,* I, 294–99.(See no. 1440.)

British factor, representing Muscovy Company, comments on market places and other economic matters in Moscow.

19. Killingworth, George. "The letter of M. George Killingworth the companies first agent in Moscovie, touching their interteinement in their second voyage. Anno 1555, the 27. of November in Mosco." In Hakluyt, *Principal navigations,* I, 307–13. (See no. 1440.)

Muscovy Company factor describes trading arrangements and comments on the court life of the czar and his relations with the Company.

20. Burrough, Steven. "The navigation and discoverie toward the river of Ob, made by Master Steven Burrough, Master of the Pinesse called the Serchthrift, with divers things worth the noting passed in the year 1556." In Hakluyt, *Principal navigations,* I, 333–52. (See no. 1440.)

Burrough describes the discovery of the strait south of Novaya Zemlya into the Kara Sea, in July and September, and comments on the Samoyeds and their religious practices.

21. Johnson, Richard. "Certaine notes unperfectly written by Richard Johnson servant to Master Richard Chancelour,

which was in the discoverie of Vaigatz and Nova Zembla, with Steven Burrowe in the Serchthrift 1556. and afterwarde among the Samoedes, whose devilish rites he describeth." In Hakluyt, *Principal navigations,* I, 352–56. (See no. 1440.)

Johnson comments on a journey made from July to September.

22.   Burrough, Steven. "The voyage of the foresaid M. Steven Burrough, An. 1557, from Colmogro to Wardhouse, which was sent to seeke the Bona Esperanza, the Bona Confidentia, and the Philip and Mary, which were not heard of the yeere before." In Hakluyt, *Principal navigations,* I, 367–77. (See no. 1440.)

Burrough outlines the journey he made east along the Siberian coast searching for lost ships in May and June.

23.   Best, Robert. *Early voyages and travels to Russia and Persia.* E. Dalmar Morgan and C. H. Coote, editors. London, Hakluyt Society, 1886. II, 355–57.

Interpreter to Joseph Napea, Muscovite ambassador to England, journeys to Moscow, where he observes the "maners, usages and ceremonies of the Russes" between July 13, 1557, and April 14, 1558.

24.   Jenkinson, Anthony. *Early voyages and travels to Russia and Persia.* E. Dalmar Morgan and C. H. Coote, editors. London, Hakluyt Society, 1886. I, 1–176. II, 1–351.

Muscovy Company agent and ambassador from Queen Elizabeth to Moscow describes his several journeys from Moscow to Persia by way of the Volga River and Astrakhan, 1557–72. This account is a basic document for understanding Britain's first contacts with the Russia of Ivan IV.

25.   Lane, Henry. "The maner of justice by lots in Russia, written by Master Henrie Lane, and executed in a controversie betweene him and one Sheray Costromitskey in

Mosco. 1560." In Hakluyt, *Principal navigations,* I, 406–8. (See no. 1440.)

One of the earliest comments on Russian justice.

26. Edwards, Arthur. "A letter of Arthur Edwards to M. Thomas Nicols, Secretarie to the worshipful company trading into Russia and other the North parts, concerning the preparation of their voyage into Persia." In Hakluyt, *Principal navigations,* II, 33–34, 53–57. (See no. 1440.)

Merchant of the Muscovy Company outlines trade routes and distances within the territories ruled by Moscow in 1565.

27. Southam, Thomas. "The way discovered by water by us Thomas Southam and John Sparke, from the town of Colmogro, by the western bottome of the Baie of S. Nicholas, unto the citie of Novgorod in Russia, containing many particulars of the way, and distance of miles, as hereafter foloweth, Anno. 1566." In Hakluyt, *Principal navigations,* II, 57–65. (See no. 1440.)

British sailor, "servant of Muscovie Company," provides details of mileage (versts) and of conditions along the trading routes.

28. Webbe, Edward. *Edward Webbe, Chief Master Gunner, his trauailes, 1590.* Edward Arber, editor. Westminster, Constable, 1902. pp. 17–19.

Unlettered British sailor with Jenkinson, 1566–71, describes Moscow and his life as a prisoner of the Tartars and Turks.

29. Randolfe, Thomas. "The Ambassage of the right worshipfull Master Thomas Randolfe, Esquire, to the Emperour of Russia, in the year 1568, briefly written by himselfe." In Hakluyt, *Principal navigations,* II, 80–95. (See no. 1440.)

In July, 1568, Elizabeth sent a trade commission of forty, led by Thomas Randolfe, to persuade Ivan IV to renew the trading privileges he had withdrawn. One year later, the company returned to report success. Here the ambassador comments on his mission and his relations with the people and rulers of Muscovy.

30.   Turberville, George. "Certain letters in verse, written by Master George Turberville out of Moscovia, which went as Secretarie thither with Master Thomas Randolph, her Majesties Ambassadour to the Emperour 1568, to certeine friends of his in London, describing the maners of the countrey and people." In Hakluyt, *Principal navigations,* II, 99–108. (See no. 1440.)

Homesick observer perceptively observes customs and manners of the Muscovites, using the unflattering medium of doggerel, written during his year of service as secretary to Randolph, July, 1568, to July, 1569. He comments on everything he sees and hears about— housing, entertainment, treatment of women by Russian men, hunting, etc.

31.   Horsey, Jerome. "A relacion or Memoriall abstracted owt of Sir Jerom Horsey his travells, imploiments, services, and negociacions. Observed and written with his owne hand; wherein he spent the most part of eighteen years tyme." In Purchas, *Hakluytus posthumus,* XXVII, 114–32. (See no. 1462.)

Russian Company representative in Moscow and later special envoy from Elizabeth, 1575–91, describes his activities in trading and diplomacy.

32.   * Staden, Heinrich von. *Concerning the Moscow of Ivan the Terrible. Notes of a German Opricknik.* Translated from the German by I. Polosin. Moscow, 1925.

Experiences in Ivan IV's Russia, about 1575.

33.   Broniovius de Biezerfedea, Martin. "Collections out of Martin Broniovius de Biezerfedea sent ambassadour from Stephen King of Poland to the Crim Tartar: Containing a description of Tartaria, or Chersonesus Taurica, and the regions subject to the Perecop or Crim Tartars with their

customs private and public in peace and warre." In Purchas, *Hakluytus posthumus,* XIII, 461–91. (See no. 1462.)

Ambassador describes the various activities of the Tartars in 1579.

34.   Bowes, (Sir) Jerome. "A briefe discourse of the voyage of Sir Jerome Bowes knight, her Majesties ambassadour to Ivan Vasilivich the Emperour of Muscovia, in the year 1583." In Hakluyt, *Principal navigations,* II, 251–63. (See no. 1440.)

Sir Jerome outlines his journey to Moscow and the treatment he was accorded there by royalty.

35.   Fletcher, Giles. "The Ambassage of M. Giles Fletcher, Doctor of the Civil Law, sent from her Majestie to Theodor the Emperour of Russia, Anno 1588." In Hakluyt, *Principal navigations,* II, 284–327. (See no. 1440.)

Queen Elizabeth's special ambassador, commissioned to secure trade treaty, inaccurately describes what he saw in Moscow, 1588–89. The account was suppressed to avoid Russian displeasure. In spite of its deficiencies, it is a first-class source.

36.   Barents, William. "Voyage to the northeast." In Pinkerton, *Voyages and Travels,* I, 81–127. (See no. 1461.)

Dutch sailor-trader seeking the northeast passage to China in 1594 describes his brief contacts with Russia and its inhabitants.

37.   De Veer, Gerrit. *The three voyages of William Barents to the Arctic regions (1594, 1595, and 1596).* London, Hakluyt Society, 1876. 272 pp. illus. map. index.

Second mate on Barents' ship provides enormous detail on the three journeys. Pidgin Russian-Dutch is used when contact is made with the Russians near Novaya Zemlya.

38.   Merick, John. "A branch of a letter from M. John Merick, agent unto the Muscovie company in Russia, closed up in the Mosco the 14 of March, Anno 1597. touching the death

of Pheodor Ivanovich late Emperor of all Russia, etc." In Hakluyt, *Principal navigations,* II, 362–63. (See no. 1440.)

Circumstances around Feodor I's death as seen through eyes of Muscovy Company agent.

39.   Smith, (Captain) John. *Travels and works of Captain John Smith. President of Virginia, and Admiral of New England. 1580–1631. [a new edition with bibliography and critical introduction by A. G. Bradley].* Edward Arber, editor. Edinburgh, John Grant, 1910. II, 853–69. biblio.

In 1603 John Smith was captured by the Tartars while fighting as a mercenary in the army of the Holy Roman Emperor. Here he describes Tartar life and his escape through northwest Russia.

40.   Smith, (Sir) Thomas. *Voiage and entertainment in Rushia. With the tragicall ends of two Emperors and one empress, within one month of his being there; and the miraculous preservation of the now reigning Emperor, esteemed dead for 18 years.* London, Butter, 1605. 100 pp.

First governor of English East India Company travels from Archangel to Yaroslavl in search of trade and provides what amounts to an anonymous account based on materials furnished to him by company members during 1604–5.

41.   Dutch Merchant. "The Reporte of a Bloudie and Terrible Massacre in the City of Mosco, with a fearfull and tragicall end of Demetrius the last Duke, before him raigning at this present." Translated and edited by William Russell. London, Sims, Macham, Cooke, 1607. In Howe, *The False Dmitri,* pp. 27–62. illus. (See no. 1445.)

Trader describes Dmitri's short reign from April 13 to June 15, 1605.

42.   Gilbert, (Captain). "Report of Captain Gilbert, of Dmitri's bodyguard." In Howe, *The False Dmitri,* pp. 63–68. (See no. 1445.)

Captain Gilbert describes Dmitri's death and what took place immediately afterward in June and July, 1605.

43. Zolkiewski, (Hetman) Stanislas. *Expedition to Moscow, a Memoir.* Translated from the Polish by M. W. Stephen. London, Polonica Publications, 1959. pp. 39–129. illus. map.

Hero of the Polish invasion of Muscovy in 1610–12 describes the activities of his army and the reaction of the Russians. He provides valuable data that helps us to understand the lasting friction between Poles and Russians.

44. Finch, Richard. "A letter of Richard Finch to the Right Worshipfull Sir Thomas Smith, Governour; and to the rest of the Worshipfull companie of English merchants, trading in Russia: touching the former voyage, and other observations." In Purchas, *Halkuytus posthumus,* XXVI, 205–22. (See no. 1462.)

British merchant describes what he considers to be the best ways to appeal to the Russians in trading operations, from experiences gained between April 11 and September 21, 1611. See no. 40 for Sir Thomas Smith.

45. Gourdon, William (of Hull). "A voyage made to Pechora, 1611. Written by Wm. Gourdon of Hull, appt'd chief pilot, for discoverie to Ob, etc." In Purchas, *Hakluytus posthumus,* XXVI, 194–205. (See no. 1462.)

Chief pilot observes customs and business manners of Russian and English traders and provides details on harbors, etc. He makes his voyage between April 11 and September 21.

46. Pursglove, William. "A briefe relation of a voyage to Pechora and wintering there, began in the yeare 1611. Written by William Pursglove." In Purchas, *Hakluytus posthumus,* XXVI, 239–55. (See no. 1462.)

British trader-explorer lists items needed for Russian trade and includes a discussion of useful routes after his journey between April 11 and September 21. See no. 45 on William Gourdon.

47.   Logan, Josias. "The voyage of Master Josias Logan to Pechora, and his wintering there, with Master William Pursglove, and Marmaduke Wilson." In Purchas, *Hakluytus posthumus,* XXVI, 222–38. (See no. 1462.)

Another trader-explorer comments on the Pechora voyage between April and September, 1611. See nos. 45 and 46. He also provides some comment on the great rivers to the east—the Ob, etc.

48.   Gourdon, William (of Hull). "Later observations of William Gourdon, in his wintering at Pustozera, in the yeares 1614. and 1615. with a description of Samoyeds life." In Purchas, *Hakluytus posthumus,* XXVI, 255–64. (See no. 1462.)

Gourdon's day-to-day journal, November, 1614, to August, 1615.

49.   Tradescant, John-the elder. "Journey to Archangel." In Hamel, *England and Russia,* pp. 258–98. (See no. 1441.)

Amateur Dutch biologist comments on peoples' way of life in June, 1618.

50.   Olearius, Adam. *The voyages and travels of the Ambassadors sent by Frederick, Duke of Holstein, to the Grand Duke of Muscovy and to the King of Persia.* Translated from the German by John Davies. London, Dring & Starkey, 1662. pp. 1–181. map. port.

Saxon member of trade commission on two journeys to the Black Sea and to Moscow between 1633–39 provides a detailed description of everything he found worth noting, especially emphasizing the negative characteristics of the Russians. He includes a map that locates the wall built of wood, trees, stakes, and brush to slow down the upward thrust of the Tartars to the south, running across the northern Ukraine from north of Astrakhan, northwest to Smolensk.

51.   La Vasseur de Beauplan, (Sieur) William. "A description of Ukraine containing several provinces of the kingdom of Poland, lying between the confines of Muscovy, and the

borders of Transylvania. Together with their customs, manners of life, and how they manage their wars." In Churchill, *Voyages and Travels,* I, 571–610. (See no. 1433.)

Seventeen years in the Ukraine as engineer in the service of the king of Poland, Sieur William describes Tartar and Cossack life and manners about 1640. Some items he discusses are the relationship between the nobility and the peasants, religion, courting, housing, hunting, and the election of their king. He observes: "Tartars are libertines, they obey no one."

52. Paul of Aleppo. *The travels of Macarius. Extracts from the diary of the travels of Macarius, Patriarch of Antioch, written in Arabic by his son Paul, Archdeacon of Aleppo; in the years of their journeying, 1652–1660.* Lady Laura Ridding, editor. Translated from the Arabic by F. C. Balfour. London, Oxford University Press, 1836. pp. 1–90.

The Archdeacon describes his father's journey to Moscow to beg alms from Czar Alexis and comments on Nikon's reform of the Orthodox ritual and ceremonies. Special reference is made to the Holy Week ceremonies with all their colorful display.

53. Danish Gentleman. "Muscovy". In Harris, *Voyages and travels,* II, 467–87. illus. port. (See no. 1442.)

Merchant, located in Moscow in 1653, describes life there and in western Siberia.

54. Collins, Samuel. *The present state of Russia, in a letter to a friend at London; written by an eminent person residing at the Great Tsars court at Mosco for the space of nine years.* London, Dorman Newman, 1671. 141 pp. illus.

Physician to, and favorite of, Alexis from 1660 to 1669, British medical doctor describes funerals, music, marriage, law, caviar, and the "barbarous Russe."

55. Gordon, Patrick. *Passages from the diary of General Patrick Gordon of Auchleuchries, A.D. 1635–A.D. 1699.* Aberdeen, The Spalding Club, 1859. pp. 40–193. index.

Twenty-six-year-old British mercenary enters service with Alexis and remains with the Russians until the end of the seventeenth century. His diary records his friendly impressions of court and people.

56. Miège, Guy. *A relation of three embassies from his Sacred Majestie Charles II, to the Great Duke of Muscovie, the King of Sweden, and the King of Denmark. Performed by the Right Honorable Earl of Carlisle, in the years 1663–1664. Written by an attendant on the embassies.* London, John Starkey, 1669. 330 pp. port.

Some rather naïve observations by a Swiss attendant who sees the masses of people debauched by drink and sodomy.

57. Struys, John. *The voiages and travels of John Struys through Italy, Greece, Muscovy, Tartary, Media, Persia, E. India, Japan and other countries in Europe, Africa, and Asia.* London, Abel Swalle, 1684. pp. 113–206. illus. map.

Dutch adventurer-traveler journeys to Novgorod and Moscow, September, 1668, to June, 1670. He describes the drinking and eating habits of the people, along with their religious life and ways of entertaining themselves. A brief reference is made to the rebellion of Stenka Razin.

58. La Martiniere, Pierre Martin de. *A new voyage to the north: containing a full account of Norway; the Laplands, both Danish, Swedish and Muscovite; of Borandia, Siberia, Samojedia, Zemblya and Iseland. With the description of the religion and customs of the several nations. To which is added. A particular relation of the court of the Czar, of the religion and customs of the Muscovites; and a short history of Muscovy.* London, Thomas Hodgson, 1706. pp. 22–258. illus.

Russian-speaking Frenchman employed by company of merchants trades north from Copenhagen, 1670. His observations are considered to be rather superficial by some critics.

59. Chardin. "Journey into the Caucasus." In Murray, *Discoveries and Travels,* III, 61–64. (See no. 1457.)

Expert on Persia describes journey to the Caucasus in 1673. He finds the Georgians to be "civil and friendly, though fickle, turbulent, and mutinous."

60. Spathary, Nicholai Gabrilovich. "Journal of Embassy to China." In Baddeley, *Russia, Mongolia, China,* II, 242–86. map. biblio. (See no. 1428.)

Adventurer of noble family, born in Moldavia, serves in many eastern European courts before arriving in Moscow in 1671 to serve Alexis as ambassador to China. Spathary recounts the passage by water and portage over the Siberian rivers, the manner of life of the Siberian natives, the natural resources, etc., February, 1675–January, 1676.

61. C.T. *The new Atlas; or travels and voyages in Europe, Asia, Africa and America, thro' the most renowned parts of the world.* London, Cleave & Roper, 1698. pp. 168–87.

An observant tourist notes every aspect of life coming into range of his eyes in Muscovy, along the Volga River and around the Caspian Sea, 1684.

62. Avril, Philippe. *Travels into divers parts of Europe and Asia, undertaken by the French King's order to discover a new way by land into China, containing many curious remarks in Natural Philosophy, Geography, Hydrography, and History. Together with a description of Great Tartary, and of the different people who inhabit there.* London, Timothy Goodwin, 1698. Book 2, pp. 103–36. Book 4, pp. 1–98.

Jesuit father journeys to Moscow by way of the Black Sea and the Volga River in 1686.

63. Gerbillion, (Father) John Francis. "Travels into western Tartary, by order of the Emperor of China, or in his retinue,

between the years 1688, and 1698." In Astley, *Voyages,*
IV, 664–750. (See no. 1426.)

The Jesuit spokesman for the emperor of China supplies details
of the making of the Treaty of Nerchinsk in 1689 and its aftermath.

64.   La Neuville, Foy de (pseudonym of Adrian Baillet). *An*
       account of Muscovy, as it was in the year 1689. In which
       the troubles that happened in that empire from the present
       Czar Peter's election to the throne, to his being firmly
       settled in it, are particularly related. With a character of
       him, and his people. London, Land & Castle, 1699. 119 pp.

Envoy extraordinary to Moscow from the king of Poland describes
how Peter secured his power. Observes: "The Muscovites, to
speak properly, are Barbarians, Suspicious, and mistrustful, Cruel,
Sodomites, Gluttons, Covetous, Beggars, and Cowards." The Envoy sees them as dull and "British" and unable to accomplish anything without the aid of the Germans.

65.   Ides, E. Ysbrants. *Three years' travels from Moscow over-*
       land to China through Great Ustiga, Sirinia, Perma, Sibi-
       ria, Daour, Great Tartary, etc., to Peking. London, Free-
       man, et al., 1706. pp. 1–110. illus. map.

Peter's ambassador, a Dutch employee, journeys to the Chinese
emperor, 1692–95. In his travels through Siberia he describes its
people and resources and reflects on its potentials for trade by
listing routes and river systems.

66.   Brand, Adam. *A journal of an embassy from their majesties*
       John and Peter Alexowits, Emperors of Muscovy, etc., into
       China through the provinces of Ustuigha, Siberia, Dauri,
       and the Great Tartary to Peking, the capital city of the
       Chinese Empire. Translated from the German by H. W.
       Ludolf. London, Brown & Godwin, 1698. 117 pp. illus.

German secretary of the embassy describes the journey from
March, 1692, to January, 1695. Related to the period after the
making of the Treaty of Nerchinsk, the account is useful as an
early example of Russian diplomatic activity.

67. Allison, Thomas. *An account of a voyage from Archangel in Russia in the year 1697.* London, Brown, 1699. 96 pp. map.

Ship's commander describes North Cape way of life in 1697–98.

68. Gentleman from Germany. "An abstract of a letter written by a person of quality, a native of Germany residing in Muscovy, concerning the present state of that Kingdom." In Harris, *Voyages and Travels,* pp. 223–28. (See no. 1442.)

This "person of quality" describes Peter's return to Moscow and the destruction of the Streltsy in 1698.

69. Korb, Johann Georg. *Scenes from the court of Peter the Great; based on the Latin diary of John G. Korb, a secretary of the Austrian Legation at the court of Peter the Great.* F. L. Glaser, editor. Translated from the Latin by Count McConnell. New York, Nicholas L. Brown, 1921. 164 pp. app.

Secretary Korb's real mission was to intervene for the Jesuits in 1698–99. While doing so, he observes the customs and practices of the Russian Orthodox church and comments decisively on "the manners of the Muscovites." The nature of his comments brought down the wrath of the czar's government on him, and an attempt was made to destroy the diary before he could take it out of the country.

70. Perry, (Captain) John. *The state of Russia under the present Czar, in relation to the several great and remarkable things he has done, as to his naval preparations, the regulating his army, the reforming his people, and improvement of his country. Particularly those works on which the author was employed, with the reasons of his quitting the Czar's service, after having been fourteen years in the country. Also an account of those Tartars, and other people who border on the eastern and extreme northern parts of the Czar's dominions, their religion, and manner of life; With many other observations.* London, Tooke, 1716. 280 pp. map.

Former British naval officer in czar's army, and an engineer of canals and military works, provides a detailed account of Peter's regime between 1698–1712. It is an extremely important document for understanding the period.

71.   * Deane, John. *A letter from Moscow to the Marquess of Carmarthen relating to the Czar of Muscovys forwardness in his great navy.* London, 1699.

Peter the Great's navy, about 1699.

72.   Strahlenberg, (Captain) Philip John von. *An historico-geographical description of the north and eastern parts of Europe and Asia; But more particularly of Russia, Siberia, and Great Tartary; Both in their ancient and modern state: Together with an entirely new polyglot-table of the dialects of 32 Tartarian nations: And a vocabulary of the Kalmuck-Mungalian tongue. As also a large and accurate map of those countries; and variety of cuts, representing Asiatik-Scythian antiquities.* London. Brotherton, et al., 1738. 455 pp. illus. map. app.

Swedish officer captured at Poltava and sent to Siberia between 1700 and 1713 provides what is considered to be a basic study of the early eighteenth-century Russian regime.

73.   Bruyn, Cornelius le. *Travels into Muscovy, Persia, and part of the East Indies. Containing, An accurate description of whatever is most remarkable in those countries. And embellished with above 320 copper plates, representing the finest prospects, and most considerable cities of those parts; the different habits of the people; the singular and extra-ordinary Birds, Fishes, and Plants which are there to be found: As likewise the antiquities of those countries, and particularly the noble ruins of the famous palace of Perse-polis, called Chelminar by the Persians. The whole being deliniated on the spot, from the respective objects.* London, Bettesworth & Hitch, 1737. I, 1–95. II, 169–93. illus. map. port. index.

Dutch painter obtains first permit to sketch antiquities in two visits, September, 1701—July, 1703, and August, 1707—August, 1708. Sketches are original, the text based on earlier travelers' accounts. Bruyn includes a magnificent map of Moscow, sketches of Samoyed tents exactly like those of American Indians, and copper plates of children being carried like papooses.

74.   La Mottraye, Aubry de. *The voyages and travels of A. de la Mottraye, in several provinces and places of the kingdoms and dukedoms of Prussia, Russia, Poland, etc.* London, Symon, 1732. III, 54–224. illus.

French traveler's journeys to southern Russia in 1707, and to the northern parts in 1714 and 1726. Dull but informative, his account is one of the first about Crimea and the Black Sea region.

75.   Whitworth, Charles. *An account of Russia as it was in the year 1710.* Twickenham, Strawberry Hill, 1758. 158 pp.

British ambassador extraordinary describes Peter as great *in spite of* his people, although he is unscrupulous, violent, and extravagant. Some nobility he sees as full of "modesty, sense and honor."

76.   Bruce, Peter Henry. *Memoirs of Peter Henry Bruce, esq., a military officer in the services of Prussia, Russia, and Great Britain. Containing an account of his travels in Germany, Russia, Tartary, Turkey, the West Indies, etc., as also several interesting private anecdotes of the Czar, Peter I, of Russia.* London, Payne & Sons, 1782. pp. 33–374.

British mercenary in Peter's employ provides a historically accurate, but very poorly organized, account of military operations, 1711–24.

77.   Weber, Friedrich Christian. *The present state of Russia. Being an account of the government of that country, both civil and ecclesiastical; of the Czar's forces by sea and land, the regulation of his finances, the several methods he made use of to civilize his people and improve the country, his*

transactions with several eastern princes, and what hap-
pened most remarkable at his court, particularly in relation
to the late czarewitz, from the year 1714, to 1720. London,
Taylor, 1723. vol. I, 352 pp. map.

Foreign minister of Hanover, who lived in Moscow from 1714 to
1719, provides an informative and reliable account of Peter's Russia
with the first published description of St. Petersburg.

78.   Bell, John. *Travels from St. Petersburg in Russia to di-*
         verse parts of Asia. London, Homer, 1764. vol. I, 387 pp.
         vol. II, 499 pp. map.

British expatriate and embassy gentleman, Russian-speaking,
travels throughout most of Russia, 1715–38. He provides useful
and very detailed information on Russian expansion to the south
and east.

79.   Manstein, (General) Christoff Hermann von. *Memoirs of*
         Russia, historical, political and military, from the year
         MDCCXXVII, to MDCCXLIV. A period comprehending
         many remarkable events. In particular the wars of Russia
         with Turkey and Sweden. With a supplement, containing
         a summary account of the state of the military, the marine,
         the commerce, etc., of that great empire. London, Beckett
         & De Hondt, 1770. 425 pp. illus. map. index.

German mercenary in Russian service describes the part he played
in the accession to power of Anna Ivanovna in 1730. General
Manstein served the Russian state from 1727 to 1744.

80.   Vigor, Mrs. William. *Letters from a lady who resided*
         some years in Russia, to her friend in England. With his-
         torical notes. London, Dodsley, 1775. 207 pp. app.

The widow of a Muscovy Company merchant marries Claudius
Rondeau, negotiator of the commercial treaty of 1734, living in
Russia altogether from 1728 to 1739. In her delightful letters she
says nothing about diplomacy and commerce but a great deal about
life in St. Petersburg and its people, the death of the emperor, and
the reign of Anna Ivanovna.

81. Locatelli, (Count) Francesco. *Lettres Moscovites: or, Muscovian letters. Containing, an account of the form of government, customs, and manners of that great empire. Written by an Italian officer of distinction.* Translated from the French by William Musgrave. London, Symon, 1736. 190 pp.

Soldier-adventurer journeys to St. Petersburg in reign of Anna Ivanovna, 1733, and comments on the ways of war and peculiarities of the Muscovites. Entire account suffers from a somewhat petty tone of criticism, which may be illustrated by the remark: "A shameful practice, to oblige people to pay for a pass!" (a visa).

82. Waxell, (Lieutenant) Sven. *The American expedition.* Translated from the Danish by M. A. Michael. London, Hodge, 1952. pp. 39–212. illus. map. port. app. biblio. index.

Swedish, Russian-speaking officer on Bering's second expedition from St. Petersburg to the Pacific Ocean, 1733–43, provides a detailed description of Kamchatka and the Sea of Okhotsk.

83. Justice, (Mrs.) Elizabeth. *A voyage to Russia: Describing the laws, manners, and customs of that great empire, as governed at this present by that excellent princess the czarina. Shewing the beauty of her palace, the grandeur of her courtiers, the forms of building at St. Petersburgh, and other places: with several entertaining adventures that happened in the passage by sea and land. To which is added four letters, wrote by the author when at Russia to a gentleman in London.* London, printed for the author, 1746. 63 pp.

Governess to children of St. Petersburg merchant writes a brief but informative account of food, customs, houses, and manners, 1734–37.

84. Cook, John. *Voyages and travels through the Russian empire, Tartary, and part of the kingdom of Persia.* Edinburgh, printed for the author, 1770. vol. I, 467 pp. vol. II, 628 pp.

Scottish medical officer in the Russian army from 1736 to 1750 records observations with wry humor and a sense of detail. Valuable because of his extensive journeys into the interior.

85.   Algarotti, (Count) Francesco. *Letters from Count Algarotti to Hervey and the Marquis Scipio Maffei, containing the state of the trade, marine, revenues, and forces of the Russian Empire: with a history of the late war between the Russians and the Turks, and observations on the Baltic and the Caspian Seas.* London, Johnson & Payne, 1769. vol. I, 205 pp. vol. II, pp. 7–72.

Voltaire's Italian friend finds court life under Anna Ivanovna sumptuous and gay in 1739. He comments in detail on the army and its life but provides little on the general manners and customs of the Russian people.

86.   Spilman, James. *A journey through Russia into Persia; by two English gentlemen, who went in the year 1739, from Petersburg, in order to make a discovery how the trade from Great Britain might be carried on from Astracan over the Caspian. To which is annexed, a summary account of the rise of the famous Kouli Kan, and his successes, till he seated himself on the Persian throne.* London, Dodsley, 1742. 65 pp.

British businessman concentrates on economic aspects and how entrepreneurs are protected by various arrangements.

87.   Steller, Georg Wilhelm. *Bering's voyages. An account of the efforts of the Russians to determine the relation of Asia and America. Steller's journal of the sea voyage from Kamchatka to America and return on the second expedition, 1741–1742.* F. A. Golder, editor. New York, American Geographical Society, 1925. 249 pp. illus. index.

German physician and botanist describes his journey through Siberia to the Bering Strait.

88. Hanway, Jonas. *An historical account of the British trade over the Caspian Sea: with the author's Journal of travels from England through Russia into Persia; and back through Russia, Germany and Holland. To which are added, The revolutions of Persia during the present century, with the particular history of the great usurper Nadir Kouli.* London, Dodsley, 1753. I, 71–399. II, 1–173. illus. map, app. index.

British trader operating out of St. Petersburg, 1743–50, describes Anglo-Russian commerce with an almost religious conviction of the universal utility of trade. His account provides valuable and essential information on eighteenth-century British and Russian trading relations. Included is Captain (and merchant-trader) John Elton's journey from Moscow to Persia, March, 1739–January, 1740, who comments on items related to the movement of goods. See pp. 16–42.

89. Chappé d'Auteroche, (Abbé) Jean. *A journey into Siberia made by order of the King of France.* London, Jefferys, 1770. 395 pp. illus. map. app.

Between January and August, 1761–62, the French astronomer travels to Tobolsk, Siberia, by way of St. Petersburg and observes the transit of Venus over the sun. His account provides a mass of detail on drinking, science, mercantile exports, religion, etc. His criticisms provoked a rebuttal, written "By a Lover of Truth," *The Antidote: or an enquiry into the merits of a book entitled A journey into Siberia . . . In which many essential errors and misrepresentations are pointed out and confuted.* Translated into English by a lady dedicated to the Czarina of Russia. London, Leacroft, 1772. 202 pp.

90. Rulhière, Claude Carolman de. *A history or anecdotes of the Revolution in Russia in the year 1762.* London, Beauvalet, 1797. 200 pp.

A rather frivolous account in which a member of the French Academy who witnessed Catherine's ascent to power in 1762–63 depicts Russians as servile and resigned.

91. Hobart, John, Earl of Buckinghamshire. *The despatches and correspondence of John, second Earl of Buckinghamshire, Ambassador to the court of Catherine II, 1762–1765.* Adelaide D'Arcy Collyer, editor. London, Longmans, Green, 1900–1901. I, 71–238. II, 2–288. app. index.

British ambassador provides description of negotiations for Anglo-Russian agreement to offset French influence. His comments are especially useful to specialists in diplomacy. Appendix includes copies of dispatches.

92. Macartney, (Sir) George. *An account of Russia.* London, privately printed, 1768. 230 pp. illus. map.

British diplomat in St. Petersburg, 1764–67, provides authoritative and detailed information on the army, navy, resources, trade, and church of Russia under Catherine II.

93. Macartney, (Sir) George. *Some account of the public life, and a selection from the unpublished writings of the Earl of Macartney.* John Barrow, editor. London, Cadell & Davis, 1807. I, 413–27. II, 2–93. port.

Sir George was envoy extraordinary to St. Petersburg from August, 1766, to February, 1767. Much of the content of these letters is critical of Anglo-Russian diplomatic relations.

94. Casanova de Seingalt, Giovanni Jacopo. *The memoirs of Jacques Casanova de Seingalt in London and Moscow.* Translated from the Italian by Arthur Machen. New York, Putnam, n.d. V, 501–60.

Casanova recounts his journey to St. Petersburg and Moscow, where he consorts with nobility and adventurers in 1765. He observes life in and out of court and refers to Catherine as a "monarch in petticoats." He claims to have advised her to adopt the Gregorian calendar.

95. Tott, (Baron) Francis de. *Memoirs of the Baron de Tott, on the Turks and the Tartars.* London, Jarvis, 1785. I, 288–532. index.

French tourist in St. Petersburg in 1767 comments on manners and customs of court and people.

96. Richardson, William. *Anecdotes of the Russian Empire. In a series of letters written a few years ago from St. Petersburg.* London, Strahan & Cadell, 1784. 478 pp.

Tutor to the sons of Lord Cathcart, British ambassador to Russia, writes lively and amusing letters in which he describes the court life, weather, theater, national character, etc., 1768–72.

97. Benyowsky, Mauritus Augustus (Count) de. *The memoirs and travels of Mauritus Augustus Count de Benyowsky in Siberia, Kamchatka, Japan, the Liukiu Islands and Formosa.* Pasfield Oliver, editor. Translated from the French by William Nicholson. London, Fisher Unwin, 1893. 392 pp. illus. map. port. app. index.

Hungarian soldier in the Polish army is captured by the Russians and sent along the exile road to Kamchatka, 1769–71. Here he describes his experiences among the Siberians. There is some question about the veracity of this traveler.

98. Marshall, Joseph. *Travels through Holland, Flanders, Germany, Denmark, Sweden, Lapland, Russia, The Ukraine and Poland, in the years 1768, 1769, and 1770. In which is particularly minuted The Present State of those countries, reflecting their agriculture, population, manufactures, commerce, the arts, and useful undertakings.* London, Almon, 1773. III, 103–233.

British businessman in Russia during the summer of 1770 attempts a serious and objective survey of economic resources.

99. Tooke, William. *A view of the Russian Empire during the reign of Catherine the Second and to the close of the eighteenth century.* London, Longmans, 1800. vol. I, 630 pp. vol. II, 574 pp. vol. III, 575 pp. map. app. index.

Chaplain of the English church in Kronstadt writes an account of Catherine's and Paul's reigns between 1771 and 1798. His personal experiences are included in his dull but informative description.

100.   Wraxall, Nathaniel, Jr. *Cursory remarks made in a tour through some of the northern parts of Europe, particularly Copenhagen, Stockholm and Petersburgh.* London, Cadell, 1775. pp. 202–88.

On a six weeks' journey during the summer of 1774, a twenty-three-year-old British baronet describes court life around Catherine, characterizing her as corpulent, but dignified.

101.   * John (second Lord Henniker). *A northern tour in the years 1775 and 1776 through Copenhagen and Petersburg to the River Swir, joining the lakes of Onega and Ladoga. In a series of letters, from John, second Lord Henniker, to whom letters are addressed.*

102.   Richard, John. *A tour from London to Petersburgh and thence to Moscow.* Dublin, William Wilson, 1781. pp. 7–131. illus.

In a series of letters to a friend in London, British tourist describes life in St. Petersburg and Moscow in 1776, commenting on trade, the nobility, shopkeepers, women and courtship, the Orthodox church, etc. Observes Russians to be "rustic and unpolished," but not addicted to the custom of dueling as are their British contemporaries.

103.   Harris, (Sir) James. *Diaries and correspondence of James Harris, first Earl of Malmesbury.* James Howard Harris, editor. London, Richard Bentley, 1845. vol. I.

British plenipotentiary in St. Petersburg, 1777–83, writes on a wide variety of subjects related to problem of armed neutrality of 1780.

104.   Coxe, William. *Travels into Poland, Russia, Sweden and Denmark. Interspersed with historical relations and political*

inquiries. Dublin, S. Price, et al., 1784. I, 285–498. II, 501 pp. III, 1–76. app. biblio. index.

Cambridge scholar-historian journeys through European Russia, August, 1778–February, 1779. He combines historical background with his diary comments in which he objectively and without contempt describes the life of peasant and noble, playing down Peter's impact on institutions. Highly recommended as a basic document for the period.

105. Ledyard, John. *A journal of Captain Cook's last voyage to the Pacific Ocean, and in quest of a northwest passage, between Asia and America; Performed in the years 1776, 1777, 1778, 1779.* Hartford, Nathaniel Patten, 1783. pp. 164–91. map.

Ledyard comments on Cook's coasting along the Kamchatka peninsula toward the Bering Strait, April–October, 1779.

106. Ligne, (Prince) Charles Joseph de. *The Prince de Ligne. His memoirs, letters, and miscellaneous papers.* Translated and edited by Katherine Prescott Wormeley. Boston, Hardy, Pratt, 1902. I, 302–11. II, 8–70. illus. port. app. index.

A journey to St. Petersburg in 1780 to arrange for his son's wife's dowry extends into a long visit that ends with his service under Potemkin against Turkey in 1787–88. Writing in a romantic style, he comments in friendly fashion on his life in court and on the battlefield.

107. Howard, John. *Memoirs of Howard. Compiled from his diary, his confidential letters, and other authentic documents.* James Baldwin Brown, editor. Boston, Lincoln & Edmonds, 1831. pp. 178–84, 322–31.

Capture and imprisonment by a French privateer early in his life led Britisher John Howard to a deep interest in prison reform. In 1781–82 he visits St. Petersburg and Moscow, where he sees and describes the use of the *knoot* (knout), wooden cages, and instruments of torture and punishment. He died on a second visit to Moscow in 1789.

108. Dana, Francis. *Francis Dana. A Puritan diplomat at the court of Catherine the Great.* William Penn Cresson, editor. New York, Dial Press, 1930. pp. 154–397. illus. port. biblio. index.

American diplomat sent to Catherine's court to secure recognition of the United States, 1781–83, fails in his mission but does manage to arouse some unofficial sympathy for the American rebels among the nobility.

109. Forster, George. *A journey from Bengal to England, through the northern part of India, Kashmire, Afghanistan, and Persia, and into Russia, by the Caspian Sea.* London, Faulder, 1798. II, 204–97. map.

Member of the Indian Civil Service tours the Volga River to Moscow and St. Petersburg in 1783–84. He comments chiefly on Russian seamen and their way of life.

110. Bentham, Jeremy. *The works of Jeremy Bentham, published under the superintendence of his executor, John Bowring.* John Bowring, editor. Edinburgh, William Tait, 1843. X, 147–79.

Between 1785 and 1787 Bentham assists Potemkin in improving agriculture, trading, and manufacturing. He also comments on Catherine II and her court.

111. Ségur, (Count) Louis-Philippe de. *Memoirs and recollections of Count Ségur. Ambassador from France to the courts of Russia and Prussia, etc., etc. Written by himself.* London, Henry Colburn, 1825. II, 153–352. III, 1–441. port. app.

Count Ségur describes the court of Catherine II and her journey to the Crimea, 1785–89. Emphasizes diplomatic procedures.

112. Billings, (Commodore) Joseph. *An account of a geographical and astronomical expedition to the northern parts of Russia, for ascertaining the degrees of latitude and longitude of the mouth of the river Kovima; of the whole coast*

of the Tshutski, to east cape; and of the islands in the eastern ocean, stretching to the American coast. Martin Sauer, editor. London, Cadell, 1802. 332 pp. illus. map. app.

Englishman serving in Catherine's navies sails and rides horseback along the north Russian coast, 1785–94. He provides a valuable description of the land and the natives by word and sketch.

113.   Masson, Charles François Philibert. *Secret memoirs of the court of St. Petersburg, particularly toward the end of the reign of Catherine II and the commencement of that of Paul I.* London, Nichols, 1895. 382 pp. illus. app.

In 1786 this French middle-class poet entered Russian military service, and in 1795 he married Baroness Rosen and became secretary to the Grand Duke Alexander. When Paul succeeded, Masson was expelled. Accordingly, this work is highly critical of Paul but otherwise is fairly impartial and very good on court life.

114.   Craven, Elizabeth. *A journey through the Crimea to Constantinople in a series of letters from the Right Honorable Elizabeth Lady Craven, to His Serene Highness, the Margrave of Brandenburg, Anspach, and Bareith. Written in the year 1786.* Vienna, R. Sammer, 1800. pp. 5–468.

English lady tourist journeys from St. Petersburg to the Crimea during January–April, 1786. She writes amusing and witty letters devoid of political content. She admires Catherine greatly but deplores French influence in her court, and observes the Russians generally as gay, amiable, and lacking prejudice. She characterizes the peasants by the phrase "happy simplicity." Highly recommended as a useful picture of the period.

115.   Ledyard, John. *Travels and adventures of John Ledyard; comprising his voyage with Captain Cook's third and last expedition; his journey on foot 1300 miles around the Gulf of Bothnia to St. Petersburgh; his adventures and residence in Siberia; and his exploratory mission to Africa.* Jared Sparks, editor. London, Richard Bentley, 1834. pp. 236–379.

American adventurer-explorer describes his famous journey across Siberia, his arrest in Yakutsk, and his return, 1786–88. His account includes observations on the native tribes and their relations with the Russian administrators, on animal life, and on transportation.

116.   * Sinclair, (Sir) John. *General observations regarding the present state of the Russian Empire.* London, 1787.

After a journey in 1787, Sir John warns the British government about Russian expansion to the south and states that eventually all Europe will need to unite to put a stop to the ambitions generating in St. Petersburg. See no. 1425, Anderson, *Britain's discovery of Russia,* p. 151.

117.   La Pérouse, (Count) Jean François de Galaup. *A voyage around the world in the years, 1785, 1786, 1787, and 1788, by the "Boussole" and "Astrolabe", under the command of J.F.G. de la Pérouse: pub. by order of the National Assembly under the superintendence of L.A.Milet-Mureau.* London, Johnson, 1798. III, 1–37. map. port.

French explorer, commissioned by Louis XVI to circle the earth, visits Kamchatka and the Sea of Okhotsk in September, 1787.

118.   Lesseps, Jean Baptiste-Barthelemy. *Travels in Kamtschatka during the years, 1787–1788.* London, Johnson, 1790. I, 1–283. II, 1–382.

Interpreter to La Pérouse (see no. 117) carries dispatches from him to Paris across Siberia. His observing eye misses little, and his style adequately conveys his impressions.

119.   Damas D'Antigney, (Count) Joseph Elizabeth Roger de. *Memoirs of the Comte Roger de Damas (1787–1806).* Jacques Rambaud, editor-annotator. Translated from the French by Mrs. Rudolph Stowell. London, Chapman & Hall, 1913. 151 pp. port.

French officer in Potemkin's army, 1787–91, describes his life at court and on the battlefield. In discussing Catherine, he concludes that Russians are "suspicious, envious, and not very frank."

120. Chantreau, Pierre Nicholas. *Philosophical, political and literary travels in Russia during the years 1788 and 1789.* London, Vernor & Hood, 1794. vol. I, 321 pp. vol. II, 515 pp. map.

French traveler with commercial motives details every aspect of life in St. Petersburg and Moscow. Historical backgrounds underscore his friendly analysis.

121. Jones, John Paul. *Memoirs of John Paul Jones, late Rear-Admiral in the Russian service.* London, Henry Washburne, 1893. vol. I, 331 pp. vol. II, pp. 1–241. app.

Admiral Jones describes his service under Catherine II, asking only to be trusted and not to be "condemned unheard." 1788–89.

122. Jones, John Paul. *John Paul Jones in Russia.* F. A. Golder, editor. Garden City, New York, Doubleday, 1927. pp. 148–220.

Letters to Catherine in which Kontradmiral Pavel Ivanovich Jones complains about his shabby treatment.

123. Swinton, Andrew. *Travels into Norway, Denmark and Russia in 1788, 1789, 1790, 1791.* London, Robinson, 1792. pp. 126–496. app.

Informal travel diary by Englishman visiting in St. Petersburg and Moscow, October, 1788–January, 1791. Describes peasant life and land cultivation and charges misunderstanding and bias underlie the account by Chappé d'Auteroche (see no. 89).

124. ** Letters from the continent describing the manners and customs of . . . Russia . . . in years 1790, 1791, 1792.* London, 1812.

125. Thomson, William. *Letters from Scandinavia on the past and present state of the northern nations of Europe.* London, Robinson, 1796. I, 1–351. II, 44–279.

British businessman describes 1791–92 journey to St. Petersburg, refering to the invidious account by Chappé d'Auteroche (see no. 89). Details way of life from weddings to use of the knout.

126. Pallas, Peter Simon. *Travels through the southern provinces of the Russian Empire in the years 1793–1794.* Translated from the German by P. S. Pallas. London, Longmans, 1812. vol. I, 541 pp. vol. II, 510 pp. illus. map. index.

As an employee of the Russian crown, Pallas, eminent German naturalist, travels throughout the realm, describing the flora and fauna with Teutonic thoroughness. He includes colored plates of peoples, animals, scenes, etc., by the Leipzig artist, C. G. H. Geissler.

127. Guthrie, (Mrs.) Marie. *A tour, performed in the years 1795–6, through the Taurida, or Crimea, the Antient Kingdom of Bosphorus, the once-powerful Republic of Tauric Cherson, and all the other countries on the north shore of the Euxine, ceded to Russia by the peace of Kainardgi and Jassy.* London, Cadell, 1802. 308 pp. illus. map. app.

Wife of British physician in St. Petersburg court writes series of letters making chiefly historical observations, 1795–96. The appendix includes copies of coins, monuments, etc.

128. Kotzebue, Augustus von. *The most remarkable year in the life of Augustus von Kotzebue; containing an account of his exile into Siberia, and of the other extraordinary events which happened to him in Russia.* London, Richard Phillips, 1802. vol. I, 278 pp. vol. II, 271 pp. vol. III, 216 pp. port.

Soldier of fortune, who has been suspected of never letting the truth interfere with a good story, describes his arrest, exile, and restoration to favor in 1800. See no. 97 for a similar experience by Benyowsky.

129. Clarke, Edward Daniel. *Travels in various countries of Europe, Asia and Africa.* London, Cadell & Davies, 1816. vol. I, 446 pp. vol. II, 381 pp. illus. map. port. app. index.

After a journey of 4,086 miles throughout European Russia, from St. Petersburg to the Sea of Azov, British scholar-geologist-tutor presents an extremely critical account of Paul's regime, April 3 to October 31, 1800. He claims that the droshky first appeared about this time.

130. Atkinson, John Augustus and James Walker. *A picturesque representation of the manners, customs, and amusements of the Russians in one hundred coloured plates; with an accurate explanation of each plate in English and French.* London, Bulmer, 1803–4. Three volumes, each 2 x 3 feet.

Magnificent colored plates prepared between 1800–1803.

131. Campenhausen, (Major) Pierce Balthaser. *Travel through several provinces of the Russian Empire; with an historical account of the Zaporog Cossacks, and of Bessarabia, Moldavia, Wallachia and the Crimea.* London, Phillips, 1808. pp. 1–60.

German major of cavalry serving under Alexander I, 1800–1807, collects and records a mass of information, much of which comes under the class of trivia.

132. * Reuilly, Jean. *Travels in the Crimea, and along the shores of the Black Sea, performed during the year 1803.* London, Phillips, 1807. 84 pp. illus. map.

133. Wilmot, Martha and Catherine. *The Russian journals of Martha and Catherine Wilmot. Being an account by two Irish ladies of their adventures in Russia as guests of the celebrated Princess Daschkaw, containing vivid descriptions of contemporary court life and society, and lively anecdotes of many interesting historical characters, 1803–1808.* The

Marchioness of Londonderry and H. M. Hyde, editors.
London, Macmillan, 1934. 415 pp. illus. port. index.

The two Irish ladies see only rottenness in the government, with
Machiavellian cruelty below the surface. Includes two long letters
on her impressions of Russia by Eleanor Cavanaugh, maid to
Catherine Wilmot.

134. D'Wolf, (Captain) John. *A voyage to the North Pacific and
a journey through Siberia more than half a century ago.*
London, Cambridge, 1861. 147 pp.

New England sea captain journeys across Siberia to St. Petersburg
in 1804 to get a bill of sale honored. His remarks are typically
tourist-like.

135. Carr, John. *A northern summer: or Travels around the
Baltick through Denmark, Sweden, Russia, Prussia and
part of Germany, in the year 1804.* Philadelphia, Samuel F.
Bradford, 1805. pp. 125–286.

English tourist visiting St. Petersburg and environs, May–November, 1804, makes observations that cover a wide range of subjects
from dogs, beards, and punishments, through kissing, horses with
false hair, and dwarfs, to famine and the theater.

136. Rochechouart, (Count) Louis Victor Léon de. *Memoirs of
the Count de Rochechouart in France, in southern Russia,
the Napoleonic wars, 1812–15 and as commandant of Paris,
1788–1816.* Translated from the French by Francis Jackson.
New York, Dutton, 1920. pp. 38–172. port.

French mercenary who served under Richelieu at Odessa and with
Alexander I against Napoleon, 1804–15, provides an unusual point
of view on the Russian attitude toward Napoleon.

137. Reinbeck, Georg. *Travels from St. Petersburgh through
Moscow, Grodno, Warsaw, Breslaw, etc., to Germany in
the year 1805: in a series of letters.* London, Phillips, 1807.
pp. 5–146.

German businessman of St. Petersburg records flourishing Russia under Alexander the Good, May–June, 1805. Delightfully written letters on a variety of subjects, all complimentary.

138. Seume, Johann Gottfried. *A tour through parts of Germany, Poland, Russia, Sweden, Denmark, etc., etc., during the summer of 1805.* London, Phillips, 1807. pp. 31–53.

A typical and disgruntled tourist, Seume speaks caustically about everything on his July, 1805, journey to St. Petersburg—especially the mineral waters.

139. Heber, Amelia. *The life of Reginald Heber, D.D.* New York, Protestant Episcopal Press, 1830. pp. 89–238.

Includes Reginald Heber's "A journal of his tour in Norway, Sweden, Russia, Hungary and Germany." As a twenty-two-year-old Oxford student, Heber and classmate (John Thornton) journey to St. Petersburg and Moscow, October 9, 1805–April 20, 1806. In a series of letters to his mother and others in his family he describes the land and the people, characterizing Moscow as a "vast over-grown village."

140. Green, George. *An original journal from London to St. Petersburgh by way of Sweden; and, proceeding from thence, to Moscow, Riga, Mittau, and Berlin: with a description of the post towns, and everything interesting, in the Russian and Prussian capitals, etc., to which are added, the names, distances, and price of each post; and a vocabulary of the most useful terms, in English and Russian.* London, Boosey, 1813. pp. 1–147.

Russian-speaking British businessman in St. Petersburg and Moscow for many years provides valuable advice for carrying on trading activities. 1805–7.

141. Porter, Robert Ker. *Travelling sketches in Russia and Sweden during the years 1805, 1806, 1807, 1808.* London, Phillips, 1809. vol. I, 303 pp. vol. II, pp. 1–77. illus.

Between 1805–7 this British painter was commissioned by the Russian government to paint canvases for the new Admiralty in St. Petersburg. Before he is forced to leave by the Treaty of Tilsit, he produces paintings of peasants, the nobility, and the land.

142.   * MacGill, Thomas. *Travels in Turkey, Italy and Russia, during the years 1803–1806. With an account of some of the Greek islands.* Edinburgh, 1806. 2 vols.

143.   Campbell, Archibald. *A voyage around the world from 1806 to 1812: In which Japan, Kamschatka, the Aleutian Islands were visited.* Charleston, S.C., Duke and Browne, 1822. pp. 24–29.

British sailor describes his brief visit to Kamchatka, July, 1807.

144.   Everett, Alexander Hill. *Critical and miscellaneous essays to which are added a few poems.* Boston, James Munroe, 1845. Two volumes in which there are scattered references to Russia.

Secretary to John Quincy Adams in St. Petersburg, 1809 (see no. 145).

145.   Adams, John Quincy. *Memoirs of John Quincy Adams, comprising portions of his diary from 1795–1848.* Charles Francis Adams, editor. Philadelphia, Lippincott, 1874–77. II, 3–602.

First United States minister in St. Petersburg after recognition in 1809 remains until 1814. Gets along famously with Alexander I and describes Russian way of life, in court and out, with Adamsian felicity.

146.   Coggeshall, George. *Second series of voyages to various parts of the world, made between the years 1802 and 1841.* New York, Appleton, 1852. pp. 80–108. illus. port.

Sea captain from Connecticut describes winter in the Riga harbor during Napoleon's continental blockade, 1810–11.

147. Freygan, Fredericka Kudriavskaia von. *Letters from the Caucasus and Georgia; to which are added the account of a journey into Persia in 1812, and an abridged history of Persia since the time of Nadir Shah.* London, John Murray, 1823. 414 pp. illus. map.

Daughter-in-law of German physician in Alexander I's service stationed in Tiflis. This may be the joint effort of lady and gentleman travelers.

148. * Labaume, Eugene. *A circumstantial narrative of the campaign in Russia, embellished with plans of the battles of the Moskwa and Malo-Jaroslavitz.* Hartford, Sheldon & Goodrich, 1816. 365 pp.

149. Caulaincourt, Armand de (Duke of Vicenza). *With Napoleon in Russia. The memoirs of General de Caulaincourt, Duke of Vicenza.* G. Libaire and J. Honateau, editors. New York, William Morrow, 1935. pp. 45–323. map. port. index.

A somewhat prejudiced traveler describes his journey to, and away from, Moscow, June–November, 1812.

150. Bonaparte, Napoleon. *Talks with Napoleon at St. Helena with General Baron Gourgard: Together with the journal kept by Gourgard on their journey from Waterloo to St. Helena.* Translated and edited by Elizabeth Wormeley Latimer. Chicago, McClurg, 1904. pp. 154–62.

Reminiscing on his Moscow campaign, Napoleon claims that it was Russia's menacing attitude that forced him to invade. He regrets the burning of a "superb city" but considers "Moskwa" to be his most brilliant battle.

151. Bonaparte, Napoleon. *The Corsican. A diary of Napoleon's life in his own words.* R. M. Johnston, editor. Boston, Houghton Mifflin, 1910. pp. 347–66.

A few excerpts can best illustrate Napoleon's experience at Moscow: September 15. "The fire of Moscow begins." September 20.

"[To the Emperor Alexander] *Monsieur mon Frère:* The beautiful and splendid city of Moscow no longer exists. Rostopchin has burnt it down. . . . Such conduct is atrocious and aimless. . . . I have conducted the war against Your Majesty with no animosity."

152.   Bonaparte, Napoleon. *Napoleon speaks.* Albert Carr, editor. Translated from the French by Julia van Huele. New York, Viking, 1941. pp. 285–92.

From official documents, a few dispatches and a letter from Napoleon to Alexander I on the burning of Moscow.

153.   Ségur, (Count) Philippe-Paul de. *Napoleon's Russian Campaign.* Translated and edited by J. David Townsend. Boston, Houghton Mifflin, 1958. 300 pp. map.

Napoleon's loyal quartermaster general writes a not completely uncritical description of his superior, the army, the campaign, and its failure. He observes of the suffering Russian soldiers : " . . . They were less sensitive in both body and mind, as a result of living in a more primitive civilization and having their constitution hardened by a harsh climate."

154.   Walter, Jakob. *A German conscript with Napoleon. Jakob Walter's recollections of the campaigns of 1806–1807, 1809, and 1812–1813. According to a manuscript found at Lecompton, Kansas.* Otto Springer, editor, with historical collaboration by Frank E. Melvin. Lawrence, University of Kansas, Department of Journalism Press, 1938. pp. 17–109. illus. port.

An unforgettable description of conditions along the road as Napoleon's army journeys from the Niemen River to Moscow and returns, June–December, 1812.

155.   Dobbell, Peter. *Travels in Kamchatka and Siberia with a narrative of a residence in China.* London, Colburn & Bentley, 1830. vol. I, 351 pp. vol. II, pp. 1–124. illus.

British counselor at Alexander's court journeys from Kamchatka to the Ural Mountains, August–November, 1812. He provides a mass of detail about Siberia, its peoples, its resources, and the road that serves as the connection between the east and west limits of the Empire.

156. Wilson, (Sir) Robert Thomas. *Private diary of travels, personal services, and public events during mission and employment with the European armies in the campaigns of 1812, 1813, 1814. From the invasion of France to the capture of Paris.* Herbert Randolph, editor. London, John Murray, 1861. I, 144–250.

British general describes his experiences with the Russian army during Napoleon's invasion and retreat, August 14, 1812, at Smolensk, and then to St. Petersburg, Moscow, and Vilna by December 17, 1812.

157. Wilson, (Sir) Robert Thomas. *General Wilson's journal. 1812–1814.* Anthony Brett-James, editor. London, William Kimber, 1964. pp. 28–97. map.

Wilson describes the harrowing sights he saw as Napoleon retreated from Moscow, September–December, 1812.

158. Roeder, (Captain) Franz. *The ordeal of Captain Roeder. From the diary of an officer in the first battalion of Hessian Life-Guards during the Moscow Campaign of 1812–13.* Translated and edited by Helen Roeder. London, Methuen, 1960. pp. 89–218. illus. map. port. index.

Officer tells the story of his journey to Viazma (west of Moscow) and the retreat, July, 1812–March, 1813. Along with his descriptions of pain and suffering on every side, he provides excellent sketches of the soldier's equipment.

159. Bourgogne, (Sergeant) Adrien Jean Baptiste François. *Memoirs of Sergeant Bourgogne, 1812–1813. Compiled from the original MSS.* Paul Cottin, compiler. New York, Doubleday & McClure, 1899. 356 pp. illus. port.

The son of a French cloth merchant, whose father bought him a commission in Napoleon's Guard, describes the psychology of soldiers depressed by a succession of defeats, in the retreat from Moscow, August, 1812–January, 1813.

160.   Choiseul-Gouffier, (Countess) Sophie (de Tisenhaus). *Historical memoirs of the Emperor Alexander I and the court of Russia.* Translated from the French by Mary B. Patterson. Chicago, McClurg, 1900. pp. 23–308. illus. index.

Remaining behind to save the family estates when her Polish father deserts Alexander I, Sophie de Tisenhaus gradually elevates the emperor to heroic role and thus describes his regime from 1812 to 1825.

161.   Bayard, James Asheton. *Letters of James Asheton Bayard, 1802–1814.* Henry C. Conrad, editor. Wilmington, Historical Society of Delaware, 1901. pp. 31–34. port.

Bayard served on the commission to negotiate the terms of the Treaty of Ghent with Great Britain, and in the two letters here he describes his reception in St. Petersburg in 1813.

162.   James, John Thomas. *Journal of a tour in Germany, Sweden, Russia, Poland, during the years 1813 and 1814.* London, John Murray, 1817. I, 383–454. illus.

Oxford student journeys to Moscow shortly after Napoleon's sojourn there, 1813. Emphasizes economics with special attention given to the Anglo-French struggle to dominate Russia.

163.   Pinkerton, Robert. *Russia; or, Miscellaneous observations on the past and present state of that country and its inhabitants.* London, Seeleys, 1833. 410 pp. illus. app.

Agent of British and Foreign Bible Society observes religious and related conditions, 1813–22, from Petersburg to Odessa. The appendix includes examples of the sermons used by the Orthodox clergy.

164.   Johnston, Robert. *Travels through part of the Russian Empire and the country of Poland; along the southern*

shores of the Baltic. London, Stockdale, 1815. pp. 79–369. illus. map.

British scholar journeys from St. Petersburg through Moscow to Smolensk shortly after Napoleon passed there, June–October, 1814. Friendly to Russia, he laments the destruction in Moscow.

165. Holderness, Mary. *New Russia. Journey from Riga to the Crimea, by way of Kiev; with some account of the coloni- zation, and the manners and customs of the colonists of new Russia. To which are added notes relating to the Crim Tatars.* London, Sherwood, Jones, 1823. 314 pp. illus. app.

A study of Russian rural customs by a British gentlewoman who lives in the village of Karagoss in the Crimea, 1816–20. She pro- vides a woman's viewpoint on items never seen by any ordinary tourist.

166. Johnson, (Lieutenant Colonel) John. *A journey from India to England, through Persia, Georgia, Russia, Poland and Prussia, in the year 1817.* London, Longman, Hurst, 1818. pp. 236–349. illus.

Professional soldier makes some rather commonplace observations on his journey, with one possible exception—when he describes the catacombs of Kiev.

167. Macmichael, William. *Journey from Moscow to Constanti- nople, in the years, 1817, 1818.* London, John Murray, 1819. pp. 1–71. illus. app.

Oxford scholar and medical doctor describes Moscow's rebuilding after 1812.

168. Taitbout de Marigny, E. *Three voyages in the Black Sea to the coast of Circassia: including descriptions of the ports, and the importance of their trade: with sketches of the manners, customs, religion, etc., etc., of the Circassians.* London, John Murray, 1837. 277 pp. illus. map. app.

Netherlands consul at Odessa makes three journeys to Circassia, 1818–24. The nature of his comments may be surmised from the knowledge that the early edition of his work was rigorously censored by St. Petersburg.

169. Gordon, Peter. *Fragment of the journal of a tour through Persia, in 1820.* London, Ford, 1833. pp. 3–42. app.

Commercial traveler is very critical as he describes voyage to and from the Sea of Okhotsk, 1819–20. Appendix includes "ranks and terms of Russia."

170. Van Halen, (Don) Juan. *Narrative of Don Juan van Halen's imprisonment in the dungeons of the Inquisition at Madrid, and his escape in 1817 and 1818; to which are added, his journey to Russia, his campaign with the army of the Caucasus, and his return to Spain in 1821.* New York, Harper, 1828. pp. 190–374. app.

Spanish soldier of fortune describes his experiences in Russia, 1819–21. The account may be compared with those of Benyowsky (see no. 97) and Kotzebue (see no. 128).

171. Cochrane, John Dundas. *Narrative of a pedestrian journey through Russian and Siberian Tartary from the frontiers of China to the frozen sea and Kamchatka.* London, Charles Knight, 1824, vol. I, 428 pp. vol. II, 278 pp. illus. map. app.

Setting out to retrace Ledyard's route (see no. 115), Royal Navy captain walks, except for short cart and sledge rides, from St. Petersburg to Kamchatka, 1820–21. Believing in the natural goodness of peasants, he depended on them for food and shelter and was not disappointed—altogether he spent less than five pounds of his own money. His description of peasant life is detailed but does get repetitious and monotonous.

172. Henderson, Ebenezer. *Biblical researches and travels in Russia; including a tour in the Crimea, and the passage of the Caucasus: with observations on the state of the Rabbinical and Karaite Jews, and the Mohammedan and pagan tribes, inhabiting the southern provinces of the Rus-*

sian Empire. London, James Nisbet, 1826. 534 pp. illus. map. app.

British member of Russian Bible Society describes his tour of duty, January, 1821–February, 1822.

173. Kolbe, Eduard. *Recollections of Russia during thirty-three years residence, by a German nobleman.* Translated from the German by L. Wraxall. Edinburgh, Constable, 1855. 328 pp.

After a long residence, 1821–54, in and around St. Petersburg, the author, engaged in business, judges the Russian to be part of "a horde not possessing a will." Discusses the evils of serfdom, police and bureaucracy, prisons, public and private life.

174. Lyall, Robert. *Travels in Russia. The Krimea, the Caucasus, and Georgia.* London, Cadell, 1825. vol. I, 527 pp. illus. app.

British Russian-speaking medical doctor and secretary-guide to Italian travelers visiting south Russia, 1822–23, describes journey in such detail as to cover the events almost day by day.

175. Jones, (Captain) George Matthew. *Travels in Norway, Sweden, Finland, Russia, and Turkey. Also on the coasts of the Sea of Azov and of the Black Sea: with a review of the trade in those seas and of the systems adopted to man the fleets of the different powers of Europe, compared with that of England.* London, John Murray, 1827. vol. I, pp. 247–565. vol. II, 443 pp. illus. map.

Royal Navy captain describes his visit in Russia, October, 1822–June, 1823, placing much of his emphasis on matters relating to the sea but not forgetting the sights, such as performing dwarf, dogs, etc.

176. Holman, James. *Travels through Russia, Siberia, Poland, Austria, Saxony, Prussia, Hanover, etc., etc., undertaken during the years 1822, 1823, and 1824, while suffering from total blindness, and comprising an account of the author*

being conducted a state prisoner from the eastern parts of Siberia. London, G. B. Whittaker, 1825. vol. I, 408 pp. vol. II, 235 pp. illus. port. app.

Captain Cochrane (see no. 171) raised questions about Holman's entire story, and this led to a bitter exchange of letters, included in the appendix to Holman's account.

177.   Moore, John (of Paris). *A journey from London to Odessa, with notices of New Russia, etc.* Paris, privately printed, 1833. pp. 77–201. app.

Friendly British tourist, visiting in Odessa in the summer of 1824, describes the city in detail, paying special tribute to the work of the Duc de Richelieu, who raised the city from a village to an important center of New Russia during his governor generalship of the Crimea, 1805–13.

178.   Webster, James. *Travels through the Crimea, Turkey, and Egypt; performed during the years 1825–1828: including particulars of the last illness and death of the Emperor Alexander, and of the Russian conspiracy of 1825.* London, Colburn and Bentley, 1830. I, 42–101. illus. app.

Brief description of Odessa and Sebastopol in 1825 by British tourist.

179.   Wilson, William Rae. *Travels in Russia.* London, Longman, et al., 1828. I, 219–383. II, 1–145. illus.

Professional traveler counsels patience in 1825: Criticism of Russians' behavior toward travelers should take into consideration the type of government under which they live.

180.   Bloomfield, (Lord) Benjamin. *Memoirs of Benjamin, Lord Bloomfield.* Georgiana Bloomfield, editor. London, Chapman & Hall, 1884. II, 1–105.

British diplomat journeys from St. Petersburg to Nizhni-Novgorod, June 29–September 7, 1825. Tourist impressions.

181. Schnitzler, J. H. *Secret history of the court and government of Russia under the Emperors Alexander and Nicholas.* London, Richard Bentley, 1847. vol. I, 307 pp. vol. II, 435 pp. app. index.

An employee of the British embassy, Russian-speaking, devotes two volumes to a detailed analysis of the rebellion of 1825. He argues that full details of the rebellion should be exposed to the world and spends four years, 1825–29, in travel and research for his book.

182. Westminister, Elizabeth Mary (Leveson-Gower) Grosvenor. *Diary of a tour in Sweden, Norway, and Russia, in 1827, with letters.* London, Hurst & Blackett, 1879. pp. 136–245.

British Lady in St. Petersburg, July–August, 1827, provides a full account of her activities, most of them of slight importance to one interested in Russia.

183. Granville, Augustus Bozzi. *St. Petersburgh. A Journal of travels to and from that capital; through Flanders, the Rhenish provinces, Prussia, Russia, Poland, Silesia, Saxony, The Federated States of Germany, and France.* London, Colburn, 1828. I, 373–577. II, 1–524. illus. map. app. index.

British medical doctor fulfils professional engagement in St. Petersburg during 1827. He provides a minute account of his residence at court and his activities in and about the city. He sets out to design a future travelers' guide to the capital.

184. Morton, Edward. *Travels in Russia and a residence at St. Petersburgh and Odessa in the years 1827 and 1829, intended to give some account of Russia as it is and not as it is represented to be.* London, Longmans, et al., 1830. 469 pp. app. index.

Physician, resident in Odessa and ousted under protest, champions British subjects sent to Siberia. Critical of what he terms the "misled" English travelers, he is especially informative on the visit of Nicholas I to Odessa in 1828.

185.   Erman, (Georg) Adolph. *Travels in Siberia: including
        excursions northwards, down the Obi, to the Polar circle,
        and southwards, to the Chinese frontier.* Translated from
        the German by William D. Cooley. London, Longman,
        Brown, 1848. I, 34–495. II, 1–221.

Scientist-explorer (compared to Humboldt) journeys to Irkutsk
with Professor Christopher Hansteen (see no. 186) in 1828–29
on an expedition to study the magnetic pole. Describes the exile
road thus: women are not forced to walk but are carried in carts;
there are no fetters on the prisoners when they are marching;
and Irkutsk (chief political exile city) is a beautiful place with
much personal freedom within its limits.

186.   * Hansteen, (Professor) Christopher. *Travels in Siberia.*
        London, Leisure Hour, 1879.

Norwegian professor of magnetic observations. (see no. 185)

187.   Armstrong, T. B. *Journal of travels in the seat of war dur-
        ing the last two campaigns of Russia and Turkey; intended
        as an itinerary through the south of Russia, the Crimea,
        Georgia, and through Persia, Koordistan, and Asia Minor,
        to Constantinople.* London, A. Seguin, 1831. pp. 1–108.
        illus. map. app. index.

Armstrong's account includes a great deal of detail on Jewish
life, although his main purpose was to provide useful information
on travel conditions, 1828–29.

188.   Alexander, (Sir) James Edward. *Travels to the seat of
        war in the East, through Russia and the Crimea, in 1829.
        With sketches of the imperial fleet and army, personal ad-
        ventures, and characteristic anecdotes.* London, Colburn &
        Bentley, 1830. vol. I, 308 pp. vol. II, 285 pp. illus. map. app.

Captain of the Sixteenth Lancers, British armed services, describes
the way of life in and out of the army on a journey from St. Petersburg to the Black Sea in 1829.

189.   Mignan, (Captain) Robert. *A winter journey through
        Russia, the Caucasian Alps, and Georgia: thence across*

Mount Zagros by the pass of Zenophon and the ten thousand Greeks into Koordistaun. London, Bentley, 1839. pp. 1–63. illus.

British officer (Indian army), wife, children, and two servants make journey in 1829. Describes sights in typical tourist fashion.

190. * Raikes, Thomas. *A visit to St. Petersburg, in the winter of 1829–1830.* London, Bentley, 1838. 383 pp.

191. Slade, (Lieutenant) Adolphus. *Records of travels in Turkey, Greece, etc., and of a cruise in the Black Sea with the Captain Pasha, in the years 1829, 1830 and 1831.* London, Saunders & Otley, 1833. I, 485–519. illus.

British Royal Navy military observer describes his visits to Sevastopol and Odessa during the aftermath of the Russo-Turkish war.

192. Barrow, John, Jr. *Excursions in the north of Europe, through parts of Russia, Finland, Sweden, Denmark and Norway.* London, John Murray, 1835. pp. 29–127. illus. map.

British tourist and friend (John Rouse) see the sights of St. Petersburg, including the royal family, then journey to Moscow by coach along the route made famous by Alexander Radishchev in his *Journey from St. Petersburg to Moscow* (1790), July–August, 1830.

193. Elliott, Charles Boileau. *Letters from the north of Europe; or, a journal of travels in Holland, Denmark, Norway, Sweden, Finland, Russia, Prussia and Saxony.* London, Colburn & Bentley, 1832. pp. 265–413. illus.

Tourist journey by member of the Indian Civil Service to St. Petersburg, Moscow, and Nizhni-Novgorod, September 13–October 16, 1830. Remarks emphasize religion, economics, and manners of the people.

194. Bruce, William Cabell. *John Randolph of Roanoke, 1773–1833. A biography based largely on new material.* New York, Putnam, 1922. I, 634–61. port.

Appointed to be United States minister to Russia in 1830, Randolph resigned almost immediately because of ill health. Here he describes his reception in St. Petersburg and his endurance of the vile climate during summer and winter, 1831.

195. Frankland, (Captain) Charles Colville. *Narrative of a visit to the courts of Russia and Sweden, in the years 1830 and 1831.* London, Colburn & Bentley, 1832. vol. I, 118–382. vol. II, 448 pp. illus. map.

British Royal Navy captain describes life of court and of the military during journey, September–July, with a special note on cholera and its impact.

196. Buchanan, James. *The works of James Buchanan, comprising his speeches, state papers and private correspondence.* John Bassett Moore, collector-editor. London, Lippincott, 1908. II, 173–382. index.

United States envoy extraordinary and minister plenipotentiary journeys to St. Petersburg, Moscow, and Nizhni-Novgorod, June 3, 1832–August 8, 1833. The purpose of his visit was to arrange a treaty of commerce, and he concludes that Russians are "not fit for political freedom." He considers Nicholas I to be "the very beau ideal of a sovereign for Russia."

197. * Connolly, Arthur. *Journey to the north of India overland from England through Russia, Persia and Afghanistan.* 1834.

198. Tietz, Frederick von. *St. Petersburgh, Constantinople, and Napoli di Romania in 1833 and 1834: A characteristic picture, drawn during a residence there.* Translated from the German by J. D. Haas. London, Adolphus Richter, 1836. I, 1–190.

Prussian counselor of his St. Petersburg legation, 1833, describes Nicholas I as benevolent and enlightened. In addition to his comments on the life of the court, he provides data on trading activities.

199. Stephens, James Lloyd. *Incidents of travel in Greece, Turkey, Russia and Poland.* New York, n.p., 1938. pp. 59–138.

English lawyer travels from the Black Sea to St. Petersburg overland by tarantasse (a vehicle with four wheels and no springs) during the spring of 1835. Except for some rather specific comments on travel by tarantasse, his remarks are commonplace.

200. Ritchie, Leitch. *A journey to St. Petersburg and Moscow through Courland and Livonia.* London, Longman, Rees, 1836. pp. 1–166. illus.

A guidebook-type account of a journey in April, 1835, by British professional traveler.

201. * Elliott, Charles Boileau. *Travels in the three great empires of Austria, Russia and Turkey.* London, Richard Bentley, 1838. 2 vols. map.

See no. 193.

202. Bremner, Robert. *Excursions into the interior of Russia; including sketches of the character and policy of the Emperor Nicholas, scenes in St. Petersburg, etc.* London, Henry Colburn, 1839. vol. I, 500 pp. vol. II, 525 pp. illus. index.

British tourist contrasts the way of life of noble and serf in a summer visit, 1836. He includes observations on trade and advice to travelers.

203. Vane, Charles William Stewart (Marquis of Londonderry). *Recollections of a tour in the north of Europe in 1836–1837.* London, Bentley, 1838. I, 80–275. II, 1–31. illus. map. app.

The marquis hoped to be appointed as ambassador to Russia but was disappointed in his ambition. In 1836–37 he traveled to St. Petersburg, Moscow, and Odessa as the guest of his friends among the nobility. His account describes the social life of his hosts, their games, summer sports, entertainment, and other activities.

204.   Spencer, (Captain) Edmund. *Travels in Circassia, Krim-Tartary, etc., including a steam voyage down the Danube, from Vienna to Constantinople, and round the Black Sea.* London, Henry Colburn, 1839. vol. I, 392 pp. vol. II, 406 pp. illus. map. app.

British journalist describes what he claims is the first travel account of Circassia, 1836–38.

205.   Spencer, (Captain) Edmund. *Turkey, Russia, the Black Sea, and Circassia.* London, George Routledge, 1854. pp. 221–404. illus. map.

This account, based on Spencer's 1836–38 journey (see no. 204), proposes to acquaint the reader with the "dangerous designs" of Russia.

206.   Demidoff, Anatole de. *Travels in southern Russia, and the Crimea; through Hungary, Wallachia, and Moldavia, during the year 1837.* London, John Mitchell, 1853. I, 289–370. II, 1–318. illus. map.

Russian-speaking French scientist dedicates his survey of Russian trade and industry to Nicholas I. His account is a very detailed song of praise for the emperor and all his works.

207.   Kohl, Johann George. *Russia. St. Petersburg, Moscow, Kharkoff, Riga, Odessa, the German provinces on the Baltic, the steppes, the Crimea, and the interior of the Empire.* London, Chapman & Hall, 1842. 530 pp.

This German traveler, seasoned by many visits to other lands, including the United States, provides a detailed description of the Russian way of life, omitting little and including even the place of cucumbers in the Russian diet. His 1837 journey left him with a deep admiration for the Slavic peoples.

208.   Wilbraham, (Captain) Richard. *Travels in the Trans-Caucasian provinces of Russia and along the southern shore of the Lakes of Van and Urumiah in the Autumn and Winter of 1837.* London, John Murray, 1839. pp. 112–282. illus. map.

British soldier-tourist describes his journeys out of Tiflis into Georgia and notes that often Russian governors in the provinces do not have a knowledge of the non-Russian languages.

209. Venables, Richard Lister. *Domestic scenes in Russia: in a series of letters describing a year's residence in that country, chiefly in the interior.* London, John Murray, 1839. 348 pp. app.

British pastor and his wife journey to St. Petersburg and Moscow in 1837–38 to visit her relatives in rural area. His account is valuable because he uses his special opportunity to observe and associate with the peasants.

210. Bell, James Stanislaus. *Journal of a residence in Circassia during the years 1837, 1838, 1839.* London, Edward Moxon, 1840. vol. I, 453 pp. vol II, 428 pp. illus. map. app.

British merchant describes people and trade prospects with an appendix of letters on the impact of Russian control over the Circassians.

211. Dallas, George Mifflin. *Diary of George Mifflin Dallas: while U. S. Minister to Russia, 1837–1839, and to England, 1856–1861.* Susan Dallas, editor. Philadelphia, Lippincott, 1892. pp. 1–214.

In his diary Dallas tells how well he got along with the nobility and how he enjoyed the society in the capital but was shocked by the plight of the serfs. He observes the extreme paternalism of the czar and concludes that behind the secretiveness of the armed forces is an army not as strong as generally believed in the West.

212. Longworth, J. A. *A year among the Circassians.* London, Colburn, 1840. vol. I, 312 pp. vol. II, 351 pp. illus.

British writer aiding the patriotic Circassians against the Russians in 1838–39 accuses the British of deserting them.

213. Cameron, George Poulett. *Personal adventures and excursions in Georgia, Circassia, and Russia.* London, Colburn, 1845. vol. I, 349 pp. vol. II, 271 pp.

British lieutenant colonel on special mission to Persia describes journey from the Caucasus to St. Petersburg, 1838–40. Cameron liked the Russians, from czar all the way down to serf; and he did not hesitate to say so, although he could be critical and commented with brutal frankness on the prevalence of bribery in government. He and Custine (see no. 215) were in Russia at the same time. They exchanged verbal blows over their respective interpretations.

214.   Hommaire de Hell, Xavier. *Travels in the steppes of the Caspian Sea, the Crimea, the Caucasus, etc.* London, Chapman & Hall, 1847. 436 pp.

French civil engineer investigates geology of the Crimea and New Russia, 1838–43. His wife writes most of the description.

215.   Custine, (Marquis) Astolphe Louis Leonard de. *Journey for our time: The journals of Marquis de Custine.* Translated and edited by Phyllis Penn Kohler. New York, Pellegrini & Cudahy, 1951. 338 pp.

The marquis, a French aristocrat and a firm believer in monarchy, journeys to St. Petersburg, Moscow, and Nizhni-Novgorod during July–October, 1839. In his account he states: "I went to Russia in search of arguments against representative government. I returned from Russia a partisan of constitutions." His account was used as ammunition against the Russian Empire by the Soviet Union and against the communists by the United States in the cold war. See no. 213.

216.   Abbott, (Captain) James F. *Narrative of a journey from Heraut to Khiva, Moscow, and St. Petersburgh, during the late Russian invasion of Khiva; with some account of the court of Khiva and the kingdom of Khaurism.* London, William H. Allen, 1856–84. II, 55–232, 260–74. illus. map. app.

Returning from his journey to Khiva in 1839–40, Captain Abbott (British army) visits Moscow and St. Petersburg, comparing them to London. Appendix includes information on the Caspian and Aral seas and on the Russian army.

217. Jesse, (Captain) William. *Notes of a half-pay in search of health: or, Russia, Circassia, and the Crimea, in 1839–1840.* London, James Madden, 1841. I, 39–298. II, 2–306. map. app.

English gentleman-soldier and his wife journey from Odessa to St. Petersburg. His comments are on the level of a typical tourist except when he states firmly that he believes Russia to be the lowest nation on the scale of power.

218. Nolte, Vincent. *Fifty years in both hemispheres; or, Reminiscences of the life of a former merchant.* New York, Redfield, 1854. pp. 438–47.

Journey to Odessa by American businessman in 1840 to collect delinquent accounts results in humorous comments on passport and quarantine restrictions he encountered.

219. Cottrell, Charles Herbert. *Recollections of Siberia.* London, John W. Parker, 1842. 410 pp.

British businessman on tour from Moscow to Irkutsk and back to St. Petersburg, 1840–41, presents Siberia as low in refinement but very high in hospitality. The exiles, whom he met and described near Lake Baikal, thought him very eccentric.

220. Eastlake, (Lady) Elizabeth (Rigby). *Letters from the shores of the Baltic.* London, John Murray, 1842. vol. I, 293 pp. vol. II. 286 pp. illus.

British noblewoman, wife of the president of the Royal Academy, journeys from St. Petersburg south in 1841. Feminine point of view illuminates much that would be missed by a man.

221. Motley, John Lothrop. *The correspondence of John Lothrop Motley.* George William Curtis, editor. London, John Murray, 1889. I, 72–99. port.

Secretary to the United States legation in St. Petersburg, November, 1841, amusingly describes his reception by Nicholas I and the boring life of the diplomat.

222. Todd, (Colonel) Charles S. *Memoir of Col. Charles S. Todd.* G. W. Griffin, author. Philadelphia, Claxton, Remsen, and Haffelfinger, 1873. pp. 84–112.

This is the first instance of a United States minister traveling to the east of Moscow. He provides brief but excellent summaries on export-import tariffs, sugar, resources, religion, etc., 1841–46.

223. Simpson, (Sir) George. *Narrative of a journey around the world, during the years 1841–1842.* London, Henry Colburn, 1847. II, 215–469. map. port.

Governor-in-chief of the Hudson's Bay Company journeys through Siberia, June–October, 1842, and writes an account that supplies detailed information on economic resources. He describes his contact with the exile system while traveling up the Lena River from Yakutsk towards Irkutsk.

224. Haxthausen-Abbenburg, (Baron) Franz August Maria von. *The Russian Empire. Its people, institutions, and resources.* Translated from the German by Robert Farie. London, Chapman and Hall, 1856. vol. I, 432 pp. vol. II, 451 pp. index.

Baron Haxthausen, a Westphalian economist and student of rural institutions, was commissioned by Nicholas I to survey European Russia. This he did in 1843, examining and describing everything, and finding most of it commendable. This account is considered a classic. See no. 225.

225. Haxthausen-Abbenburg, (Baron) Franz August Maria von. *Transcaucasia. Sketches of the nations and races between the Black Sea and the Caspian.* Translated from German by J. E. T. London, Chapman and Hall, 1854. 448 pp. illus.

In this account, which emphasizes the area east of the Black Sea, Baron Haxthausen emphasizes the primeval relations of man and soil. See no. 224.

226. *Harrison, Joseph, Jr. *The Iron Worker and King Solomon.* Philadelphia, Lippincott, 1868, pp. 29–35. illus. map.

American manufacturer of locomotives describes the years, 1843–49, he spent in Russia as co-worker with Major George Washington Whistler, consulting engineer of the St. Petersburg and Moscow Railroad. See Babey, *Americans in Russia* (no 1427).

227. Whistler, Mrs. George Washington. *The life of James McNeill Whistler.* London, Heinemann, 1908. pp. 11–23.

Whistler's mother, wife of Major George Washington Whistler, consulting engineer on the St. Petersburg and Moscow Railroad, kept a diary of their life in Russia (most of the diary is still unpublished). In these few pages she concerns herself with the state of "Jamie's" health, 1844–48.

228. Harrison, Robert. *Notes of a nine years' residence in Russia from 1844 to 1853. With notices of the Tsars Nicholas I and Alexander II.* London, Newby, 1855. 310 pp. illus.

British businessman analyzes the Russian character and concludes that (1) they always show off before foreigners, and (2) they are taught from birth to submit to authority. He describes Simbirsk on the Volga River (where Lenin was born in 1870).

229. Englishwoman in Russia. *Englishwoman in Russia, impressions of the society and manners of the Russians at home, by a lady ten years resident in that country.* London, John Murray, 1855. 350 pp. illus.

Wife of British businessman living and trading in European Russia about 1844–54. She writes a simple but very interesting account of the people and of her relations with them. She includes tales of wolves attacking and eating families traveling in open vehicles.

230. Mayo, Richard Southwell Bourke. *St. Petersburg and Moscow: a visit to the court of the Czar.* London, Colburn, 1846. vol. I, 274 pp. vol. II, pp. 1–241. app.

Young man, forced to leave the "London season," journeys to St. Petersburg and Moscow in 1845. He writes an extremely detailed account of what he sees and hears in cafe society and on the street.

231. Thompson, Edward P. *Life in Russia: or, the discipline of despotism.* London, Smith, Elder, 1848. 344 pp. illus.

Homesick Englishman, in St. Petersburg and Moscow, 1847, gives a strong clue to his impressions: ". . . display and external grandeur give the appearance of substantial wealth and happiness, but, alas, it is a hollow mockery. . . ."

232. *Burrows, Silas E. *America and Russia.* See Babey, *Americans in Russia* (no. 1427).

233. Ditson, George Leighton. *Circassia; or, a tour to the Caucasas.* London, Newby, 1850. 453 pp.

Massachusetts lawyer claims to be the first foreigner in Circassia after its penetration by Russia. During his journey, 1847–48, he sees Russia's march south as a sign of progress.

234. Hill, S. S. *Travels in Siberia.* London, Longman, et al., 1854. vol. I, 452 pp. vol. II, 432 pp. map. app.

Journey from Moscow to Irkutsk, down the Lena River to Yakutsk and northeast overland to the Sea of Okhotsk, 1847–50. In addition to a vast amount of detail on trading possibilities in Siberia, Hill comments on the exile colony in Irkutsk.

235. Pfieffer, Ida Reyer. *A woman's journey around the world from Vienna to Brazil, Chili, Tahiti, China, Hindostan, Persia, and Asia Minor.* London, National Illustrated Library, n.d. pp. 300–328.

Brief contact with Russia on the Black Sea coast, August, 1848.

236. Maxwell, John S. *The Czar; his court and people: including a tour in Norway and Sweden.* Dublin, James M'Glashan, 1849. pp. 79–306.

Touring businessman returns from a journey to St. Petersburg and Moscow, August–September, 1848, and writes a glowing account of Nicholas I and his regime. In Chapter VIII he describes the work of Major George Washington Whistler in building the railroad from St. Petersburg to Moscow. See nos. 226 and 227.

237. Atkinson, Mrs. Thomas Witlam. *Recollections of Tartar steppes and their inhabitants.* London, John Murray, 1863. 351 pp. illus. app.

Wife of British scientist-explorer (see no. 238) pays special attention to the Siberian exile system, March, 1848–September, 1853.

238. Atkinson, Thomas Witlam. *Oriental and Western Siberia: A narrative of seven years' explorations and adventures in Siberia, Mongolia, The Kirghis Steppes, Chinese Tartary, and part of central Asia.* Philadelphia, Bradley, 1859. pp. 13–346. illus. index.

British scientist-explorer-artist provides 560 sketches of Siberian people and scenery after a long visit, 1848–55. He believes himself to have been the first westerner in many of the areas, and he writes a detailed account with special emphasis on travel difficulties, weather conditions, resources, and the manners and customs of the people. See no. 237 for his wife's account of part of the journey.

239. Atkinson, Thomas Witlam. *Travels in the regions of the upper and lower Amoor and the Russian acquisitions on the confines of India and China. With adventures among the mountain Kirghis, and the Manjours, Manyargs, Toungoutz, Goldi and Gelyaks: The hunting and pastoral tribes.* London, Hurst & Blackett, 1860. 496 pp. illus. map. app. index.

Here Atkinson provides more material from his journey, 1848–55, and issues a special warning to the British about Russian ambitions in the area.

240. * Monteith, (Lieutenant Colonel) William. *Notes on Georgia and the new Russian conquest beyond the Caucasus.* London, n.p., 1853. 40 pp.

Caption title: "Description of the frontier of Russia and Persia as settled by the Commissioners in the years 1828 and 1829."

241. * Venning, John. *Memorials of John Venning, Esq. (formerly of St. Petersburgh), with num. notices from his manuscripts relative to the Imperial Family of Russia.* T. S. Henderson, editor. London, 1862. 320 pp. illus.

242. Oliphant, Laurence. *The Russian shores of the Black Sea in the Autumn of 1852 with a voyage down the Volga and a tour through the country of the Don Cossacks.* London, Blackwood, 1853. 366 pp. illus. map.

British tourist journeys from St. Petersburg to Moscow and then down the Volga to enlighten the world on the menace of Russia. He describes places and people in an informative way, especially the long journey down the Volga River, with its peculiar means of transportation and the peoples along its banks.

243. Vitzthum von Eckstaedt, Karl Friedrich. *St. Petersburg and London in the years 1852–1864. Reminiscences.* Henry Reeve, editor. Translated from the German by Edward Fairfax Taylor. London, Longmans, Green, 1887. I, 1–51.

Saxon chargé d'affaires in St. Petersburg, 1852–53, describes the court intrigue surrounding the beginnings of the Crimean War. His verbal sketch of Nicholas I paints a natural leader of his people, a little larger than human.

244. Smith, Mary Ann Pellew. *Six years' travels in Russia by an English Lady.* London, Hurst & Blackett, 1859. vol. I, 359 pp. vol. II, 357 pp. illus.

Point of view is upper-class British diplomatic family, 1852–58. Lady Mary describes rural life in such detail that includes pig-raising, danger from wolves, and other aspects of great importance to the peasant.

245. * Boyer, Alfred. *The English prisoners of Russia.* London, 1854.

246. MacGavock, Randall W. *A Tennessean abroad, or, Letters from Europe, Africa and Asia.* New York, Redfield, 1854. pp. 365–82.

Nashville lawyer journeys to St. Petersburg and Moscow in 1853 and writes light, frothy letters home of tourist spots, all with a sense of humor that laughs at irritating incidents, such as having his pocket picked.

247. Hill, S. S. *Travels on the shores of the Baltic. Extended to Moscow.* London, Hall, Virtúe, 1854. pp. 117–286.

British businessman makes another journey (see no. 234), this time to Russia's second capital, in the summer of 1853. His account is a friendly one in which he describes the customs of the Muscovites as a "mixture of devotion and drunkenness."

248. Scott, Charles Henry. *The Baltic, the Black Sea, and the Crimea: comprising travels in Russia, a voyage down the Volga to Astrachan, and a tour through Crim Tartary.* London, Bentley, 1854. 346 pp.

The account of a strenuous journey made during the summer of 1853 by a British traveler interested in seeing the impact of the beginning of the Crimean War.

249. Evelyn, George Palmer. *A diary of the Crimea.* Cyril Falls, editor. London, Gerald Duckworth, 1954. pp. 1–139. illus. port.

British mercenary describes his part in the Crimean War, 1853–55. He is especially informative on the layout of the battlefields.

250. Whishaw, James. *Memoirs of James Whishaw.* Maxwell S. Leigh, editor. London, Methuen, 1935. 288 pp. illus. port. app. index.

British medical doctor in St. Petersburg from 1853 to 1917 illuminates the life led by foreign businessmen and professional men in pre-1917 Russia.

251. Seymour, Henry Dabny. *Russia on the Black Sea and Sea of Azof; being a narrative of travels in the Crimea and bordering provinces; with notices of naval, military, and commercial resources of those countries.* London, John Murray, 1855. 361 pp. map.

British journalist describes his experiences in the winter of 1854, comparing conditions he encounters with earlier visits in 1844 and 1846.

252.   White, Andrew Dickson. *Autobiography.* New York, Century, 1905. I, 447–75. II, 1–116. illus. port. index.

American educator and college president (Cornell, 1868–85) and diplomat (minister to Germany, 1879–81; to Russia, 1892–94; ambassador to Germany, 1897–1902) describes his life in St. Petersburg and reflects on his associations with Pobedonostzev and Tolstoi.

253.   Clifford, (Brevet-Major) Henry. *Henry Clifford, v.c.: his letters and sketches from the Crimea.* London, Michael Joseph, 1956. pp. 47–282. illus. port. index.

Major Clifford sketches, in words and paint, the horror and drama of the Crimean campaign as he encounters them between September 18, 1854, and April 18, 1856.

254.   Habersham, A. W. *My last cruise; or, where we went and what we saw; being an account of visits to the Malay and Loo-Choo islands, the coasts of China, Formosa, Japan, Kamchatska, Siberia, and the mouth of the Amoor River.* Philadelphia, Lippincott, 1857. pp. 317–495.

American naval officer-merchant describes various coastal towns touched on in an 1855 cruise gathering data for new charts.

255.   * Lake, A. *Kars and our captivity in Russia: with letters from W. F. Williams.* London, 1856.

256.   McClellan, (Major General) George B. *The armies of Europe: comprising descriptions in detail of the military systems of England, France, Russia, Prussia, Austria, and Sardinia, adapting their advantages to all arms of the U. S. Service; and embodying the report of observations in Europe during the Crimean War, as military commissioner*

from the United States Government, 1855–1856. Philadelphia, Lippincott, 1861. pp. 9–35, 85–294. illus. port.

McClellan presents a very detailed report, with drawings and charts of the organization of the Russian army—an army designed for instant action and continual service.

257. Tronson, J. M. *Personal narrative of a voyage to Japan, Kamtschatka, Siberia, Tartary, and various parts of coast of China: in H.M.S. Barracouta.* London, Smith, Elder, 1859. pp. 85–167, 294–340. illus. map.

Officer on the "Barracouta" in waters near Japan just after Commodore Perry's journey describes brief visit to Petropavlovsk along with other shore trips, March, 1855–July, 1856. Tronson notes the economic potentials of the areas.

258. Edwards, Henry Sutherland. *The Russians at home and the Russians abroad: Sketches, unpolitical and political of Russian life under Alexander II.* London, William H. Allen, 1879. vol. I, 328 pp. index.

British writer-tourist writes sympathetic account of his journey between 1855 and 1859.

259. Bunbury, Selina. *Russia after the war. The narrative of a visit to that country in 1856.* London, Hurst & Blackett, 1857. vol. I, 326 pp. vol. II, 385 pp.

Professional traveler, British, describes in detail the coronation of Alexander II and offers strong criticism of the existing system of serfdom.

260. Sala, George Augustus. *A journey due north; being notes of a residence in Russia in the summer of 1856.* London, Richard Bentley, 1859. 378 pp.

English nobleman writes cynically humorous remarks about a journey in which the ridiculous is brought out in every situation. For a twentieth-century account of similar nature, see no. 982.

261. Moltke, (Count) Helmuth Karl Bernard von. *Field Marshall Count Moltke's letters from Russia.* Translated from the German by Robina Napier. London, Paul, 1878. 163 pp.

Chief of the Prussian army general staff attends the coronation of Alexander II, August 15–September 8, 1856, and writes a series of eloquent letters reflecting the observations of an intelligent tourist.

262. Spottiswoode, William. *A tarantasse journey through eastern Russia in the autumn of 1856.* London, Longman, et al., 1857. 258 pp. illus. map. app.

English gentleman journeys from St. Petersburg to Astrakan and provides useful information on travel conditions and what it is like to ride posthaste in a "tear and toss" (his name for the vehicle).

263. Train, George Francis. *An American merchant in Europe, Asia and Australia: A series of letters from Java, Singapore, China, Bengal, Egypt, the Holy Land, the Crimea, and its battlegrounds, England, Melbourne, Sidney, etc., etc.* New York, Putnam, 1857. pp. 311–41.

Boston author-businessman visits the Crimean battlefields in 1856 and describes his contacts with members of the Russian nobility.

264. Train, George Francis. *My life in many states and in foreign lands. Dictated in my seventy-fourth year.* New York, Appleton, 1902. pp. 215–21, 249–59. port.

Train recalls 1856–57 when he was in St. Petersburg, Moscow, and the Crimea, where Alexander II's brother gave him a friendly reception.

265. Collins, Perry McDonough. *A voyage down the Amoor: with a land journey through Siberia, and incidental notices of Manchooria, Kamschatka, and Japan.* New York, Appleton, 1860. 390 pp. illus.

In his capacity as commercial agent of the United States for the Amoor River, the author studies the resources of the area, May, 1856–August, 1857. In his account is a description of the way of life along the route from St. Petersburg and Moscow, east to Irkutsk, and southeast to the Amoor River. The future railroad connection between Chita and the river valley is projected. He makes the 3,545-mile journey from Moscow to Irkutsk in thirty-five days, sleeping all but three nights in a sleigh.

266. Latrobe, John Hazelhurst Boneval. *John H. B. Latrobe and his times, 1803–1891*. John E. Semmes, editor. Baltimore, Norman, Remington, 1917. pp. 473–528. illus. port. index.

Philadelphia lawyer with railroad interests journeys to St. Petersburg and Moscow. He describes court life in the capital and tells about his journey by railroad from the capital to Moscow.

267. Hume, George. *Thirty-five years in Russia*. London, Simpkin, et al., 1914. 314 pp. illus. map. port. index.

British businessman, dealing in steamships and farm machinery, locates in the Ukraine, 1857–92. His account excels in its descriptions of peasant life and is filled with objective and friendly comments.

268. Dumas, Alexandre Davy de la Pailleterie. *Adventures in Czarist Russia*. Translated and edited by A. E. Murch. London, Owen, 1960. 193 pp. illus.

For nine months in 1858 Dumas journeys from St. Petersburg to the Caucasus as the guest of the nobility. Among his remarks he includes: aspects of life to the guest of a noble, the roguery of officials, corruption in the officialdom of the czar, the character of the Russians, etc.

269. Gautier, Théophile. *Travels in Russia*. Translated and edited by F. C. de Sumichrast. New York, George D. Sproul, 1902. XIII, 100–358. XIV, 1–214. illus.

In 1858, with the purpose of bookmaking in mind, French poet and novelist journeys to St. Petersburg and Moscow and then down the Volga River. His impressions are rather romantic, but sensitively written.

270.   Heywood, Robert. *A journey in Russia in 1858.* Manchester, England, privately printed, 1918. 41 pp.

Typical tourist comments by British businessman on June–July journey. Comments especially on the dress of the common people.

271.   Pearson, Charles Henry. *Russia, by a recent traveller: A series of letters, originally published in "The Continental Review."* London, William Francis Graham, 1859. 156 pp. illus. app. index.

Using "tourist Russian," British traveler journeys from St. Petersburg to Nizhni-Novgorod by way of Moscow in 1858. Concludes that Russia is a "coming power" and observes the approaching emancipation and thinks it must be gradual to be effective.

272.   Taylor, James Bayard. *Travels in Greece and Russia, with an excursion to Crete.* New York, Putnam, 1859. pp. 315–426.

Perceptively written account of 1858 summer journey to Moscow and St. Petersburg by American poet, novelist, and traveler. He states as his purpose " . . . an attempt to sketch the gay, bizarre, incongruous *external* forms of Russian life."

273.   Smyth, Charles Piazzi. *Three cities in Russia.* London, Lovell Reeve, 1862. vol. I, 484 pp. vol. II, 528 pp. illus. map. index.

Two packed volumes of detailed observations by royal astronomer of Scotland, whose trained eye and ear join with his wife's womanly curiosity, July–October, 1859. They claim to have lived like Russians in St. Petersburg, "Moskva," and Novgorod.

274.   Tilley, Henry Arthur. *Japan, The Amoor, and the Pacific; with notices of other places comprised in a voyage of cir-*

*cumnavigation in the imperial Russian corvette "Rynda",
in 1858-1860.* London, Smith, Elder, 1861. pp. 203–49.
illus.

Tilley claims to be the first Englishman to land at the Russian
settlements in the mouth of the Amur River. He accompanies
Commodore Popoff and a squadron of three ships visiting Japanese
waters soon after Perry's visit. His account describes events in
September–October, 1859.

275. Barry, Herbert. *Russia in 1870.* London, Wyman & Sons,
     1871. 418 pp.

Russian-speaking British head of Vladimir iron works describes
his life in Russia, 1859–71, and concludes that Russia is passing
from backwardness to progress.

276. * Ely, (Marchioness) Jane (Hope-Vere) Loftus. *Mafeesh,
     or nothing new; the journal of a tour in Greece, Turkey,
     Egypt, the Sinai-Desert, Petra, Palestine, Syria, and Russia.*
     London, W. Clowes, 1870. 2 vols.

277. Thornbury, George Walter. *Criss-cross journeys.* London,
     Hurst & Blackett, 1873. II, 245–342.

Thornbury made a long trip to the United States and then paid
a brief visit to Moscow, where he was chiefly interested, in 1860,
in seeing the Siberian exiles leave for the east. His account, which
offers comparisons of Americans and Russians, may be associated
with those of Guild in 1886 (see no. 364) and Jones in 1961 (see
no. 1393).

278. English Travelers Three. *The Northern Circuit, or, brief
     notes of Sweden, Finland, and Russia.* London, Macmillan,
     1862. pp. 82–122.

Three British travelers, probably from Cambridge University,
journey to St. Petersburg and Moscow in 1861, finding the people
to be kind, courteous, and charitable, if money is not involved.
Observe that police are the terror of all respectable people and
that the government apparently encourages drinking in order to
keep control and to augment income.

279.   Clay, Cassius Marcellus. *The life of Cassius Marcellus Clay.
       Memoirs, writings and speeches, showing his conduct in
       the overthrow of American slavery, the salvation of the
       Union, and the restoration of the autonomy of the states.*
       Cincinnati, J. Fletcher Brennan, 1886. I, 293–96, 326–450.
       port.

The U.S. minister to Russia, 1861–62, 1863–69, writes a colorful
report of his experiences in the court of St. Petersburg, with which
he was favorably impressed.

280.   Laurie, William Ferguson Beatson. *Northern Europe (Den-
       mark, Sweden, Russia) local, social and political in 1861.
       With a succinct continuation down to May, 1862.* London,
       Saunders, Otley, 1862. pp. 171–254. app.

Traveling with his father in 1861–62, British tourist remarks:
"Russia is gradually becoming enlightened and liberal." Appendix
includes humorous account of "Russian wife show."

281.   Tilley, Henry Arthur. *Eastern Europe and Western Asia.
       Political and social sketches on Russia, Greece and Syria
       in 1861-2-3.* London, Longmans, et al., 1864. 247 pp.
       illus.

After his journey to the Far East (see no. 274) Tilley returned to
St. Petersburg and Moscow, and later to the Ukraine, where he
commented on the the results of emancipation.

282.   Moor, Henry. *A visit to Russia in the autumn of 1862.*
       London, Chapman and Hall, 1863. 234 pp. illus.

British aristocrat, guest of the nobility, describes life on their
estates around St. Petersburg, Moscow, and Nizhni-Novgorod—
especially, the impact of emancipation.

283.   Dixon, William Hepworth. *Free Russia.* London, Hurst &
       Blackett, 1870. vol. I, 352 pp. vol. II, 344 pp. illus.

Friendly account of a journey to the Ural Mountains area in 1863
by British scholar-traveler interested in the state of the Orthodox

church. Compares impressions of people with those from earlier visits.

284. Michie, Alexander. *The Siberian overland route from Peking to Petersburg, through the deserts and steppes of Mongolia, Tartary, etc.* London, John Murray, 1864. pp. 203–402. illus. map.

Inspired by John Bell (see no. 78) and his journey across Siberia eastward, British tourist journeys westward from China, September, 1863–January, 1864. Discusses travel modes and conditions, the Polish exiles, and the impact of emancipation on the Russian and Siberian peasantry.

285. Forsyth, William. *The great fair of Nijni-Novgorod, and how we got there.* London, Clowes, 1865. 117 pp.

British businessman and brother on tour, August, 1864, provide excellent description of the physical layout, the trading activities, and the general atmosphere of the fair.

286. Pumpelly, Raphael. *Across America and Asia. Notes of a five years' journey around the world.* New York, Leypoldt & Holt, 1870. pp. 388–427. map. index.

American geologist journeys west by sleigh across Siberia, 3,112 miles in 352 hours, December, 1864–February, 1865. A lost passport brings him into intimate contact with authorities. (Raphael Pumpelly, *My Reminiscences* [New York, Holt, 1898], II, 505–46, includes most of this account.)

287. Curtin, Jeremiah. *Memoirs of Jeremiah Curtin.* Joseph Shafer, editor. Madison, State Historical Society of Wisconsin, 1940. pp. 78–293, 662–82, 767–833. illus. port. index.

United States anthropologist, author, traveler, and one-time legation secretary in St. Petersburg, 1864–70. In these *Memoirs* Curtin describes his journeys to Russia and Siberia in various capacities, 1864–1900.

288.   Whymper, Frederick. *Travel and adventure in the territory of Alaska. Formerly Russian America—now ceded to the United States—and in various other parts of the north Pacific.* London, John Murray, 1869. pp. 84–127. illus. map. app.

British explorer and mountain climber describes journeys into Bering Strait area in 1865 and 1866. He creates a negative impression by his reference to the dirty forts of the Russians and the thievery of the Tchuktchis (Russian Eskimos).

289.   Pollington, Viscount. *Halfway around the world. Being some account of a tour in Russia, the Caucasus, Persia, and Turkey, 1865–66.* London, Edward Moxon, 1867. pp. 1–174. app. index.

A simple tourist journal by a British nobleman of a journey from St. Petersburg south to Moscow, down the Volga River, east to the Caucasus from Astrakhan, and then south, August, 1865– April, 1866.

290.   Bush, Richard J. *Reindeer, dogs and snowshoes: A journal of Siberian travel and explorations made in the years 1865, 1866 and 1867.* New York, Harper, 1871, 518 pp. illus. map. app.

Surveyor for the Western Union Telegraph Company journeys over a proposed route for a line to run between Europe and North America across Russia. Bush writes a straightforward chronological account of his travels from the Kamchatka Peninsula to Sakhalin Island to the Sea of Okhotsk, down the Anadyr River, and on to the Bering Strait. See no. 291.

291.   Kennan, George. *Tent life in Siberia and adventures among the Karaks and other tribes in Kamchatka and northern Asia.* London, Low, Son, and Marston, 1870. 425 pp. map.

Expedition by employee of Russian-American Telegraph Company to survey projected line to Europe by way of Alaska, August, 1865–January, 1868. Kennan learns Russian and acquires an acquaintanceship with native dialects, and is thus able to intelligently describe the people, customs, and scenery. See no. 290.

292. Dicey, Edward. *A month in Russia during the marriage of the Czarevich.* London, Macmillan, 1867. 72 pp.

High and low life in St. Petersburg is described by member of the Prince of Wales' party that attended the wedding of Alexander (III) to Princess Dagmar of Denmark, November, 1866.

293. Loubat, (Duke) Joseph Florimond. *Narrative of the mission to Russia, in 1866, of the Hon. Gustavus Vasa Fox.* John D. Champlin, Jr., editor. New York, Appleton, 1873. 424 pp. illus. app.

In 1866 Alexander II escaped assassination and the people of the United States, having just lost their leader by a successful attempt, were so strongly moved that Congress passed a joint resolution and commissioned Fox to carry a message of congratulation to Alexander II. Loubat, his secretary, describes the voyage of the clumsy Civil War monitor and its escorts to the capital city, the riotous receptions accorded Fox and the United States officers and sailors, and various other peculiarities of the trip in St. Petersburg and later in Moscow, including the *Miantonomah Galop,* a piece of music dedicated to Fox.

294. Appleton, (Brevet Captain) Nathan. *Russian life and society. As seen in 1866–67 by Appleton and Longfellow, two young travelers from the United States of America, who had been officers in the Union Army, and a journey to Russia with General Banks in 1869.* Boston, Murray and Emery, 1904. 226 pp. illus. index.

A series of letters written from Russia describes experiences of many kinds, including tea drinking, horse racing, railroad travel, the city of Moscow and its environs, etc.

295. Twain, Mark (pseudonym of Samuel Langhorne Clemens). *The Innocents Abroad, or, the new Pilgrims' Progress:*

*being some account of the Steamship Quaker City's pleasure
excursion to Europe and the Holy Land; with descriptions
of countries, nations, incidents and adventures, as they
appeared to the Author.* Hartford, Connecticut, American
Publishing Company, 1870. pp. 381–402. illus.

Missouri-born humorist and author describes a brief contact with
Russia, July–August, 1867. Considers Odessa to be "like an
American city" and, after meeting him, likens Alexander II to
"a tinsel king."

296.   Carroll, Lewis (pseudonym of Charles Lutwidge Dodgson).
        *The Russian Journal and other selections from the works
        of Lewis Carroll.* John Francis McDermott, editor. New
        York, Dutton, 1935. pp. 71–121.

Typical tourist's remarks by author of *Alice in Wonderland,* July–
August, 1867. He travels the new railroad from St. Petersburg to
Moscow, witnesses a wedding, describes a meal, and rides in a
tarantasse. Especially interested in religion, he describes many
religious sites in detail.

297.   Montgomery, James Eglinton. *Our Admiral's flag abroad.
        The cruise of Admiral D. G. Farragut, commanding the
        European squadron in 1867–68 in the flag-ship Franklin.*
        New York, Putnam, 1869. pp. 47–99. illus.

Private secretary to the United States admiral writes a detailed
account of his visit to St. Petersburg and Moscow, of his reception
by Emperor Alexander II, and of the attempt to cement relations,
"which have always existed," between the two countries.

298.   Freshfield, Douglas William. *Travels in the Central Cau-
        casus and Bashan, including visits to Ararat and Tabreez
        and ascents of Kazbek and Elbruz.* London, Longmans,
        Green, 1869. pp. 141–496. app.

British mountain climber, fellow of the Royal Geographical
Society, describes the non-political aspects of his journey in 1868.
Returning home, he visits St. Petersburg and Moscow, as well as

Tiflis. Appendix includes a catalog of plants and the heights of peaks.

299. Lamont, James. *Yachting in the Arctic Seas; or notes of five voyages of sport and discovery in the neighborhood of Spitzbergen and Novaya Zemlya.* London, Chatto & Windus, 1876. pp. 1–198. illus. map.

British businessman discusses commercial possibilities after May, 1869, journey.

300. Whyte, William Athenry. *A land journey from Asia to Europe: being an account of a camel and sledge journey from Canton to St. Petersburg through the plains of Mongolia and Siberia.* London, Sampson, Low, 1871. pp. 188–336. illus. map.

Whyte's account is detailed but with little on Russian contacts, winter, 1869–70.

301. Knox, Thomas W. *Overland through Asia. Pictures of Siberian, Chinese, and Tartar life. Travels and adventures in Kamchatka, Siberia, China, Mongolia, Chinese Tartary and European Russia, with full accounts of the Siberian exiles, their treatment, condition, and mode of life, a description of the Amoor River, and the Siberian Shores of the Frozen Ocean.* Hartford, Connecticut, American Publishing Co., 1870. 608 pp. illus. map. port.

Member of United States surveying expedition planning route for future line journeys from Kamchatka across Siberia to St. Petersburg revealing the severe treatment accorded the exiles. (See especially Lansdell, no. 334, and Kennan, no. 359.)

302. Wallace, Donald Mackenzie. *Russia.* New York, Holt, 1881. 609 pp. index. Paperback edition: (Sir) Donald Mackenzie Wallace. *Russia on the eve of war and revolution.* Cyril E. Black, editor. New York, Random House (Vintage Books), 1961. 528 pp.

British doctor of laws, studying in Germany, accepts a private invitation to visit Russia after reading Haxthausen-Abbenburg's works (see nos. 224, 225). Wallace learned Russian and remained in Russia for five years, 1870–75, immediately after the emancipation. His work is a classic treatment that examines every aspect of European Russia, with special emphasis on the rural scene.

303.   Cunynghame, (Sir) Arthur Augustus Thurlow. *Travels in the Eastern Caucasus, on the Caspian and Black Seas, especially in Daghestan, and on the frontiers of Persia and Turkey, during the summer of 1871.* London, John Murray, 1872. 355 pp. illus. map. app.

British lord and his son, tourist-observers, record a sympathetic visit, July–September, to the Black Sea fortifications.

304.   Wellesley, (Colonel) Frederick Arthur. *With the Russians in peace and war.* London, Eveleigh Nash, 1905. 324 pp. illus. port.

British military attaché in St. Petersburg, 1871–78, describes activities common to his office, with some mention of the Nihilists.

305.   Prime, Samuel Irenaeus. *The Alhambra and the Kremlin. The south and the north of Europe.* New York, Randolph, 1873. pp. 284–370.

Presbyterian clergyman-author from the United States journeys to St. Petersburg and Moscow in 1872. Claims to have identified himself with the lower classes, but does not claim knowledge of the Russian language.

306.   Proctor, Edna Dean. *A Russian journey.* Boston, Osgood, 1873. 321 pp. illus.

Friendly and favorable tourist impressions of journey from St. Petersburg to Kishinev to the Volga River through the Crimea, summer, 1872. A somewhat rhapsodic description of wonderful Russia and its czar, whom she saw from a distance.

307. Harvie-Brown, John Alexander. *Travels of a naturalist in northern Europe, Norway, 1871, Archangel, 1872, Petchora, 1875.* London, Fisher Unwin, 1905. I, 125–260. II, 261–477. illus. map. port. app. index.

Study of bird life around the White and Kara seas by British ornithologist, who describes in addition the people he met and their way of life.

308. Atkinson, Joseph Beavington. *An art tour to northern capitals of Europe.* London, Macmillan, 1873. pp. 149–448. index.

British art critic journeys to St. Petersburg, Moscow, and Kiev in 1873. His work concerns his study of the art treasures, but he does include some remarks on the way of life.

309. Baker, Valentine. *Clouds in the East: Travels and adventures on the Perso-Turkoman frontier.* London, Chatto & Windus, 1876. pp. 312–76. illus. map.

Some remarks on a journey from Tiflis to St. Petersburg by British colonel in 1873. Includes "A political and strategical report on Central Asia."

310. Carrington, George. *Behind the scenes in Russia.* London, George Bell, 1874. 224 pp.

British writer comments on difficulties facing a foreigner teaching in Russia in 1873, a land where there is a strong drive to be educated. He is very critical of the Orthodox church.

311. Ker, David. *On the road to Khiva.* London, Henry S. King, 1874. 359 pp. illus. map.

London *Daily Telegraph* special correspondent uses a United States passport to bypass restrictions on Englishmen attempting to enter the area in 1873. Describes Russian threat to British-dominated Afghanistan.

312. MacGahan, Januarius Aloysius. *Campaigning on the Oxus and the fall of Khiva.* London, Sampson, Low, 1874. 438 pp. illus. map.

Correspondent of the New York *Herald* is present when Khiva becomes a Russian protectorate, on April 19, 1873.

313. Schuyler, Eugene. *Turkistan. Notes of a journey in Russian Turkistan, Khokand, Bukhara, and Kuldja.* New York, Scribner, Armstrong, 1877. vol. I, 335 pp. vol. II, 389 pp. illus. map. app.

Scholarly first secretary of United States legation in St. Petersburg journeys down the Volga River and through Central Asia, March 23–November 15, 1873, by train, boat, and sledge to study the sociopolitical conditions of the regions recently annexed by Russia.

314. Guthrie, (Mrs.) Katherine Blanche. *Through Russia from St. Petersburg to Astrakan and the Crimea.* London, Hurst & Blackett, 1874. vol. I, 324 pp. vol. II, 287 pp. illus.

Observations by a British art critic who journeys from St. Petersburg to Odessa studying art collections and people, summer, 1873.

315. Buckham, George. *Notes from the journal of a tourist.* New York, Gavin Houston, 1890. II, 385–421. index.

American tourist and his wife visit St. Petersburg and Moscow, July 21–August 8, 1873. His comments are casual and typical, although he does make some observations about the religious devotion of the people and their strict observance of the law, due to fear of extreme punishment.

316. Meignan, Victor. *From Paris to Pekin over Siberian snows. A narrative of a journey by sledge over the snows of European Russia and Siberia, by caravan through Mongolia, across the Gobi desert and the great wall, and by mule palanquin through China to Pekin.* Translated and edited by William Conn. London, Sonnenschein, 1889. pp. 1–284. illus. app.

Journey by a French traveler who wanted to see Siberia in wintertime. On the whole, he writes favorably of the land and its people, although he denounces the exile system by indirection. November, 1873–March, 1874.

317. Rae, Edward. *The land of the north wind, or, Travels among the Laplanders and the Samoyeds.* London, John Murray, 1875. pp. 144–352. illus. map.

British fellow of the Royal Geographic Society comments on his encounters with Russians in his study of the Arctic peoples in 1874.

318. Wood, Herbert. *The shores of Lake Aral.* London, Smith, Elder, 1876. 352 pp. map.

Major in the Royal Engineers accompanies 1874 expedition of the Imperial Russian Geographical Society to explore the economic possibilities of newly annexed area.

319. Johnson, Henry. *The life and voyages of Joseph Wiggins, F.R.G.S. Modern discoverer of the Kara Sea route to Siberia based on his journals and letters.* New York, Dutton, 1907. pp. 22–255, 268–300, 317–25. illus. port. index.

Between 1874 and 1896 Wiggins made many journeys to the Arctic and had many encounters with the Russians. Excellent illustrations of people and the land.

320. Reed, (Sir) Edward James. *Letters from Russia in 1875.* London, John Murray, 1876. 90 pp.

British marine engineer's letters in 1875 describing Russian naval stations and ironclads on the Black Sea.

321. * Seebohm, Henry. *Siberia in Europe: a visit to the valley of the Petchora in northeast Russia: with descriptions of the natural history, migration of birds, etc.* London, John Murray, 1880. 311 pp. illus. map.

322.   Burnaby, Frederick Gustavus. *A ride to Khiva. Travels and adventures in Central Asia.* London, Cassell, Petter & Galpin, 1877. 365 pp. map. app.

Captain of the British Horse Guards journeys from St. Petersburg to Transcaspia, December, 1875–March, 1876, to check on czarist plans for Central Asia. He provides a detailed description of the way of life in, and out of, the cities. A useful appendix includes data on the Russian advance to the east, the suppression of Anglican missionary efforts, Russian immorality in Asia, etc.

323.   * W. R. (pseudonym of G. W. R. Pigott). *Savage and civilized Russia.* London, Cambridge, 1877. 216 pp.

324.   Bryce, (Lord) James. *Transcaucasia and Ararat: being notes of a vacation tour in the autumn of 1876.* London, Macmillan, 1878. 420 pp.

British political philosopher and traveler describes his journey down the Volga River to Mt. Ararat and his ascent and return to Europe by way of the Black Sea, August–October, 1876. Very well written, with many historical comparisons between the United States and Russia.

325.   Telfer, (Commander) John Buchan. *The Crimea and Transcaucasia, being the narrative of a journey in the Kouban, in Gouria, Georgia, Armenia, Ossety, Imertia, Swannety, and Mingrelia, and in the Tauric range.* London, Henry S. King, 1876. vol. I, 297 pp. vol. II, 230 pp. illus. map. app.

British naval officer and his wife take a 92-day journey in 1876 with the purpose of encouraging tourism. Detailed appendixes are supplied on timetables, routes, food, wines, etc.

326.   Eyre, Selwyn. *Sketches of Russian life and customs made during a visit in 1876–7.* London, Remington, 1878. 337 pp.

Notes on the English colony in Moscow, July, 1876–August, 1877, by British correspondent, during Russo-Turkish War.

327. Seebohm, Henry. *Siberia in Asia: A visit to the valley of the Yenesay in E. Siberia. With description of the natural history, migration of birds, etc.* London, John Murray, 1882. 298 pp. illus. map. index.

Comments on birds and people by British ornithologist in 1877. See no. 321.

328. Greene, Francis Vinton. *Sketches of army life in Russia.* New York, Scribner's, 1881. 326 pp.

Military attaché, United States legation in St. Petersburg, describes the czar, the Russian soldiers, their campaigns, war correspondents, and other military matters in 1877–78.

329. Hoffman, Wickham. *Leisure hours in Russia.* London, George Bell, 1883. pp. 1–30.

Secretary of United States legation, St. Petersburg, 1877–82, writes a brief description of middle-class Russian life, with an added item on superstition.

330. Christie, (Reverend) James. *Men and things Russian, or, Holiday travels in the lands of the Tsar.* Edinburgh, Andrew Elliot, 1879. 216 pp.

With "nothing in prejudice, or to serve any end but that of truth" acting chaplain to British forces in Europe tours St. Petersburg, Moscow, and Kiev in the autumn of 1878, and writes a sympathetic account of people and their lives. Also notes the growth of Nihilism.

331. Young, John Russell. *Around the world with General Grant: A narrative of the visit of General U. S. Grant, ex-president of the United States to various countries in Europe, Asia, and Africa in 1877, 1878, 1879. To which are added certain conversations with General Grant on questions connected with American politics and history.* New York, American News Co., 1879. pp. 464–94. illus.

Young, secretary to General Grant and correspondent of the New York *Herald,* describes the receptions for Grant in St. Petersburg and Moscow, July–August, 1878. A typical tourist's account.

332. Nordenskjold, Nils Adolf Erik. *The voyage of the Vega around Asia and Europe.* Translated from the Swedish by Alexander Leslie. London, Macmillan, 1883. pp. 1–377. illus. map. port.

Swedish explorer sails across the Arctic Ocean from the Kara Sea to the Bering Strait, July 21, 1878–August 14, 1879. He reports on life among the Chukchis, on the resources of northern Siberia, and on his journey up and down the Yenisei River.

333. Cushman, (Mrs.) Mary Ames. *She wrote it all down.* Alice Dalgliesh, editor. New York, Scribner's, 1936. pp. 62–69. illus. port.

Thirteen-year-old's impressions of St. Petersburg during the Christmas holidays, December, 1879.

334. Lansdell, Henry. *Through Siberia.* Boston. Houghton Mifflin, 1882. vol. I, 376 pp. vol. II, 373 pp. illus. port. app. biblio.

Lansdell, an Anglican minister and very much interested in prison reform, journeys through Siberia, May–September, 1879, distributing religious tracts. He describes the exile system as an effective and fair system, but was accused of being nothing but an agent of government propaganda (see Buel, no. 346). See also Kennan, no. 359.

335. Dufferin and Ava, (Marchioness) Hariot. *My Russian and Turkish journals.* London, John Murray, 1916. pp. 1–123. illus. index.

British ambassador's wife describes her social life, 1879–81, from immediately after the Congress of Berlin to the assassination of Alexander II. Much trivia along with an awareness of political events and activities of the Nihilists. She says nothing about her husband's work or the activities of other embassies.

336. O'Donovan, Edmond. *The Merv oasis. Travels and adventures east of the Caspian during the years 1879–80–81. Including five mo. residence among the Tekkes of Merv.* London, Smith, Elder, 1882. vol. I, 502 pp. vol. II, 475 pp. illus. map. app.

Irish correspondent for American and English newspapers describes the significance of the Merv political situation, February 5, 1879–November 26, 1881.

337. Bliss, Richard W., compiler. Revised by Raymond Lee Newcomb. *Our lost explorers: The narrative of the Jeannette Arctic expedition as related by the survivors; and in the records and last journals of Lieutenant de Long.* San Francisco, Bancroft, 1882. 479 pp. illus. map. port.

In 1879 Gordon Bennett, owner of the New York *Herald,* stirred by Nordenskjold's (see no. 332) journeys to the Arctic, equipped the "Jeannette" with three years' provisions to explore northwest of the Bering Strait. Lt. George Washington de Long, United States Navy, was to command the vessel, with Lt. John W. Danenhower as navigator. A special act of Congress made it a national undertaking. Lt. De Long and his ship were last heard from on September 3, 1879. Later, it was learned that the "Jeannette" had sunk in 1881. Some of her crew survived after crossing the ice to the Siberian shore. Melville (see no. 338) found the accounts herein in 1882. See nos. 345 and 348.

338. Melville, George W. *In the Lena delta. A narrative of the search for Lieut.-Commander DeLong and his companions, followed by an account of the Greely relief expedition and a proposed method of reaching the North Pole.* Melville Philips, editor. Boston, Houghton Mifflin, 1885. 497 pp. illus. map. port. app.

Chief engineer of the "Jeannette" (see no. 337) describes its voyage to the Arctic, its sinking, and his search for Lt. De Long and others who survived to reach the Lena River delta, but died there. Melville then tells how he and his companions survived through the kindly offices of the Siberians. See also nos. 345 and 348.

339. Baddeley, John F. *Russia in the "Eighties." Sport and politics.* London, Longmans, Green, 1921. 466 pp. illus. map. index.

Special correspondent to the *London Standard* and protégé of Count Peter Schouvaloff describes hunting and other sports as well as court life, 1879–88.

340. Foster, John W. *Diplomatic memoirs.* Boston, Houghton Mifflin, 1909. I, 146–238. illus. port.

Envoy extraordinary and minister plenipotentiary, American embassy, 1880–81 and 1897, presents an excellent account of embassy and court life, with a detailed description of the assassination of Alexander II, his funeral, and the treatment accorded the assassins by Alexander III.

341. Cox, Samuel S. *Arctic sunbeams: or From Broadway to the Bosphorus by way of the North Cape.* New York, Putnam, 1882. pp. 219–341. illus.

Professional writer of travel books from the United States presents a somewhat above-average description of his journey to St. Petersburg, Moscow, Kiev, and Odessa, 1881.

342. Huntly, Charles Gordon. *Travel, sport and politics in the east of Europe.* London, Chapman & Hall, 1887. pp. 46–207.

British nobleman-journalist describes his journey to the Crimea and the Caucasus in 1881, where he saw increased Russo-Turkish tension.

343. Tissot, Victor. *Russians and Germans.* Translated from the French by Stephen L. Simeon. London, Remington, 1882. 293 pp.

Tour of St. Petersburg, Moscow, and the Ukraine in 1881 by French writer who observes that a country like Russia, with its backwardness, corruption and political inefficiency, will naturally be host to something like Nihilism.

344. Gallenga, Antonio Carlo Napoleone. *A summer tour in Russia.* London, Chapman & Hall, 1882. 426 pp. map.

Journey from St. Petersburg to Tiflis, summer, 1881, by British professional traveler-writer. He writes on rural economic conditions, the exile system, Nihilism, etc., and paints a vivid verbal picture of the poor Russian workingman.

345. Gilder, William Henry. *Ice-pack and tundra. An account of the search for the "Jeannette" on a sledge journey through Siberia.* New York Scribner's, 1883. 334 pp. illus. map. port.

New York *Herald* correspondent describes search around Wrangel Island from July, 1881–August, 1882. See nos. 337, 338, and 348 for details on the voyage of the "Jeannette."

346. Buel, James William. *Russian Nihilism and exile life in Siberia. A graphic and chronological history of Russia's bloody nemesis, and a description of exile life in all its true but horrifying phases. Being the results of a tour through Russia and Siberia made by the author, who carried with him letters of commendation from both the American and Russian governments.* Philadelphia, Historical Publishing Co., 1883. 574 pp.

Implications of Illinois author-journalist's account are to be seen in the title of his book, based on a journey made in 1882. His account concludes with a description of the mistreatment of the Jews.

347. Lansdell, Henry. *Russian Central Asia including Kuldja, Bokhara, Khiva and Merv.* London, Row,, Marston, Searl & Rivington, 1885. vol. I, 676 pp. vol. II, 505 pp. illus. map. app. biblio. index.

This journey of June through December was considered by Lansdell to complete the philanthropic work begun in 1879 (see no. 334). Again, he gives the exile system a clean bill of health. See Buel, no. 346, and Kennan, no. 359.

348.　Schuetze, William Henry. *William Henry Schuetze.* Charles Deering, editor. Chicago, Donnelly, 1903. pp. 17–155. illus. map. port.

In 1882, young lieutenant-commander, United States Navy, journeys to Siberia to bring home the bodies of the "Jeannette" victims. In 1885 he returned to Siberia, carrying gifts to those who had aided the survivors of the disaster. His letters to his mother describe the journey with dignity and sympathy. See nos. 337, 338, and 345.

349.　Hunt, William H. *The life of William H. Hunt.* Thomas Hunt, editor. Brattleboro, Vt., privately printed, 1922. pp. 271–83.

United States ambassador to St. Petersburg, 1882–84, analyzes the relationship between the czar and his people in a letter dated November 6, 1883. He includes criticism of the way the Russians treat the Jews.

350.　McCagg, Ezra Butler. *Six weeks of vacation in 1883.* Chicago, McDonnell, 1884. pp. 5-113.

A typical tourist, a lawyer from the United States, describes his journey to the Volga River and Tiflis.

351.　Waddington, Mary King. *Letters of a diplomat's wife. 1883–1900.* New York, Scribner's, 1903. pp. 92–120. illus. port.

Granddaughter of Rufus King describes the coronation of Alexander III in 1883. She also includes the court life in St. Petersburg and the Moscow Kremlin by moonlight.

352.　Wells, (Mrs.) Sara Furnas. *Ten years around the world, or, from land to land, isle to isle, and sea to sea, embracing twenty tours.* West Milton, Ohio, Morning Star Publishing Co., 1885. pp. 593–609. illus.

American tourist describes the coronation of Alexander III in May, 1883.

353.   Buckley, James Monroe. *The midnight sun. The Tsar and the Nihilist. Adventures and observations in Norway, Sweden and Russia.* Boston, Lothrop, 1886. pp. 149–396. illus.

Methodist clergyman from the United States studies the "burning question" of Nihilism on a standard tour in 1884. He observes that Nihilism is inherent in Russian autocracy, and only the overthrow of the government will end it.

354.   Hare, Augustus John Cuthbert. *Studies in Russia.* London, Smith, Elder, 1885. 482 pp. index.

British tour director–artist produces guide to sites from St. Petersburg to Kiev, 1884. He is especially detailed on "The New Jerusalem" monastery near Moscow.

355.   Lewis, Alexander Leonard. *Life of Alonzo Taft.* New York, Hawke Publishing Co., 1920. pp. 183–88.

United States ambassador to Russia notes some of his impressions during 1884–85.

356.   Leland, Lilian. *Traveling alone. A woman's journey around the world.* New York, American News Co., 1890, pp. 269–79.

"Russia is dirty, her people are likewise," but it is "a holy land and a pious people," concludes this tourist after seven days in St. Petersburg and Moscow, July 13–20, 1885.

357.   Meriwether, Lee. *A tramp trip. How to see Europe on fifty cents a day.* New York, Harper, 1887. pp. 203–30. port.

Missouri lawyer-author, commissioned by the United States secretary of the interior to report on labor conditions in Europe, briefly visits Russia on his journey in 1885–86. He attempts an analysis of the socioeconomic condition of the humble Russian.

358.   Yate, Arthur Campbell. *England and Russia face to face in Asia. Travels with the Afghan Boundary Commission.* London, Blackwood, 1887. 452 pp. map. app.

British correspondent of London *Daily Telegraph* describes way of life along the Oxus River in 1885–86, along with his very detailed account of the negotiations attending the boundary settlement.

359.   Kennan, George. *Siberia and the exile system.* New York, Century, 1891. vol. I, 409 pp. vol. II, 471 pp. illus. port. app. biblio. index.

Kennan, hoping to refute the allegations of brutality in the Russian exile system, journeys to Siberia with George Frost, a *Century Magazine* journalist. After an 8,000-mile journey from June, 1885–March, 1886, with the full support and help of the St. Petersburg authorities, he shocks the world and angers the Russians by his full description of venality, harshness, brutality, and inefficiency as he found them. See nos. 346 and 347.

360.   Lothrop, Almira (Strong). *The court of Alexander III.* William Prall, editor. Philadelphia, Winston, 1910. pp. 1–177. illus.

Wife of United States minister plenipotentiary and envoy extraordinary describes her life in court and home in St. Petersburg, 1885–87.

361.   Yate, (Major) Charles E. *Northern Afghanistan; or letters from the Afghan Boundary Commission.* London, Blackwood, 1888. 430 pp. map. index.

British major in Indian army writes a series of letters, 1885–88, as negotiations on the Afghanistan boundary go on between Russia and England.

362.   Hedin, Sven Anders. *My life as an explorer.* Translated from Swedish by Alfhild Huebsch. Garden City, New York, Garden City Publishing Co., 1925. pp. 1–184. illus. index.

Swedish explorer and geographer describes his experiences in climbing and hiking in the Pamirs, 1885–95. He has some comments on Anglo-Russian tension in Central Asia.

363. Gaussen, William Frederick Armytage. *Memorials of a short life. A biographical sketch of W. F. A. Gaussen with essays on Russian life and literature*. G. F. Browne, editor. London, Fisher Unwin, 1895. pp. 61–263. illus. port.

British translator of Russian literature into English, who loves Russia and hopes to further East-West friendship by his work, makes two journeys: in 1886 to see the Baku oil fields, and in 1890–91 to study Russian in St. Petersburg and Moscow. Although he knew the language, his remarks are those of the typical tourist.

364. Guild, Curtis. *Britons and Muscovites, or, Traits of two empires*. Boston, Lee & Shepard, 1888. pp. 90–230.

Guild, editor and writer from the United States, journeys to Britain and Russia, and compares the two. His journey followed the familiar path from St. Petersburg to Moscow and then to Nizhni-Novgorod, and return, but he is observant. See Jones, no. 1393, for a traveler from Britain who compares his journeys to the United States and the U.S.S.R.

365. Stevens, Thomas. *Around the world on a bicycle*. New York, Scribner's, 1887. pp. 250–68. illus. port.

New York *World* correspondent, riding large-front-wheel, small-rear-wheel bicycle, touches briefly in southern Caucasus in 1886.

366. Ballou, Maturin Murray. *Due North or glimpses of Scandinavia and Russia*. Boston, Ticknor, 1887. pp. 193–352.

Massachusetts author and journalist travels to St. Petersburg, Moscow, and Niznhi-Novgorod in the summer of 1886 and returns to castigate the venality of officials.

367. * Davis, Sarah Matilda Henry. *Norway nights and Russian days*. New York, Fords, Howard & Hulbert, 1887. pp. 213–325. illus.

United States tourist describes shops and sights in St. Petersburg and Moscow in the summer of 1886. Claims to have been undisturbed by the evidence of Nihilist activity. See Babey, *Americans in Russia* (no. 1427).

368.   * Bouton, John Bell. *Roundabout to Moscow, an epicurian journey.* New York, Appleton Century, 1887. pp. 203–349, 419–21.

Journey to St. Petersburg and Moscow by United States tourist in July, 1886. See Babey, *Americans in Russia* (no. 1427).

369.   Curtis, William Eleroy. *The land of the Nihilist. Russia; its people, its palaces, its politics.* Chicago, Belford, Clarke, 1888. 323 pp. illus.

Chicago *Daily News* correspondent and wife journey to St. Petersburg, Moscow, and surroundings in 1887. Their account, which is otherwise ordinary, puts emphasis on press censorship.

370.   De Windt, Harry. *From Pekin to Calais by land.* London, Chapman & Hall, 1889, pp. 268–647. illus. map.

A chatty, gossipy account by a professional author-traveler-lecturer who acquires a smattering of Russian and some knowledge of prison life during a series of journeys, 1887–1906. He gives special emphasis to Irkutsk and Tomsk, two of the main exile stations in 1887, and is very critical of the treatment accorded political prisoners.

371.   Freshfield, Douglas William. *The exploration of the Caucasus.* London, Edward Arnold, 1902. I, 80–278. II, 1–20, 115–73, 191–220. illus. map. app.

British mountain climber and scientist makes two journeys in 1887 and 1889 that yield much new material. See no. 298.

372.   Brandes, (Dr.) Georg. *Impressions of Russia.* Translated from the Danish by Samuel C. Eastman. London, Walter Scott, 1889. 353 pp. port.

Danish professor of literature journeys to St. Petersburg and Moscow, invited by the Russian Authors' Association, spring, 1887.

In the first part of his account he discusses the character and life of the people. The second part is devoted to their literature.

373. Heath, Perry S. *A Hoosier in Russia. The only White Tsar—his imperialism, country and people.* New York, Lorborn, 1888. 152 pp. illus. port.

Indiana publisher and editor defends the exile system and the Russian system of passport control, then condemns Nihilism and all its implications, after his journey in the summer of 1887.

374. Aldrich, Herbert L. *Arctic Alaska and Siberia, or, Eight months with the Arctic whalemen.* Chicago, Rand, McNally, 1889, pp. 42–62. illus.

Doing research on the New Bedford whaling industry, writer from the United States sails with the fleet, through the Bering Strait into the Arctic Ocean. He describes his impressions of Siberian Eskimo life in June, 1887.

375. Cutting, Charles F. *Glimpses of Scandinavia and Russia.* Boston, Thomas Groom, 1887. pp. 55–94.

American businessman's brief remarks on journey, July–August, 1887. He makes some special comment on alcoholism.

376. Dobson, George. *Russia's railway advance into Central Asia. Notes of a journey from St. Petersburg to Samarkand.* London, Allen, 1890. 436 pp. illus. map. app.

Attending the opening of the Central Asian Railway, British political observer sees the danger of Russian advance in 1888 to English aspirations in Afghanistan and India.

377. Mummery, Albert Frederick. *My climbs in the Alps and Caucasus.* Oxford, Basil Blackwell, 1936. pp. 203–29.

Famous climber comments briefly on his contacts with the Russians in 1888.

378. Stead, William Thomas. *Truth about Russia.* London, Cassell, 1888. 457 pp. index.

The editor of *Pall Mall,* a British journal, travels to St. Petersburg and Moscow in 1888 to study the Anglo-Russian war scare. He favors friendship with Russia and interviews Tolstoy. He describes all aspects of Russian life, especially forces that he believes make for peace or war.

379.   Blackstock, E. Frazer. *The land of the Viking and the empire of the Tsar.* New York, Putnam, 1889. 213 pp. illus.

A brief account by a typical woman tourist who sees all the sights in St. Petersburg and Moscow, summer, 1888. She contrasts Russians with Americans and Europeans, always to the Russians' detriment. A phrase she uses repeatedly may characterize her attitude: "one Russian and one civilized."

380.   Abercromby, (Lord) John. *A trip through the Eastern Caucasus, with a chapter on the languages of the country.* London, Edward Stanford, 1889. pp. 1–296. illus. map. app. index.

Gentleman traveler from Britain on tour, July–August, 1888. Friendly observer writes detailed account of Caucasian life.

381.   * McConaughy, David, Jr. *Rambles through Russia.* Philadelphia, Lippincott, 1888. pp. 8–16.

United States delegate to Young Men's Christian Association conference in Stockholm, September, 1888, writes of peoples' loyalty to church and state, as he sees them, in St. Petersburg and Moscow. See Babey, *Americans in Russia* (no. 1427).

382.   Cook, Charles. *The prisons of the world. With stories of crime, criminals and convicts.* London, Morgan & Scott, 1891. pp. 160–72, 190–95. port.

On two journeys, in 1889 and in 1890, British clergyman distributes Bibles and tracts in St. Petersburg and Moscow prisons. He describes the conditions he observes as satisfactory.

383.   Howard, Benjamin Douglas. *Life with Trans-Siberian savages.* London, Longmans, Green, 1893. 209 pp.

British medical doctor and amateur anthropologist travels to Sakhalin Island in 1889, where he lives with the Russian governor on native reservation. He hears about the prison compounds while in Vladivostok and secures permission to visit Sakhalin. His comments on the exile system are very critical.

384. Sessions, Francis Charles. *From the land of the midnight sun to the Volga.* New York, Welch, Fracker, 1890. pp. 96–167. illus. port. app.

President of the Ohio Historical and Archaeological Society tours from St. Petersburg to Nizhni-Novgorod in 1889. He describes what he sees with credulity, but he does observe the growing Nihilism.

385. Newton, William Wilberforce. *A run through Russia. The story of a visit to Count Tolstoi.* Hartford, Student Publishing Co., 1894. 211 pp. illus.

Journey to St. Petersburg and Moscow by Pennsylvania Episcopal clergyman, April 2–15, 1889. He interviews Tolstoy and spends a day on the estate of Prince Ourouzeff.

386. Dillon, Emile Joseph. *Russian traits and terrors. A faithful picture of Russia today.* Boston, Tucker, 1891, 288 pp.

Professor Dillon strongly indicts the czarist regime, about 1889–90. Adviser to Count Sergei Witte, correspondent for the London *Daily Telegraph,* and instructor in comparative philology at Kharkov University, Dillon (of British ancestry and educated in Russia) discusses such traits as lying, fatalism, sloth, dishonesty, sexual immorality, along with the terrors of Russian prisons, the treatment of Jews, and censorship (see nos. 428 and 886).

387. Gowing, Lionel Francis. *Five thousand miles on a sledge. A mid-winter journey across Siberia.* New York, Appleton, 1890. pp. 33–257. illus. map.

Businessman from the United States supports Kennan's judgment of the exile system although grateful to Lansdell, who gave him letters of introduction, 1889–90. See nos. 334, 347, and 359.

388.   Oriental widow. *Light thrown on a hideous empire.* London, Neville Beeman, 1897. 143 pp. app.

Satiric diatribe against Russia by anonymous critic in the 1890's. Accuses the venal officials of treating the people like cattle, with the middle class required to purchase costly trading permits.

389.   Child, Theodore. *The Tsar and his people, or, Social life in Russia.* New York, Harper, 1891. pp. 151–97, 201–390. map.

American artist on typical tour—St. Petersburg, Moscow, Nizhni-Novgorod—about 1890.

390.   * Cohen, Joseph Jacob. *The house stood forlorn. Legacy of remembrance of a boyhood in the Russia of the late 19th century.* Paris, 1954.

391.   Howard, Benjamin Douglas. *Prisoners of Russia; a personal study of convict life in Sakhalin and Siberia.* New York, Appleton, 1902. 389 pp. illus. port.

Return visit of British medical doctor (see no. 383) to Sakhalin in 1890. Writes a detailed account of every aspect of the treatment of prisoners, including use of the knout. He claims Kennan (see no. 359) was wrong and recommends the Russian system to the world.

392.   * Morris, I. *A summer in Kieff.* London, 1891.

393.   Stoddard, Charles Augustus. *Across Russia. From the Baltic to the Danube.* New York, Scribner's, 1891. pp. 27–231. illus.

Clergyman from the United States visits St. Petersburg, etc., in 1890 and draws some conclusions of the typical tourist.

394.   De Windt, Harry. *Siberia as it is.* London, Chapman & Hall, 1892. 481 pp. illus. app.

Impressions of the exile system in the summer of 1890 in which Kennan's book (see no. 359) is challenged. De Windt claims that

Keenan was fooled by "political martyrs" and assures his readers that his assertions can be checked by any traveler to Russia. See no. 370 for another journey of De Windt.

395. Stevens, Thomas. *Through Russia on a mustang.* New York, Cassell, 1891. 334 pp. illus.

On a "Wild America" mustang, purchased in Moscow from the Carver-Whitney Show in June, 1890, American newspaperman Stevens rides south to the Black Sea, up the Don and Volga rivers to Nizhni-Novgorod by August. He describes the peasants, whom he had an excellent opportunity to meet, and decries their lack of constitutional rights. Includes some excellent illustrations.

396. Price, Julius M. *From the Arctic coast to the Yellow Sea. The narrative of a journey in 1890 and 1891, across Siberia, Mongolia, the Gobi Desert, and north China.* New York, Scribner's, 1892. pp. 1–248. illus. port. index.

Special artist for the *Illustrated London News* joins Captain Wiggins' (see no. 319) expedition to the Arctic. He describes the exile system.

397. Marsden, Kate. *On sledge and horseback to outcast Siberian lepers.* London, Record Press, 1892. 195 pp. illus. map. port. app.

Member of the Royal British Nurse Association journeys to Irkutsk and Yakutsk, Siberia, to locate an herb that, it is believed, will cure leprosy. Her search was unsuccessful, but her journey brought her into contact with the exile system. Her interpreter, Charles Davisson, concludes that the treatment of prisoners is just and fair.

398. Whishaw, Frederick J. *Out of doors in Tsarland. A record of the seeings and doings of a wanderer in Russia.* London, Longmans, Green, 1893. 380 pp. illus.

British sportsman makes a genuine attempt to describe the people of Russia outside of politics, Nihilists, and exiles during "some years duration"—1890–92? His material on sports and his characterizations of St. Petersburg "types" are very informative.

399. *Allen, Henry Tureman. *Hunting in many lands.* London, 1900.

Kentucky army officer, military attaché in St. Petersburg, 1890–95, describes "wolf hunting in Russia." See Babey, *Americans in Russia* (no. 1427).

400. Hapgood, Isabel Florence. *Russian rambles.* Boston, Houghton Mifflin, 1895. 355 pp. index.

An earnest, friendly, "truthful" account of Russia in the early 1890's by American champion of autocracy who was one of the first to translate Russian literature into English. She emphasizes how distorted the United States view of Russia is and how important to future understanding is a knowledge of languages.

401. *Biddulph, Cuthbert Edward. *Four months in Persia and visit to Trans-Caspia.* London, Kegan Paul, et al., 1892. 137 pp.

402. Frederic, Harold. *The new exodus. A study of Israel in Russia.* London, Heinemann, 1892. 286 pp. illus. app. index.

British writer journeys to Moscow, St. Petersburg, Odessa, and Kiev in 1891 to study the effects of the enforcement of Ignatieff's May Laws against the Jews. Detailed description of exile, fines, and pogrom. Refers to the "charnell house" of Berditchef.

403. Pennell, Joseph. *The Jew at home. Impressions of a summer and autumn spent with him.* New York, Appleton, 1892. pp. 64–105. illus.

Philadelphia-born illustrator, strongly anti-Semitic, caricatures Jews in Kiev and Berditchev, 1891.

404. Pennell, Joseph. *The adventures of an illustrator. Mostly in following his authors in America and Europe.* Boston, Little, Brown, 1925. pp. 222–36. illus. port.

Backward glance to 1891 by American artist, in which the "real" Jew is distinguished from the "Bolshevik" Jew. See no. 403.

405. Allen, Thomas Gaskell, Jr. *Across Asia on a bicycle. The journey of two American students from Constantinople to Peking.* New York, Century, 1894. pp. 105–44. illus. map. port.

Journey by Washington University (St. Louis) students, November, 1891. Perhaps its most unusual feature is the crossing of a great many frontiers with so little difficulty.

406. Edgar, William Crowell. *The Russian famine of 1891 and 1892: some particulars of the relief sent to the destitute peasants by the millers of America in the steamship Missouri; a brief history of the movement, a description of the relief commission's visit to Russia, and a list of subscribers to the fund.* Minneapolis, Millers and Manufacturers Insurance Co., 1893. 74 pp. illus. map. port. app.

Editor of the *Northwestern Miller* (Minneapolis) organizes a private program of famine relief that contributes 5,389,728 pounds of flour. He makes an inspection journey from Libau through St. Petersburg to Moscow in April, 1892, to the Volga River valley, where he sees and describes the destitution and hopelessness as well as the saving from death of an estimated 30,000 people.

407. Reeves, Francis Brewster. *Russia then and now, 1892–1917. My mission to Russia during the famine of 1891–1892 with data bearing upon Russia of today.* New York, Putnam, 1917. 112 pp. illus. app.

Administrator of American famine relief visits Tolstoy and the rural areas, and champions the "much maligned" nobility, 1891–92.

408. Steveni, William Barnes. *Through famine-stricken Russia.* London, Sampson, Low, Marston, 1892. 174 pp. app.

Special correspondent to London and British professor of English at College of Peter the Great, St. Petersburg, 1887–1914, journeys through the famine-stricken areas in 1891–92. He refutes the rumor that the famine was a hoax and that the grain sent in from abroad was being hoarded to supply the Russian army for an attack on Europe.

409. Bigelow, Poultney. *The borderland of Czar and Kaiser. Notes from both sides of the Russian frontier.* Illustrated by Frederic Remington. London, Osgood, McIlvaine, 1895. pp. 1–130, 237–343.

Son of John Bigelow, newspaperman, editor, and diplomat, portrays the Russian peasant as cunning and gullible, in a journey to St. Petersburg and Novgorod in 1892.

410. Talmage, Thomas de Witt. *T. de Witt Talmage. His life and work.* Lewis Albert Banks, editor. New York, Eaton & Mains, 1902. pp. 199–224. illus. port.

Presbyterian clergyman and editor of the United States *Christian Herald* escorts a shipload of food to St. Petersburg during famine of 1892. He is greatly impressed by the Russian nobility and their efforts to feed the hungry. Concludes: "Russia—America's friend."

411. Stadling, Jonas Jonsson. *In the land of Tolstoi. Experiences of famine and misrule in Russia.* Will Reason, editor. New York, Thomas Whittaker, 1897. 286 pp. illus.

Stadling works with Tolstoy during the famine of 1892. The German writer furnishes much information on the various religious sects and their treatment by the government and describes how certain German colonists gave up their wealth to live like the peasants.

412. Butterfield, (General) Daniel. *A biographical memorial of General Daniel Butterfield including many addresses and military writings.* Julia Lorrilard Butterfield, editor. New York, Grafton Press, 1904. pp. 294–301. port.

American soldier and banker visits Moscow in an attempt to get concessions on the building of the Trans-Siberian Railway, about 1893. He is extremely critical of Nihilism.

413. Dunmore, (Earl) Charles Adolphus Murray. *The Pamirs. Being a narrative of a year's expedition on horseback and on foot through Kashmir, western Tibet, Chinese Tartary,*

and Russian Central Asia. London, John Murray, 1893. I, 244–360. II, 2–340. illus. map. port. index.

Traveling north from India, July 19, 1892–January 30, 1893, British sportsman speaks highly "of the civility we received from Russians of all ranks" in the much vexed districts of Central Asia.

414.   Peel, Helen. *Polar gleams. An account of a voyage on the yacht "Blencartha".* Chicago, McClurg, 1894. pp. 1–143. illus. map. port. app.

Exploits of an unusual British woman on board a yacht convoying rails up the Yenisei River to the building site of the Trans-Siberian Railway, August–September, 1893.

415.   Hedin, Sven Anders. *Through Asia.* Translated from the Swedish by J. T. Bealby. New York, Harper, 1899. I, 1–197. II, 653–704. illus. map. port.

Swedish explorer and geographer records his impressions while on a journey to make astronomical measurements during Anglo-Russian boundary dispute, 1893–94. Supplies considerable information on peoples' way of life.

416.   Jackson, Frederick George. *The great frozen land (Bolshaia Zemelskaia Tundra). Narrative of a winter journey across the tundras and a sojourn among the Samoyeds.* Arthur Montefiore, editor. London, Macmillan, 1895. 234 pp. illus. map. app. index.

British leader of Jackson-Harmsworth Polar Expedition, September, 1893–January, 1894. Appendix includes ornithological notes, weather observations, map of the tundra, etc.

417.   Welzl, Jan. *Thirty years in the golden north.* Edvard Valenta and Bedrich Golombek, editors. Translated from the Czech by Paul Selver. New York, Macmillan, 1932. pp. 19–149.

Czech adventurer who helped to build the Trans-Siberian Railway describes life in Siberia and on the New Siberian Islands, 1893–

1923. His comments on the impact of the north on "polar outcasts" are especially good.

418.   Welzl, Jan. *The quest for polar treasures.* Edvard Valenta and Bedrich Golombek, editors. Translated from the Czech by M. and R. Weatherall. New York, Macmillan, 1933. pp. 13–352.

Continuation of Welzl's adventures. See no. 417.

419.   Logan, John A., Jr. *In joyful Russia.* New York, Appleton, 1897. 275 pp. illus.

Professional tour director and his wife guide group to participate in the festivities surrounding the coronation of Nicholas II in 1894. The title of his account indicates what he found there, although he admits to the existence of an "other Russia," he says he did not see it.

420.   Norman, (Sir) Henry. *The peoples and politics of the Far East; travels and studies in the British, French, Spanish and Portuguese colonies.* New York, Scribner's, 1895. pp. 141–66. illus. map.

British editor and Member of Parliament visits Vladivostok in 1894 and discusses the probable impact of the future completion of the Trans-Siberian Railway on the Far East.

421.   Shoemaker, Michael Myers. *Trans-Caspia. The sealed provinces of the Czar.* Cincinnati, Robert Clarke, 1895. 310 pp. illus.

Traveler-tourist from the United States describes the people and their activities, May–July, 1894. Excellent photographs.

422.   Davis, Richard Harding. *A year from a reporter's notebook.* New York, Harper, 1898. pp. 3–65. illus.

American war correspondent, novelist, and traveler reports on the coronation ceremonies of Nicholas II, May, 1894. Describes how the emperor and peasant envy each other!

423. Selfridge, Thomas Oliver, Jr. *Memoirs of Thomas Oliver Selfridge, Jr., Rear Admiral, U.S.N.* London, Putnam, 1924. pp. 229–33, 251–74. illus. map. port.

Journey to St. Petersburg and Moscow, May, 1894. Attends the coronation of Nicholas II and describes him as loved and admired by all his people.

424. Grenfell, (Baron) Francis Wallace. *Memoirs of Field Marshall Lord Grenfell.* London, Hodder & Stoughton, 1925. pp. 127–42. illus. port.

Representative of the British army at the coronation of Nicholas II describes the "Céremonial de la Proclamation Solemnelle du jour du Couronnement" in St. Petersburg and Moscow, May 18–June 8, 1894.

425. De Windt, Harry. *The new Siberia. Being an account of a visit to the penal island of Sakhalin and political prison and mines of the Trans-Baikal District, Eastern Siberia.* London, Chapman & Hall, 1896. 302 pp. illus. map. port. app. index.

De Windt (see nos. 370 and 394) claims to have been the first foreigner to be given free run of a Russian convict ship, on his journey in the summer of 1894. He accompanies his descriptions with excellent sketches.

426. Battye, Aubyn Bernard Rochfort Trevor. *Ice-bound on Kolguev. A chapter in the exploration of Arctic Europe to which is added a record of the natural history of the island.* Westminster, Constable, 1895. 375 pp. illus. map.

British explorer and ornithologist describes Samoyed life on a small island to the southwest of Novaya Zemlya, June–August, 1894.

427. Battye, Aubyn Bernard Rochfort Trevor. *A northern highway of the Tsar.* Westminster, Constable, 1898. 248 pp. illus. map. port. index.

Journey in 1894 from Kolguev Island, up the Pechora River, and then west to the White Sea. The author receives much help from the peasants when all government services, except the post office, are in suspension between autumn and winter, before freezing. Sees Nicholas II's marriage to an English bride as a "happy augury for the future of Russia."

428.   Dillon, Emile Joseph. *Eclipse of Russia.* London, Dent, 1918. 420 pp.

Here, Professor Dillon (see no. 386) includes some "personal recollections" along with an analysis of Russia's "eclipse" between 1897 and 1917. He discusses the Russian enigma and mind, rule by the bureaucrats, the lack of unity, weaknesses of Nicholas II with Rasputin as a sign of decay, and the downfall of the czar.

429.   Jefferson, Robert L. *Awheel to Moscow and back. The record of a record cycle ride.* London, Sampson Low, Marston, 1895. pp. 61–159. illus.

British adventurer and amateur cyclist makes round trip from Warsaw to Moscow in fifty days to advertise the Rover bicycle. Comments on the terrible monotony of the great Russian plain during his journey, April–June, 1895.

430.   Joubert, Carl. *Russia as it really is.* London, Eveleigh Nash, 1905. 295 pp. app.

A bitter book on Russia before 1905 by French writer who claims nine years (1895–1904) acquaintanceship with Russia, from St. Petersburg to Vladivostok.

431.   Maynard, (Sir) John. *Russia in flux.* S. Haden Guest, editor. New York, Macmillan, 1948. 529 pp. app. index.

A thorough mastery of the Russian language enables this British friend of the muzhik to record authoritative impressions obtained from four journeys in 1895–96, 1933, 1935, and 1937. Sir Bernard Pares (see no. 450) considered Maynard to be the greatest scholar on Russia.

432. Addams, Jane. *Twenty years at Hull-House, with autobiographical notes.* New York, Macmillan, 1912. pp. 262–77. port.

American social worker describes her visit with Tolstoy in 1896.

433. Kenworthy, John Coleman. *A pilgrimage to Tolstoy.* Croyden, Brotherhood Publishing Co., 1900. 45 pp. illus.

British businessman journeys to Tolstoy in 1896 and comes away with the observation: "Leo Tolstoy is singled out among men because upon him, at his height, the light of the dawn shines and glows."

434. Simpson, James Young. *Side-lights on Siberia. Some account of the great Siberian railroad, the prisons and exile system.* London, William Blackwood, 1898. 376 pp. illus. app. index.

British critic sees the exile system as all right in principle but violated in practice: it was too arbitrary, the conditions on the march were very bad, and the hospitals were unsatisfactory.

435. Fraser, (Sir) John Foster. *Round the world on a wheel. Being the narrative of a bicycle ride of nineteen thousand two hundred and thirty-seven miles through seventeen countries and across three continents, by John Foster Fraser, S. Edward Lunn, and F. H. Lowe.* London, Methuen, 1899. pp. 25–84. port.

Three British students on an "unadventurous" journey through the Ukraine, Crimea, and the Caucasus regions, 1896–98.

436. Dana, Charles A. *Eastern journeys. Some notes of travel in Russia, in the Caucasus and to Jerusalem.* New York, Appleton, 1898. 106 pp.

Travel notes, mostly trivial, by American tourist on journey through Central Asia, the Black Sea, and Moscow in 1897.

437.　Jefferson, Robert L. *Roughing it in Siberia. With some account of the Trans-Siberian Railway and the gold-mining industry of Asiatic Russia.* London, Sampson Low, Marston, 1897. 249 pp. illus. map. port. index.

Jefferson leads a party of four on a business-seeking expedition and sees Siberia as a land of promise. Journey was made by rail from Moscow to Krasnoiarsk and then down the Yenisei River, January–April, 1897.

438.　Honeyman, Abraham Van Doren, and Abbie Ranlett Mason. *From America to Russia in summer of 1897.* Plainfield, New Jersey, Honeyman & Co., 1897. pp. 88–114.

Tourist journey, with Mason writing a friendly description of St. Petersburg and its people but Honeyman presenting a critical characterization of the Muscovites, finding them to be repulsive and deserving of the strong government under which they lived.

439.　Gillis, Charles J. *A summer vacation in Iceland, Norway, Sweden and Russia.* Privately printed, 1898. pp. 36–52. illus.

American businessman visits St. Petersburg and Moscow, June–July, 1897, and records the typical tourist's impressions.

440.　Miles, Nelson Appleton. *Military Europe. A narrative of personal observation and personal experience.* New York, Doubleday & McClure, 1898. pp. 73–94. illus. port.

Major general, United States Army, observes Russian military maneuvers, August, 1897. Concludes that the army is adequately prepared and equipped for any purpose. See no. 256 for McClellan's remarks in 1855–56.

441.　* Pearson, Henry J. *Beyond Petsora eastward: Two summer voyages to Novaya Zemlya.* London, R. H. Porter, 1899. 335 pp. app.

442. Cobbold, Ralph P. *Innermost Asia. Travel and sport in the Pamirs.* London, Heinemann, 1900. 315 pp. illus. map. port. app. biblio. index.

Claiming to be first writing Englishman on the Oxus River, hunter and sportsman comments on the mineral resources and the political conditions, September, 1897–August, 1898.

443. Hammond, John Hays. *The autobiography of John Hays Hammond.* New York, Farrar & Rinehart, 1935. II, 455–78. illus. port. biblio.

Engineer and businessman surveys Russian industrial potentialities in 1898, 1910, and 1912. Invited by Count Sergei Witte, the American traveler names two serious hindrances to investment: (1) Russian laws, which do not use due process, and (2) bureaucratic red tape. He concludes that the Russians are too backward to deal intelligently with investment.

444. Stadling, Jonas Jonsson. *Through Siberia.* F. H. H. Guillemand, editor. Westminster, Constable, 1901. pp. 1–298. illus. map. app. index.

Traveling 15,000 miles, from May to December, 1898, German writer (see no. 411) accompanies an expedition to find lost explorers in the Arctic. His route begins at St. Petersburg, then to the Lena River and down to the Arctic Ocean, then along the coast to the Yenisei River. He is extremely critical of the exile system, alleging cannibalism.

445. Bookwalter, John Wesley. *Siberia and Central Asia.* New York, Frederick A. Stokes, 1899. 548 pp. illus. map.

Ohio businessman makes his journey during the summer of 1898. He intelligently comments on every aspect of life and includes hundreds of photographs.

446. Russell-Cote, (Lady) Annie Nelson (Clark). *Letters from Russia.* London, Mapp, n.d. pp. 1–40. illus.

Mother, writing in August–September, 1898, to her children at home, reacts to St. Petersburg, Moscow, and Nizhni-Novgorod like a typical tourist.

447.   Reid, Arnot. *From Peking to Petersburg*. London, Edward Arnold, 1899. pp. 131–293. map. port. index.

Businessman from Britain writes a book with a purpose—a tract against Russia—and urges Anglo-American co-operation against the ambitions of St. Petersburg's rulers. He also speculates upon the impact of the Trans-Siberian Railway after a journey by tarantasse and rail, September–October, 1898.

448.   Vanderlip, Washington B. *In search of a Siberian Klondike*. As told to Homer B. Hulbert. New York, Century, 1903. 315 pp. illus. map. port.

Gold prospector from the United States surveys resources in East Siberia, Kamchatka, and Sakhalin, 1898–1900. He comments on the way of life, the exile system, and sport, along with observations on the Trans-Siberian Railway.

449.   Baddeley, John F. *The rugged flanks of the Caucasus*. London, Oxford, 1940. vol. I, 272 pp. vol. II, 263 pp. illus. map. port. index.

British scholar and linguist, with a complete command of Russian, describes his journeys by horseback, 1898–1902. Superb photographs accompany his comments on the people, their customs and way of life, and the land.

450.   Pares, Bernard. *My Russian memoirs*. London, Jonathan Cape, 1931. 606 pp. illus. port. app. index.

Here Pares tells of his developing passion for Russia, its people, and its history. A thorough mastery of the language preceded his numerous journeys from England to Russia's capitals and country, 1898–1936, where his friendships included men and women in all

walks of life, from muzhik to priest, politician to prince. Time
and again, he was present when revolution and change occurred.

451.   Pares, Bernard. *A wandering student: the story of a purpose.* Utica, New York, Syracuse University Press, 1948.
407 pp. app. index.

Another general account of Pares' life and visits to Russia, 1898–
1936. Appendix includes a large selection of his poetry. See no.
450.

452.   Leroy-Beaulieu, Pierre. *The awakening of the East: Siberia–Japan–China.* Translated from the French by Richard
Davey. New York, McClure, Phillips, 1900. pp. 1–80.

French scholar and traveler visits Siberia, 1899, and studies the
economic potential of the area and probable results of improved
communication and transportation between east and west Russia.
He provides an excellent description of the building of the Trans-
Siberian Railway.

453.   Stoddard, John L. *John L. Stoddard's Lectures.* Boston,
Balch, 1900. VI, 227–336. illus.

Professional American traveler-lecturer journeys to St. Petersburg
and Moscow in 1899. He provides excellent pictures of the two
cities, and his description concentrates on typical tourist attrac-
tions, such as buildings, monuments, etc.

454.   Jefferson, Robert L. *A new ride to Khiva.* New York, New
Amsterdam Book Co., 1900. pp. 71–312. illus.

British adventurer (see no. 437), admirer of Frederick Burnaby
(see no. 322), rides his bicycle to Khiva, summer, 1899. Emphasizes the decay of the area since it was acquired by the Russians.

455.   Morton, (Dr.) Rosalie Slaughter. *A woman surgeon.* The
life and work of Rosalie Slaughter Morton. New York,
Frederick A. Stokes, 1937. pp. 71–84. port.

American medical doctor visits St. Petersburg and Moscow during Christmas holiday in 1899. From the vantage point of 1937 she claims she saw the making of Soviet Russia when, on a visit to Tolstoy, he informed her of vast unrest.

456. Eagar, M. *Six years at the Russian Court*. New York, Charles L. Bowman, 1906. 283 pp. illus.

British governess to the daughters of Nicholas II describes her life at the Russian court, 1899–1905, and tries to uncover all lies that she believes to have been told about the czar's family. Her account is full of details about religious practices, soldiers, education, peasants, and holidays.

457. Meakin, Annette M. B. *A ribbon of iron*. New York, Dutton, 1901. 292 pp. illus. port.

British anthropologist journeys across the partially completed Trans-Siberian Railway from Moscow to Vladivostok in 1900. She emphasizes economic possibilities in the area and provides many excellent photographs, one of a railway church.

458. Palmer, Francis H. E. *Russian life in town and country*. London, Putnam, 1904. 315 pp. illus. app. index.

British secretary to the Russian royal family and equerry to His Majesty Nicholas II describes the way of life in court, town, and country at the end of the nineteenth century. He includes data on the Jews and on the growing industrial co-operative associations.

459. Roberts, James Hudson. *A flight for life and an inside view of Mongolia*. Boston, Pilgrim, 1903. pp. 285–331. app.

American missionary, escaping from China in 1900, calls Siberia "The Land of Freedom" and refers to Russians as "a people much misunderstood." He asserts that strong nations have the right to grow because they can protect the weak.

460.   Clark, Francis Edward. *Memories of many men in many lands*. Boston, United Society of Christian Endeavor, 1922. pp. 239–56. illus. port.

Journey by the president of the World's Christian Endeavor Union across the partially completed Trans-Siberian Railway in June–July, 1900, consuming forty-two days from Vladivostok to eastern Europe. He describes the country as the train crawls slowly along with many long stops, and refers to the exile system.

461.   Curtin, Jeremiah. *A journey in southern Siberia. The Mongols, their religion and their myths*. Boston, Little, Brown, 1909. 300 pp. illus. map. port. app. index.

American anthropologist and diplomat journeys to the land of the Mongols and creates a basic work on their way of life, filled with informative photographs and 114 pages of myths and folklore, July 19–September 15, 1900. See no. 287.

462.   Digby, George Bassett. *Tigers, gold and witchdoctors*. New York, Harcourt, Brace, 1928. 341 pp. illus.

Russian-speaking British prospector writes a rather juvenile account of his encounters with Siberian bears, witchdoctors, "Indians" (Buriats), vodka, and gold-mining, 1900–1914.

463.   Petersson, C. E. W. *How to do business with Russia: hints and advice to business men dealing with Russia*. London, Isaac Pitman, 1917. 195 pp. map. app.

British merchant doing business in St. Petersburg (Petrograd) and Riga, supplies a quantity of valuable data on economic resources, 1900–1917.

464.   Ossendowski, Ferdynand Antoni. *The shadow of the gloomy East*. Translated from the Polish by F. B. Czarnomski. New York, Dutton, 1925. 198 pp. index.

Russian-speaking Polish critic writes a tract in which he lays "bare before the civilized world the true face of the Russian people"—impressions he received from associations between 1900 and 1922.

465.   Colton, Ethan Theodore. *Forty years with Russians.* New York, Association Press, 1940. 192 pp.

American Young Men's Christian Association worker makes many journeys to Russia between 1900 and 1939. He describes in detail the period, 1918–32, when the *mujak* (lighthouse) ministry to young men was struggling to survive, and which came to an end with the banning of the YMCA in 1939.

466.   Swenson, Olaf. *Northwest of the world. Forty years trading and hunting in northern Siberia.* New York, Dodd, Mead, 1944. 270 pp. illus. port.

Swedish businessman describes his relationships with the government and the people while hunting and trading, 1900–1943.

467.   Beveridge, Albert Jeremiah. *The Russian advance.* New York, Harper, 1904. 461 pp. map. app.

Indiana senator and historian tours Siberia in 1901 and comments on the impact of the increased communication and transportation between the Russian east and west.

468.   Gerrare, Wirt (pseudonym of William Oliver Greener). *Greater Russia. The continental empire of the old world.* London, Heinemann, 1903. 310 pp. illus. map. index.

Russian-speaking British traveler seeks the truth about Siberia, journeys from St. Petersburg to Manchuria on the Trans-Siberian Railway in 1901. He sees the country as a new America and discovers the English are not too welcome east of Lake Baikal.

469.   Norman, (Sir) Henry. *All the Russias. Travels and studies in contemporary European Russia, Finland, Siberia, the Caucasus, and Central Asia.* New York, Scribner's, 1902 456 pp. illus. map. app. index.

In 1901 British Member of Parliament and longtime friend of Russia journeys from St. Petersburg through Siberia, visiting Tolstoy, examining the new railroad, and studying the exile system. His economic analysis focuses on Count Sergei Witte and the future relations between England and Russia.

470. Palmer, Frederick. *With my own eyes. A personal story of battle years.* London, Jarrolds, 1934. pp. 188–93.

American war correspondent journeys from Japan to London in 1901 and sees the important implications of the completion of the Trans-Siberian Railway, especially to China and Japan. His visit to European Russia makes him aware of the weaknesses of Nicholas II.

471. Vay, (Count) Peter. *Empires and emperors of Russia, China, Korea and Japan. Notes and recollections.* New York, Dutton, 1906. pp. 1–62. illus. port.

Priest, sent by Pope Leo XIII to study Catholic institutions in the Far East and Russia in 1901, is received by Nicholas II. He describes the people and land in Siberia and his experiences on the Trans-Siberian Railway.

472. Wright, George Frederick. *Asiatic Russia.* New York, McClure, Phillips, 1902. vol. I, pp. 13–120. vol. II, 581 pp. illus. map. biblio.

Oberlin College (Ohio) "professor of the harmony of Science and Revelation" journeys through Siberia in 1901. His discussion of the exile system is a combination of what he saw combined with background from the journeys of earlier travelers.

473. Shoemaker, Michael Myers. *The great Siberian Railway from St. Petersburg to Pekin.* New York, Putnam, 1903. pp. 1–121. illus. map. index.

United States tourist (see no. 421) presents an uncomplicated description of the railroad and the country through which it runs.

He includes many excellent photographs from his journey in the spring of 1901.

474.   Holmes, Burton. *Burton Holmes Travelogues, St. Petersburgh, Moscow, the Trans-Siberian Railway.* n.p., Travelogue Bureau, 1914. vol. VIII, 336 pp. vol. IX, pp. 1–112. illus. index.

American traveler-lecturer journeys down the Amur River, then northeast to Vladivostok, May–August, 1901. He includes excellent photographs, especially of the river journey.

475.   Morgan, Christopher A. *From China by rail. An account of a journey from Shanghai to London via the Trans-Siberian Railways.* Edinburgh, Ballantyne Press, 1902. 139 pp. illus.

British tourist sets out to try the railroad and its accommodations on a journey from China to England, June 19–August 20, 1901. Most of his account deals with the portion of the trip between Vladivostok and Irkutsk.

476.   Senn, Nicholas. *Around the world via Siberia.* Chicago, Conkey, 1902. 198 pp. illus.

American surgeon on the staff of the United States Army journeys from St. Petersburg to Vladivostok, July–September, 1901. His remarks are pleasant and informative—on agriculture, forests, the Jews, seasons, the Trans-Siberian Railway, peasant life, etc.

477.   Hawes, Charles H. *In the uttermost East: Being an account of investigations among the natives and Russian convicts of the island of Sakhalin, with notes of travel in Korea, Siberia, and Manchuria.* London, Harper, 1903. 478 pp. illus. map. index.

British traveler journeys from Vladivostok to the Amur River, to Sakhalin Island, then west to Moscow, August–November, 1901. Claiming to be the first Englishman to see the prisons in the northern part of Sakhalin, he concludes that the exile system has improved since the time of Kennan's journey (see no. 359).

478. Adams, Henry. *The education of Henry Adams*. New York, Modern Library, 1931. pp. 408–12.

American historian journeys to Moscow and St. Petersburg, August 17–September 7, 1901. Analyzes the character of the Russian, whom he says "had nothing in common with ancient or modern world that history knew. . . ."

479. Adams, Henry. *Letters of Henry Adams, 1892–1918*. Worthington Chauncey Ford, editor. Boston, Houghton Mifflin, 1938. II, 339–50. illus. port.

Adams (see no. 478) writes delightful letters to his personal and political friends from Moscow and St. Petersburg, in which he sees Russia as buried in the past but able to "clean us all out" if Germany helps her.

480. Fraser, (Sir) John Foster. *The real Siberia. Together with an account of a dash through Manchuria*. London, Cassell, 1902. 279 pp. illus. port.

British critic of Russia journeys east on the nearly completed Trans-Siberian Railway, autumn, 1901. He finds much to condemn but also sees "a land capable of immense agricultural possibilities."

481. Meakin, Annette M. B. *In Russian Turkestan. A garden of Asia and its people*. London, George Allen, 1903. 304 pp. illus. map. port. index.

British fellow of Anthropological Institute describes way of life of the Sarts and Turkomans, 1901–02. See no. 457.

482. De Windt, Harry. *From Paris to New York by land*. London, George Newnes, 1904. pp. 1–193. illus. map. port. app. index.

British adventurer (see nos. 370 and 394) sets out to examine the "feasibility of constructing a railroad to connect the chief cities of France and America, Paris and New York." By rail, land vehicle, boat, and on foot, he covers the route from Moscow to the Bering Strait, December 23, 1901–April 9, 1902. He comments on the exile system and includes a log of his journey and information on the Siberian way of life.

483.   * Pearson, Henry J. *Three summers among the birds of Russian Lapland, with history of Saint Triphon's Monastery and appendices.* London, R. H. Porter, 1904. 216 pp. illus. map.

484.   Hird, John Wynne. *Under Czar and Soviet. My thirty years in Russia.* London, Hurst & Blackett, 1932. 287 pp.

Russian-speaking British businessman asks: Is it worth destroying the soul to get economic good? He concludes that it is not in this detailed comparison of economic conditions and activities, 1901–31.

485.   Cary, Clarence. *The Trans-Siberian route, or, Notes of a journey from Pekin to New York in 1902.* New York, Evening Post Job Printing Office, 1902. 53 pp. map.

American journalist reports on the Trans-Siberian Railway in 1902.

486.   * Edwards, William Seymour. *Through Scandinavia to Moscow.* Cincinnati, R. Clarke, 1906. 237 pp. illus. map. port.

West Virginia lawyer and his bride honeymoon in Russia in 1902. He prophesies the fall of the Romanovs. See Babey, *Americans in Russia* (no. 1427).

487.   Landor, Arnold Henry Savage. *Across coveted lands; or, A journey from Flushing (Holland) to Calcutta, overland.* New York, Scribner's, 1903. I, 1–28. illus. map.

American tourist comments on his journey by rail across southern Russia, from Warsaw to Kiev to Rostov-on-Don to Baku, 1902.

488.   Miles, Nelson Appleton. *Serving the Republic. Memoirs of the civil and military life of Nelson A. Miles.* New York, Harper, 1911. pp. 308–9. port.

Just before he retired in 1903, General Miles journeyed over the Trans-Siberian Railway in 1902, where army concentration appeared to indicate preparations for war. See no. 440.

489. Shoemaker, Michael Myers. *The heart of the Orient. Saunterings through Georgia, Armenia, Persia, Turkomania, and Turkestan, to the Vale of Paradise.* New York, Putnam, 1904. pp. 14–89, 209–409. illus. index.

Straightforward account by American tourist on a journey in the winter of 1902. He comments on political and social conditions.

490. Fell, E. Nelson. *Russian and nomad. Tales of the Kirghiz steppes.* New York, Duffield, 1916. 201 pp. illus.

United States director of mining company located near the Ishim River, 1902–8, describes relations between himself, the Russians, and the Kirghiz workers. He notes the beginnings of labor union activities.

491. Spring Rice, (Sir) Cecil. *The letters and friendships of Sir Cecil Spring Rice. A record.* Stephen Gwynn, editor. Boston, Houghton Mifflin, 1929. I, 362–87. II, 1–76. port. index.

Secretary, and later councilor, of the British embassy in St. Petersburg, 1903, 1905–6, Sir Cecil describes his life there and his associations with the Russians, placing his emphasis on personal affairs rather than on the emerging crisis around him.

492. Swayne, (Major) H. G. C. *Through the highlands of Siberia.* London, Rowland Ward, 1904. 232 pp. illus. map. app. index.

British hunter describes his experiences in 1903, especially his contacts with the peasants. He includes excellent photographs of his activities and of the people and land.

493. Turner, Samuel. *Siberia: A record of travel, climbing, and exploration.* London, Fisher Unwin, 1905. 361 pp. illus. map. port. app. index.

English businessman and sportsman surveys the dairy industry and climbs in the Ural Mountains, March–May, 1903. Includes information on travel conditions.

494.   Simpson, Bertram Lenox (Bertram Lennox Putnam Weale, pseudonym). *Manchu and Muscovite. Being letters from Manchuria written during the Autumn of 1903. With an historical sketch entitled "Prologue to the Crisis." Giving a complete account of the Manchurian Frontiers from the earliest days and the growth and final meeting of the Russian and Chinese Empires in the Amur Regions.* London, Macmillan, 1904. pp. 469–532. illus. index.

British correspondent predicts Russia's defeat after his journey in September–November.

495.   Bigelow, Poultney. *Seventy summers.* New York, Longmans, Green, 1925. I, 320–32. II, 100–113. port.

Bigelow (see no. 409) was finally expelled from Russia for his outspoken opinions during this journey in 1903–4.

496.   Ganz, Hugo. *The downfall of Russia; under the surface of the land of riddles.* London, Hodder & Stoughton, 1905. pp. 33–320.

Austrian correspondent surveys political conditions in 1904, just before the beginning of the Russo-Japanese War. A friend of Russia, he describes conditions in court and among the common people, with comments on Russian students and his visit with Tolstoy.

497.   Joubert, Carl. *The truth about the Tsar and the present state of Russia.* Philadelphia, Lippincott, 1905. 265 pp.

French writer (see no. 430) makes an analysis of corrupt Russia and a prediction that the Romanov dynasty will soon end, and there will be a republic—in 1904.

498.   Meakin, Annette M. B. *Russia. Travels and studies.* London, Hurst and Blackett, 1906. 312 pp. illus. map. index.

Journey from St. Petersburg to the Caucasus in 1904 is described by British anthropologist (see nos. 457 and 481).

499.   Villari, Luigi. *Russia under the great shadow.* London, Fisher Unwin, 1905. 325 pp. illus. index.

Italian correspondent journeys from St. Petersburg to the Crimea in 1904 and describes his impressions of the people and land.

500.   Stone, Melville E. *Fifty years a journalist.* Garden City, New York, Doubleday, Page, 1921. pp. 183–94, 257–96. illus.

In January, 1904, Illinois journalist and organizer of the Associated Press, journeys to St. Petersburg to seek relief from the censorship. In humorous fashion he describes how his petition to get relief had to be censored!

501.   Baring, Maurice. *With the Russians in Manchuria.* London, Methuen, 1905. 205 pp.

The author, member of a great British financial and commercial house, held diplomatic posts, was a war correspondent, wrote books on Russia and Russian literature, and mastered the Russian language early in his career. Here he describes a tour of duty, May–December, 1904, in a way sympathetic to the Russians. He believes they like the English, but consider the British government to be Machiavellian.

502.   Wilton, Robert. *Russia's agony.* London, Edward Arnold, 1918. 330 pp. illus. map. port. app. index.

An objective account of events from 1904 to 1918 by a Russian-speaking London *Times* correspondent. He illuminates his account with some remarkable pictures and includes a useful appendix of revolutionary documents.

503.   Pares, Bernard. *The fall of the Russian monarchy. A study of the evidence.* New York, Random House, 1961. 502 pp. map. app. biblio. index.

British "gentleman usher" of the first Duma, describes events from 1904 to 1919 from firsthand experience. See nos. 450 and 451.

504.   Harper, Samuel N. *The Russia I believe in. The memoirs of Samuel N. Harper, 1902–1941.* Paul V. Harper, editor, and Ronald Thompson. Chicago, University of Chicago Press, 1945. pp. 15–260.

Samuel N. Harper and Bernard Pares are considered by many students of Russian history and culture to have been most responsible for the advancement of Russian studies in the United States and Britain (see no. 450 for a summary of Pares). In this work Harper describes his ten journeys from the United States to Imperial and Soviet Russia between 1904 and 1939 in one capacity or another and for various purposes. Somehow, he always manages to be in Russia at the time of a critical change.

505.   Durland, Kellogg. *The red reign. The true story of an adventurous year in Russia.* New York, Century Co., 1907. 533 pp. illus. map. port. index.

New York socialist investigates labor conditions in 1905 on a journey from St. Petersburg to the Crimea. He visits Tolstoy and appends notes on wages.

506.   Mackenzie, Frederick Arthur. *From Tokyo to Tiflis. Uncensored letters from the war.* London, Hurst & Blackett, 1905. pp. 285–327. illus.

London *Daily Mail* special correspondent in the Caucasus, 1905, reports discontent and graft, a result of the defeat of Russia by Japan. Illustrations include a cartoon on the Russian Red Cross.

507.   Reynolds, Rothay. *My Russian year.* London, Mills & Boon, 1913. 304 pp. illus.

Analysis of Russian characteristics by Russian-speaking English traveler and writer during 1905. He especially emphasizes religion.

508.   Reynolds, Rothay. *My Slav friends.* London, Mills & Boon, 1916. 307 pp. index.

An English friend of Russia (see no. 507) verbally paints a rosy picture of Russian conditions with the intention of encouraging continuing Anglo-Russian unity.

509.   Washburn, Stanley. *The cable game. The adventures of an American press-boat in Turkish waters during the Russian Revolution.* Boston, Sherman, French, 1912. 222 pp. illus.

Coverage from the Black Sea area of the Revolution of 1905 by Chicago *Daily News* correspondent. Much of his account describes the problems faced by news-gathering agencies in and around Odessa.

510.   Winter, Nevin O. *The Russian Empire of today and yesterday. The country and its peoples, together with a brief survey of its history, past and present, and a survey of its social, political, and economic conditions.* Boston, Page, 1913. 465 pp. illus. map. app. biblio. index.

United States lawyer and writer combines history and current remarks in his special emphasis on political institutions as a result of journeys in 1905 and 1912. He also includes useful appendixes on economics, politics, and tips for travelers.

511.   Villari, Luigi. *Fire and sword in the Caucasus.* London, Fisher Unwin, 1906. 341 pp. illus. index.

Italian correspondent describes the impact of the Revolution of 1905 on the Caucasus after a journey there during the summer and autumn, 1905.

512.   Decle, Lionel. *The new Russia.* London, Eveleigh Nash, 1906. 263 pp. app.

British writer journeys to St. Petersburg to study revolutionary activities, 1905–6.

513.   Kennard, Howard P. *The Russian peasant.* London, Werner Laurie, 1907. 302 pp. illus.

Criticism of "Russia's poison—bureaucracy and church" by Russian-speaking British medical doctor working among the peasants in 1905–6.

514.   Nevinson, Henry Woodd. *The dawn in Russia, or, Scenes in the Russian Revolution.* New York, Harper, 1906. 340 pp. illus. map. index.

Correspondent of the London *Daily Chronicle* records his impressions of revolutionary activity in 1905–6. He illustrates his account with cartoons of the times.

515.   Pares, Bernard. *Russia: between reform and revolution.* Francis B. Randall, editor. New York, Schocken Books, 1962. 576 pp.

Pares (see nos. 450, 451, and 503) observes firsthand the Russian character under stress as the events of 1905–6 take place before his eyes in St. Petersburg.

516.   Baring, Maurice. *A year in Russia.* New York, Dutton, 1907. 307 pp. index.

Baring (see no. 501) attempts to present impartially the divergent points of view of groups, August, 1905–August, 1906. Creation, actions, and dissolution of the first Duma are described.

517.   Howe, M. A. DeWolfe. *George von Lengerke Meyer, his life and public services.* New York, Dodd-Mead, 1920. pp. 137–351. illus. port.

Boston merchant and ambassador extraordinary to Russia, 1905–7, emphasizes the corruption of the St. Petersburg court as a contributing cause of the Revolution of 1905.

518.   Walling, William English. *Russia's message. The people against the Czar.* New York, Knopf, 1917. 231 pp. illus. app.

This is a book with a message, a tract, in which Walling, a pro-socialist Russian-speaking American writer, critically examines the changing government. It is a diatribe against the czar, in which the author reports on conversations with hundreds of peasants and politicians. He includes an appendix with documents relating to negotiations between the czar and the Duma. 1905–7.

519. Baring, Maurice. *What I saw in Russia.* New York, Thomas Nelson, 1913. 381 pp. illus.

Baring's (see nos. 501 and 516) account of events from May, 1905 to September, 1907 during a round trip to Manchuria on the Trans-Siberian Railway and a journey down the Volga River.

520. Bullard, Arthur (Albert Edwards, pseudonym). *The Russian pendulum. Autocracy-Democracy-Bolshevism.* New York, Macmillan, 1919. 248 pp. index.

Socialist American correspondent explains Russia and her peasant communities on the basis of journeys in 1905–8 and in 1917–18.

521. Noble, Algernon. *Siberian days. An engineer's record of travel and adventure in the wilds of Siberia.* London, Witherby, 1928. 318 pp. illus. index.

British friend of czarist Russia describes copper and gold mining in the steppes, and gold prospecting in Siberia in the period 1905–14.

522. Gilliard, Pierre. *Thirteen years at the Russian court (A personal record of the last years and death of Czar Nicholas II and his family).* Translated from the French by F. Appleby Holt. New York, Doran, n.d. 304 pp. illus.

French tutor to the czarevitch describes the life of the royal family from 1905 to 1918. His is a deeply loyal and sympathetic portrait of the court, and he expresses his distress about the stories that are current about the czar, the czarina, and their relations to Rasputin and other figures.

523. Preston, Thomas. *Before the curtain.* London, John Murray, 1950. 306 pp. illus. port. index.

Musician and British embassy jack-of-all-trades describes his life, 1905–40, and is especially interesting in his comments on the Revolutions of 1905 and 1917.

524.   Bryan, William Jennings. *Under other flags. Travels, lectures, speeches.* Lincoln, Nebraska, Woodruff-Colliers Printing Co., 1904. pp. 77–85, 96–108. illus. port.

Lawyer and political leader, "The Great Commoner," had been nominated for the Presidency of the United States and twice defeated before he journeyed to St. Petersburg and Moscow in 1906. He indicates the highlights of his visit were seeing the new Duma in action and talking with Tolstoy.

525.   De Windt, Harry. *Through savage Europe; being the narrative of a journey (undertaken as a special correspondent of the "Westminster Gazette"), throughout the Balkan states and European Russia.* London, Fisher Unwin, 1907. pp. 261–89. illus. port.

Adventurer (see nos. 370 and 394) journeys to southern Russia and Odessa in 1906 with bioscope artist. Describes the venality of the people just after the Revolution of 1905.

526.   Niedieck, Paul. *Cruises in the Bering Sea. Being records of further sport and travel.* Translated from the German by R. A. Ploetz. London, Rowland, Ward, 1909. pp. 3–107. illus. map. port. app. index.

German hunter-taxidermist describes fauna, animal and human, of Kamchatka on a journey there in March, 1906

527.   Barrows, Isabel C. *A sunny life: The biography of Samuel June Barrows.* Boston, Little, Brown, 1913. pp. 192–96, 204–5, 240–41.

Daughter of Samuel June Barrows, American authority on crime and punishment and corresponding secretary of the Prison Association of New York, visits prisons in St. Petersburg and Moscow with her father in 1907 and pays a visit to Tolstoy. In 1909 she returned to Russia to organize aid for Madame Breshkovskaya, who was in prison. Her father comments favorably on prisons in the two cities on pp. 204–5.

528. Bayne, Samuel Gamble. *Quicksteps through Scandinavia, with a retreat from Moscow.* New York, Harper, 1908. pp. 17–31. illus.

American tourist on journey to St. Petersburg and Moscow, 1907, advises other travelers about the most interesting sights.

529. * Fischer, Emil Sigmund. *Overland via the Trans-Siberian. Description of a trip from the Far East to Europe and the United States of America.* Tientsin, Tientsin Press, 1908. 44 pp. illus. map.

530. Foulke, William Dudley. *A random record of travel.* New York, Oxford University Press, 1925. pp. 94–111.

American writer of travel books visits the capital and Moscow in 1907 and makes observations about the "uncanny" atmosphere of the country. Also comments on the magnificent and sinister sides of Moscow.

531. Barrett, R. J. *Russia's new era. Being notes, impressions and experiences—personal, commercial and financial—of an extended tour in the empire of the Tsar. With statistical tables, portraits, snapshots and other illustrations.* London, Financier and Bullionist, Ltd., 1908. 288 pp. illus.

British banker sees improved conditions on the horizon in the spring and summer of 1907 as a result of the impending Anglo-Russian entente.

532. Murray, Robert H. *Around the world with Taft. A book of travel, description, history.* Detroit, Dickerson, 1909. pp. 325–76. illus.

United States Associated Press correspondent with Secretary of War William Howard Taft, November 17–December 5, 1907, as

Taft's party travels on the Trans-Siberian Railway from Vladivostok to St. Petersburg. Murray comments on the threats made against Taft's life while he was on the train and describes the Secretary of War's reception by Nicholas II.

533.   Young, Charles Christian. *Abused Russia.* New York, Devin-Adair, 1915. 100 pp. illus. app.

German-American scientist born in Russia reports on Russian potentialities explored during numerous journeys, 1907–14. Provides a description of Teutonic Russia in words and in excellent photographs.

534.   * Marshall, Leslie A. *The romance of a tract and its sequel; the story of an American pioneer in Russia and the Baltic states.* Riga, Jubilee Fund Commission of the Baltic and Slavic Mission Conference of the Methodist Episcopal Church, 1928. 79 pp. illus. map.

Superintendent of the St. Petersburg (Petrograd) mission describes his work, 1907–18. See Babey, *Americans in Russia* (no. 1427).

535.   Bates, Lindon, Jr. *The Russian road to China.* Boston, Houghton Mifflin, 1910. 363 pp. illus. map.

Tourist describes journey from Moscow to China on the Trans-Siberian Railway and on sledge in 1908.

536.   Craig-McKerrow, (Mrs.) Margaret (Reibold). *Distant journeys, 1908–1928.* London, Baylis, 1930. pp. 15–37, 349–69. illus. port.

British tourist travels from Vladivostok to Moscow on the Trans-Siberian Railway in 1908. Twenty years later, visiting Leningrad and Moscow, she compares the two periods and sees improvement in the general standard of living for the mass of people. She observes that the Soviet offers a continuing challenge to all the world.

537. Hoover, Herbert. *The memoirs of Herbert Hoover: Years of adventure, 1874–1920.* New York, Macmillan, 1952. pp. 102–9.

The former President of the United States makes some critical remarks about the Communist expropriation of mining properties, especially those he had discovered by using Kennan's (see no. 359) accounts of mines worked by exiles. Mr. Hoover was in Russia as a mining engineer, 1908–14.

538. Harrison, E. J. *Peace or war east of Baikal?* Yokohama, Kelly and Walsh, 1910. pp. 63–211.

American correspondent sets out to discover the truth or falsity in rumors of impending conflict between the Russians and the Japanese or the Russians and Americans, 1909.

539. Latimer, Robert Sloan. *With Christ in Russia.* London, Hodder & Stoughton, 1910. 232 pp. index.

British writer describes the work of the Young Men's Christian Association in St. Petersburg and Moscow (where he visited Tolstoy). His account of the YMCA *miyak* (lighthouse) ministry includes a visit to the work in Kiev. The journey was made in 1909.

540. *Loew, Charles E. *Reminiscences of Russia.* New York, 1910.

541. Wood, Ruth Kedzie. *Honeymooning in Russia.* New York, Dodd, Mead, 1911. 341 pp. illus. port.

Wife of United States steel official describes their journey from St. Petersburg, Moscow, and south in 1909 with some references to revolutionists they met.

542. Taft, Marcus Lorenzo. *Strange Siberia along the Trans-Siberian Railway. A journey from the Great Wall of China to the skyscrapers of Manhattan.* New York, Eaton & Mains, 1911. 256 pp. illus. index.

Artist from the United States, with his wife and child, records the courteous treatment accorded him and his family in May–June, 1909. Although his verbal sketches are rather pedestrian, he does substantiate his observations with historical background and includes excellent photographs.

543.   Graham, Stephen. *A vagabond in the Caucasus. With some notes of his experiences among the Russians*. London, John Lane, 1911. 308 pp. illus. map. app. index.

From his writings it appears that Stephen Graham is a gentle soul who became deeply interested in Russia when he was about twenty-five years of age, learned the language, and spent the next decade in journeys that enabled him to write the books that made Russia known to his fellow Englishmen. *A vagabond in the Caucasus* is Graham's first record of the impressions received from a hobo journey in European Russia in 1909–10. He includes an appendix on "How to get about in Russia."

544.   Hubback, John. *Russian realities. Being impressions gathered during some recent journeys in Russia by John Hubback*. London, John Lane, 1915. 279 pp. illus. index.

Friendly and well-written comments by a British businessman who made eleven journeys to European Russia and the Caucasus between 1909 and 1914.

545.   Dukes, (Sir) Paul. *The unending quest: autobiographical sketches*. London, Cassell, 1950. pp. 35–115. illus. port.

Russian-speaking British music student describes life among the artists before and during World War I, 1909–17. Dukes became a Bureau of Information clerk and summarized Russian newspapers and other news sources for British Ambassador George Buchanan. From this experience he is able to provide another facet of the embassy in wartime.

546.   Curtis, William Eleroy. *Around the Black Sea, Asia Minor, Armenia, Caucasus, Circassia, Daghestan, the Crimea,*

Roumania. London, Hodder & Stoughton, 1911. 450 pp. illus. index.

Journey by Chicago *Daily Herald* correspondent in 1910 that provides a description of the people and their way of life.

547. Eddy, Sherwood. *A pilgrimage of ideas; or, the re-education of Sherwood Eddy.* New York, Farrar & Rinehart, 1934. pp. 313–36.

Comparison of journeys before (1910, 1912) and after (1923) the 1917 revolution by American sociologist friendly to Marxian-Socialist principles. He sees "Russia a new planet" with two leaders who have provided the principles for leadership in the world—Jesus of Nazareth and Karl Marx.

548. Simpson, Eugene E. *Eugene E. Simpson's travels in Russia, 1910 and 1912.* Taylorville, Illinois, published by the author, 1916. 126 pp. map. port. index.

New York *Musical Courier* publisher travels from St. Petersburg to the Crimea and Samara to savor Russian music. He greatly admires the people, the language (which he spoke), and the music—sung and whistled.

549. Crawford, Laura MacPherson. *Dear Family: The travel letters and reminiscences of Laura MacPherson Crawford.* Ruth Saunders, editor. Claremont, California, privately printed, 1946. pp. 107–16.

On a journey around the world in 1910, tourist from the United States pays a May visit to Moscow and to the Ponafidine (see no. 616) estate near there, the atmosphere of which she characterizes by the word "deadliness." She observes: " . . . There is nothing but Moscow that pays for the weary hours of travel necessary to reach Russia."

550. Lee, Helena Crumett (Mrs. John Clarence). *Across Siberia alone. An American woman's adventures.* London, John Lane, 1914. 220 pp. illus. map.

Philadelphia traveler journeys from China to the United States through Russia on the Trans-Siberian Railway, summer, 1910. An ordinary report by a tourist, with some attempt to sense ordinary life in Russia. Mrs. Clarence spends one evening with exiles.

551.   Goodrich, Joseph King. *Russia in Europe and Asia.* Chicago, McClurg, 1912. 282 pp. illus. biblio. index.

Professor from the United States teaching in the Imperial Government College in Kyoto, journeys across Siberia to Moscow in July, 1910. In this study of Russian institutions, the author includes an account of types and places he sees on his train trip. Illustrations are excellent and illuminate the text.

552.   Washington, Booker T. *The man farthest down. A record of observation and study in Europe.* Garden City, New York, Doubleday, Page, 1912, pp. 276–95.

United States Negro educator sees life in a Russian village when he and a Russian-speaking friend are permitted to cross from Poland to Russia for a brief visit without a visa. This small contact leads Washington to observe that the Russian serf is about on a level with a Mississippi Negro farmer. Journey was made in 1910, August–September.

553.   McCaig, A. *Wonders of grace in Russia.* Riga, Revival Press, 1926. 251 pp. illus. port.

Principal emeritus of Spurgeon's College, London, journeys to St. Petersburg, Moscow, and Novgorod several times between 1910–17 to observe the work of the Russian Missionary Society, especially among the Baptists.

554.   Buchanan, (Sir) George. *My mission to Russia and other diplomatic memories.* London, Cassell, 1923. vol. I, pp. 76–253. vol. II, 263 pp. illus. map. index.

Sir George served as British ambassador to Russia from 1910 to 1918, through war and revolution to the beginning of the Allied intervention. He describes his life in St. Petersburg (Petrograd) in court and in the embassy almost day by day. This account along with that of Paléologue, French ambassador to Petrograd (see no. 607), provides a basic understanding of the Anglo-French attitudes during this period.

555. Buchanan, Meriel. *Recollections of Imperial Russia.* New York, Doran, 1924. 277 pp. illus.

Daughter of the British ambassador (see no. 554) describes the life of the court, of the embassy, and of the city, 1910–18, records visits to Moscow and Kiev along with descriptions of the Russian Orthodox Church, the manners and customs of the Cossacks, and the rising spirit and activities of the Bolsheviks.

556. Buchanan, Meriel. *Diplomacy and foreign courts.* London, Hutchinson, 1928. pp. 133–243. illus. index.

Here the ambassador's daughter provides a detailed description of her father's life and activities between 1910 and 1918. She is especially informative about life in St. Petersburg (Petrograd) during war and revolution. See nos. 554 and 555.

557. Buchanan, Meriel. *The dissolution of an empire.* London, John Murray, 1932. 304 pp. illus. port. index.

In this account the social side of an ambassador's life is emphasized, 1910–18. See nos. 554, 555, 556.

558. Buchanan, Meriel. *Ambassador's daughter.* London, Cassell, 1958. pp. 89–194. illus. port. biblio.

Essentially, this account is the ambassador's daughter's defense of her father's actions while in Russia, 1910–18, and much of the material found in earlier accounts is repeated (see nos. 554, 555, 556, 557).

559. Eddy, Sherwood. *The challenge of Russia.* New York, Farrar & Rinehart, 1931. 278 pp.

Between 1910 and 1930 Eddy made many visits to Imperial and Soviet Russia, never losing his faith in the positive features of

Marxian socialism as applied to the Russian situation. He believes that Intourist guides and the statistics they quote are honest, and he is especially informative on morals and religion. See no. 547.

560.   Lied, Jonas. *Prospector in Siberia: the autobiography of Jonas Lied*. New York, Oxford University Press, 1945. pp. 52–307. illus. map. index.

Lied, a Norwegian Russian-speaking trader in Russia, was made an honorary citizen and remained active in business, chiefly in Siberia, 1910–31. The work describes Lied's life on the Kara Sea and in the north, with special emphasis on the mineral wealth.

561.   Lied, Jonas. *Return to happiness*. London, Macmillan, 1944. pp. 52–83, 97–134. port.

In this account Lied describes his activities between 1910 and 1931 in Siberia and why he finally gave up his honorary citizenship and made his "return to happiness" in Norway. See no. 560.

562.   * Tuganov, (Prince) Mussa Bey. *From Tsar to Cheka; the story of a Circassian under tsar, padishah and Cheka*. London, Low, Marston, 1936. 250 pp. app.

563.   Graham, Stephen. *Undiscovered Russia*. London, John Lane, 1912. 332 pp. illus. map. index.

In 1911 Graham (see no. 543) journeyed to Archangel, Vologda, Moscow, the Sea of Azov, and the Caucasus. He continues his purpose of making Englishmen aware of Russia and its institutions.

564.   Graham, Stephen. *A tramp's sketches*. London, Macmillan, 1912. 339 pp.

Our traveler comments along philosophic lines after his journey of 1911 (see no. 563).

565.   Herbert, Agnes. *Casuals in the Caucasus. The diary of a sporting holiday*. London, John Lane, 1912. 331 pp. illus.

British tourist comments on life in Tiflis in 1911, with a few references to the part the city is playing as a revolutionary center.

566.   Phelps, William Lyon. *Autobiography with letters.* New York, Oxford University Press, 1939. pp. 522–28. port.

Yale University professor of literature and *Scribner's Magazine* critic, Phelps helped to popularize Russian literature in the United States. In 1911 he journeys to St. Petersburg, where he visits the Tretyakov Gallery, and Moscow, where he observes little joy in the faces of the Russian passersby as he walks through the city.

567.   Wood, Ruth Kedzie. *The tourist's Russia.* New York, Dodd, Mead, 1912. 244 pp. illus. map. port. app. index.

Mrs. Wood provides future tourists with information that will make their journeys easier and more interesting by describing travel in 1911 from St. Petersburg to Odessa. See no. 541.

568.   Donner, Kai. *Among the Samoyed in Siberia.* New Haven, Human Relations Area Files, 1954. 144 pp. illus.

Swedish linguist describes his visit to the tundra area of the Ob and Yenisei rivers, 1911–14.

569.   Monkhouse, Allan. *Moscow, 1911–1933.* Boston, Little, Brown, 1934. 334 pp. illus.

Pre-revolutionary experience heightens post-1917 observations by British engineer in and out of Russia many times between his initial journey and his ousting in 1933. He describes the industrialization of the Soviet economy from October, 1917, through the New Economic Policy and into the beginning of the second Five Year Plan. After the trial of the British engineers in 1933, he was deported as an enemy of the people.

570.   Dobson, George. *Russia.* London, Black, 1913. 460 pp. illus.

Along with his partner, the Dutch painter F. de Haenen, the British commentator Dobson sets out to paint and write about the Russian Empire in 1912. The paintings, colored and uncolored, range through pope to peasant, priest to postman, royalty to commoner. The supporting text is very informative with much historical background.

571.   Graham, Stephen. *Changing Russia.* London, John Lane, 1915. 304 pp. illus. map. port. index.

In 1912 Graham set out to sound out the intelligentsia, and this led him on a walking and train journey through European Russia, the Ural Mountains, the Caucasus, and the Crimea. See nos. 543, 563, and 564.

572.   Steveni, William Barnes. *Things seen in Russia.* New York, Dutton, 1913. 258 pp. illus. index.

Professor of English at the College of Peter the Great and English news correspondent in St. Petersburg produces a volume of verbal and pictorial descriptions of Russia in 1912 that gives little hint of the existing disruptive forces.

573.   Stewart, Hugh, and F. de Haenen. *Provincial Russia.* London, Adam and Charles Black, 1913. 168 pp. illus. map. index.

British writer (Stewart) and Dutch painter team up on journey in 1912. Excellent colored and uncolored pictures and commentary covering large portions of European Russia.

574.   Wright, Richardson L., and George Bassett Digby. *Through Siberia; an empire in the making.* New York, McBride, Nast, 1913. pp. 740–48. illus.

American author and journalist briefly examines the economic resources of Siberia in 1912.

575.   * Peel, (Hon.) W. R. W. *British representative delegation to Russia, Jan. 23rd—Febr. 5th 1912 with a view to promoting good relations between Great Britain and Russia.* The Hague, Mouton & Co., 1966.

Peel, Member of Parliament, describes events in St. Petersburg and Moscow in a scrapbook compiled by him consisting of programs, menus, invitations, proclamations, speeches, visiting-cards, snapshots, etc. This data from *Catalogue Fourty Six, A collection of books on Russia in its historical aspects*. The Hague, Mouton & Co., 1966. Item # 152, p. 10.

576. Graham, Stephen. *With the Russian pilgrims to Jerusalem*. London, Macmillan, 1916. 306 pp. illus. map.

Wanderer's journey reveals peasant character and soul. Graham travels to Jerusalem with 560 Russian pilgrims in the summer of 1912 on a vessel about the size of a Thames River steamer and bases his analysis on his close associations during the journey. See nos. 543, 563, 564, and 571.

577. Lockhart, (Robert H.) Bruce. *British agent*. New York, Putnam, 1933. 346 pp. illus. index.

Lockhart began his career in Russia as British vice-consul in Moscow and St. Petersburg, 1912–17. In the summer of 1917 he returned to London on sick leave and then was posted back to Leningrad with no authority as a special agent. In 1918 he was approached by Trotsky, who urged him, as British High Commissioner, to guarantee aid to Russia against Germany in return for which the Congress of Soviets would not ratify the Treaty of Brest-Litovsk.

578. Lied, Jonas. *Siberian Arctic. The story of the Siberian Company*. London, Methuen, 1960. 199 pp. illus. map. port. app. index.

Norwegian trader (see nos. 560 and 561) describes the activities of the Siberian Steamship Manufacturing and Trading Company, Ltd., on the Kara Sea, 1912–18.

579. Johnson, William Eugene. *The liquor problem in Russia*. Westerville, Ohio, American Issue Publishing Co., 1915. 221 pp. illus. map. app. index.

In 1913, Johnson, an Anti-Saloon League member, journeys to European Russia to expose the Russian government's vodka monopoly. The photographs illustrating this account are particularly good of the royal family, especially the young czarevitch.

580.   Steveni, William Barnes. *The Russian army from within.* London, Hodder & Stoughton, 1914. 184 pp. app.

Steveni (see no. 572) journeys from Kronstadt to the Caucasus during 1913 observing the army and its backbone, the peasants. He includes two chapters on the Cossacks.

581.   Bryce, (Lord) James. *Memories of travel.* New York, Macmillan, 1923. pp. 254–97.

Lord James (see no. 324) returns to Russia in 1913 and journeys through the Altai Mountains on the Trans-Siberian Railway. He comments on the character of the country and its people.

582.   Wheeler, William Webb. *The other side of the earth.* St. Joseph, Missouri, privately printed, 1913. pp. 169–203. illus. port.

Merchant from the United States journeys west across Siberia in June, 1913, and finds travel to be as good as in the United States and much cheaper!

583.   Nansen, Fridtjof. *Through Siberia. The land of the future.* Translated from the Norwegian by Arthur G. Chater. London, Heinemann, 1914. 436 pp. illus. map. port. app. index.

Nansen, Arctic explorer, scientist, statesman, and author, had a number of contacts with Russia in a long and excitement-filled life. Between 1910 and 1914 he explored along the Siberian coast, in 1920 he arranged for the repatriation of war prisoners, and during 1921 to 1923 he had general charge of the Red Cross Russian famine relief in the Volga and South Ukraine region. This work describes a journey made by him and three other men to explore commercial possibilities in the area, August–October, 1913.

584. Shelley, Gerard. *The blue steppes. Adventures among Russians.* London, John Hamilton, 1925. 268 pp. illus.

British writer records his impressions during the years 1913–20. He comments on the influence of Rasputin and life among the nobility and depicts the country as a "red madhouse" after the Revolution of 1917.

585. Bartlett, Robert A., and Ralph T. Hale. *Northward Ho! The last voyage of the Karluk.* Boston, Small, Maynard, 1916. pp. 161–279. illus. map.

The "Karluk" was commissioned and equipped to drift along the Russian and Canadian Arctic coasts as its crew studied the currents. Here Captain Bartlett describes how the ship sank and the crew escaped through northeast Siberia, March, 1913—May, 1914. The captain's account provides some data on the Chukchis.

586. Graham, Stephen. *Russia and the world. A study of the war and a statement of the world-problems that now confront Russia and Great Britain.* New York, Macmillan, 1915. 305 pp. illus.

Between December, 1913, and December, 1914, Graham toured European Russia and penetrated east to the border of China. He describes how the war affected the remote villages and its impact on the Jews, the Germans, and the use of alcoholic liquor. See nos. 543, 563, 564, 571, and 576.

587. Anderson, Herbert Foster. *Borderline Russia.* London, Cresset Press, 1942. 238 pp.

British student of Russian affairs learns the language and makes three journeys into Russia at critical times—in 1914, 1929, and 1930–32. His description points up the problems faced by the leaders of the Soviet Union and their success in solving them.

588. Baedeker, Karl W. *Russia, with Teheran, Port Arthur and Peking: Handbook for travelers.* Leipzig, Baedeker, 1914. 590 pp. map. index.

Baedeker provides the tourist with seventy-eight plans and forty maps of Russia just before the beginning of World War I.

589.   Fraser, (Sir) John Foster. *Russia of today.* London, Cassell, 1915. 289 pp. illus. port. index.

Friend of Russia journeys to Petrograd and Moscow to observe the impact of the war on the people and the economy in 1914. He emphasizes the tendency to procrastinate on the part of Russian officials. See no. 435.

590.   Gaunt, Mary. *A broken journey; wanderings from the Hoang-Ho to the island of Saghalien and the upper reaches of the Amur River.* London, Werner Laurie, 1919. pp. 157–295.

British tourist describes anti-German demonstrations by east Siberians at the beginning of World War I, as she heads home with her small dog on the Trans-Siberian Railway.

591.   Graham, Stephen. *The way of Martha and the way of Mary.* New York, Macmillan, 1916. 296 pp.

A comparison of Russian and Western religious characteristics resulting from Graham's journey in 1914. See nos. 543, 563, 564, 571, 576, and 586.

592.   Lethbridge, Alan Bourchier. *The new Russia, from the White Sea to the Siberian steppe.* London, Mills & Boon, 1915. 309 pp. illus. map. index.

British businessman and wife explore commercial possibilities in European and Asiatic Russia after reading Kliuchevsky in translation. He describes how they heard the first rumors of the beginning of World War I in Omsk and observed the initial treatment of the Germans.

593.   Moore, Benjamin Burges. *From Moscow to the Persian Gulf. Being the journal of a disenchanted traveller in*

Turkestan and Persia. New York, Putnam, 1915. pp. 1–70. illus. map.

American tourist's impressions, February 8–11, 1914.

594. Graham, Stephen. *Through Russian Central Asia.* New York, Macmillan, 1916. 254 pp. illus. map. app. index.

From the spring of 1914 until the beginning of World War I, Graham walked through Central Asia. Here he reports on the Anglo-Russian friction over Russia's proximity to India. See nos. 543, 563, 564, 571, 576, 586, and 591.

595. Scudder, Jared Waterbury. *Russia in the summer of 1914 with discussions of her pressing problems.* Boston, Badger, 1920. 186 pp. illus. index.

Although otherwise light in content, this American tourist account describes riots against the Germans in St. Petersburg in July, 1914, and their frantic attempts to escape.

596. Merry, Walter Mansell. *Two months in Russia, July–September, 1914.* Oxford, Blackwell, 1916. 202 pp.

Vicar of St. Michael's, Oxford, makes a round-trip journey from St. Petersburg to Odessa and describes how Russia went to war and how little the masses were aware of the issues.

597. Garstin, Denis. *Friendly Russia.* London, Fisher Unwin, 1915. 248 pp.

An intimate and friendly picture of Russian home life and customs by Russian-speaking British correspondent in autumn, 1914.

598. Bury, Herbert. *Russian life today.* London, Mowbray, 1915. 267 pp. illus. map. index.

Bishop for north and central Europe visits Anglican congregations in Russia, 1914–15. Expressing high regard for Nicholas II, he tries to describe the obvious, which is usually ignored.

599.   Czaplicka, Marie Antoinette Crispine. *My Siberian year.* New York, Oxford University Press, 1916. 306 pp. illus. map. port. index.

British anthropologist on the joint expedition to western Siberia sponsored by Oxford and Pennsylvania universities, 1914–15, reports on manners and customs of the Russian Eskimos and of her meetings with political exiles.

600.   Pares, Bernard. *Day by day with the Russian army, 1914–1915.* London, Constable, 1915. 282 pp. illus. map. port. index.

Friend of Russia (see nos. 450, 451, 503, and 515) details Russian army life from firsthand experience.

601.   Washburn, Stanley. *Field notes from the Russian front.* London, Andrew Melrose, 1915. 291 pp. illus. port.

London *Times* correspondent writes report quickly for public consumption about events, October, 1914–February, 1915. Excellent illustrations by George H. Mewes of the London *Daily Mirror,* the only English photographer with the Russian army in Poland. See no. 509.

602.   Marye, George T. *Nearing the end in Imperial Russia.* Philadelphia, Dorrance, 1929. 476 pp. illus. port.

Ambassador Marye, in St. Petersburg from 1914 to 1916, provides a study of Russia at war. He describes his appointment, his journey to the capital, reception by the emperor, the activities of the Duma, the machinations of Rasputin, impact of defeat on the Russians, and his final audience with Nicholas II.

603.   Cantacuzène, (Princess) Julia Grant. *Revolutionary days. Recollections of Romanoffs and Bolsheviks, 1914–1917.* London, Chapman & Hall, 1920. 411 pp. illus. port.

The granddaughter of United States General U. S. Grant provides a very unusual picture of Russia, 1914–17, as the wife of a Russian general. She describes her life in St. Petersburg and later in south Russia when escape from the Bolsheviki becomes necessary. The account is especially valuable because it reflects the fate of the Russian nobility through foreign eyes.

604. Dieterich, Johann. *Tovarish. The odyssey of a Siberian exile.* Paul Colestin Ettighoffer, editor. Translated from the German by M. H. Jerome. London, Hutchinson, 1935. 240 pp. illus. map.

Russian-speaking German telepathist and magician describes his escape through Siberia to Japan, 1914–17, in a series of impressions not pinpointed by any chronological data.

605. Farson, Negley. *The way of a transgressor.* New York, Harcourt Brace, 1936. pp. 112–295, 509–46. illus. port.

Farson is a munitions salesman and adventurer who describes his two journeys to Russia from the United States in 1914–17 and in 1928–29. He names the frustrations he encountered on his first journey in trying to arrange contracts for war material, and later he describes how Russia has changed under communism but remains the same in its business dealings.

606. Knox, (Major General Sir) Alfred William Fortescue. *With the Russian army, 1914–1917. Being chiefly extracts from the diary of a military attaché.* New York, Dutton, 1921. vol. I, 368 p. vol. II, pp. 383–740. illus. map. app. index.

Senior British military attaché with the Russian armies, Russian-speaking, provides an objective account of events on the Polish front.

607. Paléologue, Maurice. *An ambassador's memoirs.* Translated from the French by F. A. Holt. London, Hutchinson, 1924–25. vol. I, 350 pp. vol. II, 320 pp. vol. III, 346 pp. illus.

This account, along with that of Buchanan (see no. 554), provides a basis for understanding Franco-British policy, 1914–17. Paléologue was the last French ambassador to the Imperial Russian court, and his observations cover every aspect of Russian activity in court and common, with comments on the Orthodox church, the Jews, the rising chaos back of the front lines, etc.

608.   Hanbury-Williams, (Sir) John. *The Emperor Nicholas II as I knew him.* New York, Dutton, 1923. 264 pp. illus. port. index.

The chief of the British military mission from 1914 to 1917 comments on the court life of Petrograd and the character of the royal family. His remarks about the czarevitch are somewhat sentimental, perhaps what one would expect when one member of the nobility is writing about another.

609.   Price, Morgan Philips. *War and revolution in Asiatic Russia.* London, Allen & Unwin, 1918. 296 pp. map.

Russian-speaking *Manchester Guardian* correspondent, friendly to Russian people but very critical of Bolshevism, journeys to European Russia five times between 1908 and 1959, and writes a sympathetic account of Petrograd, the Western Front, and the Caucasus, 1914–17. He gives special attention to the impact of the war on the Caucasus and how the people reacted when the 1917 revolution occurred.

610.   * Brändström, Elsa. *Among prisoners of war in Russia and Siberia.* Translated from the German by C. Mabel Richmers. London, Hutchinson, 1929. 284 pp. illus. port.

611.   Buchanan, Meriel. *Petrograd the city of trouble, 1914–1918.* London, Collins Sons, 1918–19. 262 pp.

Daughter of British ambassador (see nos. 555, 556, 557, and 558) gives an informal, non-official view of the capital city, especially after the death of Rasputin. She provides a full chapter on "Monday, March 12."

612. Kroeger, Theodor. *The forgotten village. Four years in Siberia.* London, Hutchinson, 1936. 320 pp.

German army medical officer, Russian-speaking, describes how he was caught by the war while practicing in St. Petersburg (he had been born there). His four years, 1914–18, in Siberian prisons earned him many friends among the exiles, of whom he speaks with deep affection.

613. Keeling, H. V. *Bolshevism. Mr. Keeling's five years in Russia.* London, Hodder & Stoughton, 1919. 212 pp.

Russian-speaking British photographer and mechanic works in St. Petersburg and Moscow, 1914–19. He sees Lenin and his associates as idealists using ruffians to carry out their aims.

614. Wardell, John Wilford. *In the Kirghiz steppes.* London, Galley Press, 1961. 182 pp. illus. map. port. index.

British metal engineer, stationed in the area now called Kazakhstan, April, 1914–November, 1919, recalls the way of life, the geography and climate, and the impact of the revolution on the Kirghiz.

615. Meyendorff, (Baroness) Stella Zoe (Whishaw). *Through terror to freedom; the dramatic story of an Englishwoman's life and adventures in Russia before, during and after the Revolution.* London, Hutchinson, 1929. 288 pp. illus. port.

British actress married to Russian member of the czar's military household describes life at the Imperial court from 1914 to 1920, the Revolution seen through the eyes of the aristocracy, and escape.

616. Ponafidine, Emma Cochrane. *Russia—my home. An intimate record of personal experiences before, during and after the Bolshevik Revolution.* New York, Blue Ribbon Books, 1931. 312 pp. port.

A description of the changing rural scene from 1914 to 1921 as seen through the eyes of the Russian-speaking American wife of a Russian diplomat. She gives the lie to communist allegations that the country was without resourceful leadership until after October, 1917.

617. Roberts, Carl Eric Bechhofer. *A wanderer's log; being some memories of travel in India, the Far East, Russia, the Mediterranean and elsewhere!* London, Mills & Boon, 1922. pp. 106–82. illus.

As an English tutor in Russia, Roberts learned Russian before 1914 and learned to love the country and its people. He sees Bolshevik Russia as "Russia in ruins" and refers to the famine following World War I as the "abomination of desolation." This account covers the years 1914–17.

618. Britnieva, Mary. *One woman's story.* New York, Alfred H. King, 1934. 287 pp.

An English woman, the wife of a Russian medical doctor, lives in Moscow from 1914 to 1930. She describes her way of life and her relationship to her Russian neighbors before and after the Revolution, and, being friendly to the Soviet system, presents a commentary on the constant change that took place around her.

619. Child, Richard Washburn. *Potential Russia.* New York, Dutton, 1916. 221 pp.

United States lawyer and correspondent for *Collier's* is sent to Russia in 1915 to estimate her war potential. His survey includes an examination of the Jewish question.

620. Coxwell, Charles Fillingham. *Through Russia in wartime.* New York, Scribner's, 1917. 311 pp. illus. map. index.

Journey from the White Sea (Archangel) to the Caspian Sea by an American writer in 1915 enables him to examine every aspect of life, including the sacred pigeons in Red Square, Moscow. He illustrates his account with excellent photographs.

621. McCormick, Robert Rutherford. *With the Russian army, being the experiences of a national guardsman.* New York, Macmillan, 1915. 306 pp. illus. app.

Admitted to the Russian front in 1915 as a special war correspondent, American describes conditions in the trenches and later on the home front in Petrograd and Moscow. Illustrations are excellent, especially those showing the condition of the army.

622. Thompson, Donald C. *Donald Thompson in Russia.* New York, Century, 1918. 353 pp. illus. port.

American photographs Russia during two visits, 1915 and 1917. He arrives in Petrograd from Siberia on February 26, just in time to get valuable pictures of the March Revolution.

623. Washburn, Stanley. *The Russian campaign. April to August, 1915, being the second volume of "Field notes from the Russian front."* London, Andrew Melrose, 1916. 348 pp. illus. port.

Here Washburn (see no. 601) records confidence in the Russian army as it faces the Germans in Poland. Photographs by George H. Mewes.

624. Thurstan, Violetta. *The people who run. Being the tragedy of the refugees in Russia.* London, Putnam, 1916. 164 pp. map. app. index.

British friend of Russia describes the refugees running before the German armies as they advance eastward in 1915. Observes that "pity is one of the most marked and most beautiful characteristics of the Russian people."

625. Balch, Emily G. *Women at the Hague. The International Congress of women and its results.* New York, Macmillan, 1915. pp. 103–4.

A brief note on wartime Petrograd by Wellesley College professor, delegate on peace to Scandinavia and Russia, June–July, 1915.

626.   Pierce, (Mrs.) Ruth. *Trapped in "Black Russia", June–November 1915.* Boston, Houghton Mifflin, 1918. 150 pp.

Impressions of life in Kiev by American who has journeyed there from Rumania. She describes the persecution of the Jews and concludes that there is little hope for revolution because the Russian lacks co-ordination and singleness of purpose.

627.   Christie, Ella Robertson. *Through Khiva to golden Samarkand. The remarkable story of a woman's adventurous journey alone through the deserts of Central Asia to the heart of Turkestan.* Philadelphia, Lippincott, 1925. 269 pp. illus. map. port. index.

American writer makes two journeys in 1915–16 while Russia is at war and illustrates her comments with excellent photographs.

628.   Liddell, R. Scotland. *On the Russian front.* London, Simpkin, Marshall, Hamilton, Kent, 1916. 273 pp. illus. port.

Russian-speaking British member of Polish Red Cross Volunteers describes the Russian army retreat eastward from Warsaw in 1915. He writes that in the face of defeat the high morale of the line soldier was illustrated by the question and answer: "Are we downhearted?" "No!"

629.   Grow, (Lieutenant Colonel) Malcolm Cummings. *Surgeon Grow. An American in the Russian fighting.* New York, Frederick A. Stokes, 1918. 304 pp. illus.

American officer in the Imperial Russian Army medical corps describes the action at the front from 1915 to 1917, in which there are some scattered references to the Revolution of 1917.

630.   Liddell, R. Scotland. *Actions and reactions in Russia.* New York, Dutton, 1918. 227 pp. illus.

In this account, 1915–17, Liddell (see no. 628) continues his examination of the Russian at war, this time chiefly on the home front, where he characterizes the generally slovenly conduct by the question and answer: " 'Who is responsible?' . . . 'Everybody—and nobody.' And there you have the explanation of much of the trouble in Russia." He underlines this with his comments on the magic worked by his self-identification as an "Anglaaychanyin" (Englishman) in his movements about European Russia.

631. Pollock, (Sir) John. *War and revolution in Russia. Sketches and studies.* London, Constable, 1918. 278 pp. port. index.

British writer, attached to the Russian Red Cross, Russian-speaking, visits the war fronts, 1915–17. He includes a chapter of comment on Rasputin and his influence on affairs at the front and in Petrograd.

632. Englishman's Russian diary. *The Russian diary of an Englishman. Petrograd, 1915–1917.* London, Heinemann, 1919. 210 pp. illus. app. index.

This must be an English nobleman observing the scene from Petrograd and Moscow as he views events up to just before the October Revolution. He asserts that the forced abdication of Nicholas in March grew out of the conviction by many in the Fourth Duma that the affairs of the country were falling into the hands of the czarina. In the appendix are copies of letters circulated about the murderers of Rasputin, whose killers were not yet known by December 31, 1916.

633. Dwinger, Edwin Erich. *The army behind barbed wire: A Siberian diary.* Translated from the German by Ian F. D. Morrow. London, Allen & Unwin, 1930. 341 pp.

Prisoner-of-war account of a German officer, seventeen years of age, wounded and captured in his first charge, who spent the next three years in prison, 1915–18.

634. Price, Hereward Thimbleby. *Boche and Bolshevik. Experiences of an Englishman in the German Army and in Russian prisons.* London, Murray, 1919. 247 pp. index.

Description of life in prison in Irkutsk and the horrors of revolution in Siberia after his release and escape by way of Vladivostok; an experience during the years 1915–18.

635. Pollock, (Sir) John. *Time's chariot.* London, Murray, 1950. pp. 213–35. index.

A summary of his experiences that Sir John records more fully in nos. 631 and 698.

636. Urch, Reginald Oliver Gilling. *"We generally shoot Englishmen:" An English schoolmaster's five years of mild adventure in Moscow. (1915–1920).* London, Allen & Unwin, 1936. 294 pp. illus. index.

The "mild adventure" mentioned in the title indicates the understatement of this account, which is especially informative on the miseries suffered by the Russian intelligentsia.

637. Kohn, Hans. *Living in a world revolution. My encounters with history.* New York, Trident Press, 1964. pp. 89–99, 108–17.

The internationally known historian of nationalism describes his experience as a Czech soldier in the Austrian army captured by the Russians and held prisoner from March 21, 1915 to January 12, 1920. During this time he was moved from prison camp to prison camp in Central Asia and eastern Siberia, where he learned the Russian language and cultivated his captors, whom he found to be deeply human, friendly, and outgoing.

638. Austin, Walter. *A war zone gadabout. Being the authentic account of four trips to the fighting nations during 1914, '15, '16.* Boston, Hinkley, 1917. pp. 112–54. illus. port. index.

American correspondent comments on Russia at war, the ban on alcoholic liquors, the growing criticism of governmental leadership, the hatred of Germany, and the attacks on Rasputin's baleful influence.

639. Waters, (Brigadier General) Wallscourt Hely-Hutchinson. *"Secret and confidential". The experiences of a military*

attaché. New York, Frederick A. Stokes, 1926. 376 pp. illus. map. index.

Russian-speaking British officer describes his service in various posts from St. Petersburg to Siberia between 1876 and 1916. In this account a special notice is taken of emerging socialism in Russia, and Waters strongly condemns its appearance.

640. Beable, William Henry. *Commercial Russia.* London, Constable, 1918. 263 pp. map. app. index.

Speaking commercial Russian, British businessman tours European Russia and Siberia, April–September, 1916, to explore the prospects for the postwar period. He places his emphasis on economic resources, credit, shipping, etc., with chapters on the people, their customs, and the country.

641. Graham, Stephen. *Russia in 1916.* New York, Macmillan, 1917. 191 pp.

An old and faithful friend of Russia and the Russians (see nos. 543, 563, 564, 571, 576, 586, 591, and 594) returns during summer and autumn, 1916. His are light but penetrating observations on the effects of the war on the Orthodox church, on the court and royal family, on the prohibition of alcoholic liquors, on the gay life, and so on.

642. Washburn, Stanley. *The Russian offensive. Being the third volume of "Field notes from the Russian front," embracing the period from June 15 to September 1, 1916.* London, Constable, 1917. 193 pp. illus. map.

Washburn describes the renascence of the Russian army on the Polish front. Photographs by George H. Mewes. See nos. 601 and 623.

643. Bishop, H. C. W. *A Kut prisoner.* London, John Lane, 1920. 234 pp. illus. map. app.

British soldier escapes from the Turks into southern Crimea, 1916–17. An account not of very great value.

644.   Hoare, (Sir) Samuel John Gurney. *The fourth seal; the end of a Russian chapter.* London, Heinemann, 1930. 377 pp. illus. port. index.

On-the-spot description of events from the death of Rasputin in 1916 through the Bolshevik Revolution by an unsympathetic Russian-speaking British soldier-correspondent, illustrated with reproductions of propaganda posters. Hoare sees Nihilism as the eventual winner.

645.   Keeling, Edward Herbert. *Adventures in Turkey and Russia.* London, John Murray, 1924. pp. 119–74. illus. map. port.

Escape story by British soldier imprisoned at Kut by the Turks who gets away through Russia, 1916–17.

646.   Ruhl, Arthur Brown. *White nights and other Russian impressions.* New York, Scribner's, 1917. 248 pp. illus.

Collier's reporter journeys from Petrograd to Kiev by way of the Volga river valley, 1916–17. Impressionistic and rather superficial.

647.   Harper, Florence MacLeod. *Runaway Russia.* New York, Century, 1918. 321 pp. illus. port.

Correspondent of British *Leslie's Weekly* crosses Siberia to Petrograd, December, 1916–September, 1917. Pro-czar and anti-Kerensky, she tells a story of patient heroism by the army against underground treachery.

648.   Boleslavski, Richard, and Helen Woodward. *Way of the Lancer.* Indianapolis, Bobbs-Merrill, 1932. 316 pp.

Polish officer in the Russian army tells a bloody story of war and chaos, 1916–18, in which a comparison of Kerensky's and Trotsky's leadership is made. Fact and fiction appear to be generously mixed in his account.

649. Colquhoun, James. *Adventures in Red Russia. From the Black Sea to the White Sea.* London, John Murray, 1926. 175 pp. illus. app.

The hazards of copper mining near Batum during revolutionary times, 1916–18, are listed by a British engineer, who describes how ruin comes to the industry when the workers get the upper hand. He includes a very informative foreign viewpoint of the relative leadership abilities of Lenin and Kerensky.

650. Cresson, William Penn. *The Cossacks. Their history and country.* New York, Brentano, 1919. 239 pp. illus. map.

Russian-speaking secretary of the American embassy in Petrograd journeys through Cossack country, 1916–18.

651. Fleurot, Arno Walter Dosch. *Through war to revolution. Being the experiences of a newspaper correspondent in war and revolution, 1914–1920.* London, John Lane, 1931. pp. 97–215. illus. index.

French war correspondent, in Russia to see the country of the "New Moon," records interesting but undated interviews with important revolutionary figures, 1916–18. Observes: "Trotsky won the Bolshevik Revolution."

652. Gorer, Geoffrey, and John Rickman. *The people of Great Russia. A psychological study.* New York, Chanticleer Press, 1950. pp. 21–89.

John Rickman, M.D., served as country doctor to Russian peasants with the Friends' War Victims Relief Unit, 1916–18. His account is an extremely valuable record of the impact of the war and the Bolsheviki on rural life.

653. Francis, David R. *Russia from the American Embassy, April, 1916–November, 1918.* New York, Scribner's, 1922. 349 pp. illus. port. index.

A basic document by the ambassador who represented the United States during the entire revolutionary period. He organizes his account along chronological lines, with comments in depth on significant events. The ambassador's style is excellent, and he illustrates his story with illuminating photographs and informative quotes from letters, papers, and his personal diary.

654.   Barber, Margaret H. *A British Nurse in Bolshevik Russia.* London, Fifield, 1920. pp. 1–64. illus. port. app.

Relief expedition worker in Armenia, April, 1916–December, 1919, refuses to endorse stories of atrocities allegedly committed by the Bolsheviki.

655.   Stanford, Doreen. *Siberian odyssey.* New York, Dutton, 1964. 157 pp. map.

The daughter of a British mining engineer stationed in Ulen', near the Mongolian border, 1916–20, describes village life before the 1917 Revolution. Unsympathetic to revolutionary aims, she tells how she, along with her father, mother, and dog, commandeered an abandoned train coach loaded with Red Cross supplies and escaped across Siberia.

656.   Krist, Gustav. *Prisoner in the forbidden land.* Translated from the German by E. O. Lorimer. London, Faber & Faber, 1938. 344 pp. illus. map. app. index.

Austrian soldier and adventurer, Russian-speaking, describes Russian Central Asia in his activities as a prisoner-of-war, 1916–21.

657.   Lockhart, (Robert H.) Bruce. *The two revolutions. An eyewitness study of Russia, 1917.* London, Phoenix House, 1957. 115 pp.

Lockhart's *British Agent* (see no. 577) dealt in greater detail with his experiences in 1917, experiences which he reassesses in this account after forty years have passed.

658.   Mott, John Raleigh. *America's answer to the Russian people.* Boston, Marshall Jones, 1918. pp. 105–20.

Brief comments by American Young Men's Christian Association official and member of a special diplomatic mission to Russia in 1917.

659. Reed, John. *Ten days that shook the world.* New York, Modern Library, 1935. 313 pp. illus. app.

John Reed is perhaps the best-known traveler to Russia in the twentieth century. An American journalist and a radical attached to the *Masses* after 1913, he arrives in Russia and writes a sympathetic account of events in Petrograd during the October Revolution. Without any working knowledge of Russian but possessed with a vast enthusiasm for the aims of the revolutionists, he collected handbills, copies of speeches, proclamations, and other documents that make his account a storehouse of readings on events coming under his eyes. The Bolsheviki later used this book as a textbook until it was banned by Stalin.

660. Robins, Raymond, and William Hard. *Raymond Robins' own story.* New York, Harper, 1920. 248 pp. illus. port.

Robins was the unofficial representative of the United States ambassador who had extensive dealings with Lenin. Coming into the capital from Siberia, he claims to have recognized the Petrograd Soviet as the real power. From a position of opposition to the Bolsheviki he gradually emerges as a sympathizer to their aims. He describes his activities with the Red Cross in 1917.

661. Hall, (Lieutenant) Bert. *One man's war. The story of the Lafayette Escadrille.* John Jacob Niles, editor. New York, Holt, 1929. pp. 226–76.

American aviator crosses Siberia from Petrograd on his return to the United States and comments on the March Revolution in 1917.

662. Houghteling, James Lawrence, Jr. *A diary of the Russian Revolution.* New York, Dodd, Mead, 1918. 195 pp. illus.

Member of the American embassy in March, 1917, observes: "But no one who has caught the spirit of the Revolution can doubt that the upbuilding of such a system will be duly finished—despite intervening disturbances—generously, wisely, and patriotically."

663.   Lange, Christian Louis. *Russia, the Revolution and the War. An account of a visit to Petrograd and Helsingfors in March, 1917.* Washington, D.C., Carnegie Endowment, 1917. pp. 1–26.

Norwegian correspondent to Carnegie Endowment arrives in Petrograd two days after the beginning of the March Revolution and proceeds to investigate and list the emergent problems faced by the nation.

664.   Marcossan, Isaac Frederick. *The rebirth of Russia.* London, John Lane, 1917. 208 pp. illus.

American correspondent arrives in Petrograd shortly after the March Revolution. He characterizes Kerensky as a Russian Lloyd George and considers the Root Commission from the United States to be a stabilizing influence.

665.   Rivet, Charles. *The last of the Romanoffs.* Translated from the French by Hardress O'Grady. London, Constable, 1918. 246 pp. illus.

Friendly to the purposes of the March Revolution, Russian-speaking French *Temps* correspondent seeks to apprise the world of Russia's needs.

666.   Jones, Stinton. *Russia in revolution. Being the experiences of an Englishman in Petrograd during the upheaval.* London, Herbert Jenkins, 1917. 279 pp. illus.

Resident British businessman provides a very detailed account of the five days, March 10–14, 1917. The accompanying illustrations are really unusual.

667.   Anet, Claude (Jean Schopfer, pseudonym). *Through the Russian Revolution: Notes of an eyewitness from 12th March–30th May.* London, Hutchinson, 1917. 253 pp. illus.

Russian-speaking *Petit Parisien* correspondent, a socialist extremely critical of the aims of the Bolsheviki, provides an almost hourly chronicle of events from March 12 to May 30. His comparison of Lenin and Kerensky is very informative.

668. Thompson, Donald C. *From Czar to Kaiser, "The betrayal of Russia."* Garden City, New York, Page, 1918. 199 pp. illus.

American photographer (see no. 622) records the progress of the revolution in Petrograd from March through September and then escapes by way of Siberia. Extraordinary photographs illuminate his account.

669. Steffens, Joseph Lincoln. *The autobiography of Lincoln Steffens.* New York, Harcourt, Brace, 1931. II, 747–68, 790–99. illus.

American journalist and muckraker journeys to Russia in February, 1917, and experiences what he judges to be the advantages and disadvantages of Kerensky's regime. He departs just before the October Revolution but returns to Petrograd in 1919 as a member of the Bullitt mission (see no. 731).

670. Dorr, Rheta Louise Childe. *Inside the Russian Revolution.* New York, Macmillan, 1917. 243 pp. illus.

British socialist records impressions, May–July, 1917, in Petrograd. She sees the ideals of revolution being destroyed by the emerging tyrannical working class but concludes that there will "ultimately be a return to sanity and order" and that the wise men of Russia will counter "the mad Bolsheviki."

671. Vandervelde, Emile. *Three aspects of the Russian Revolution.* Translated from the French by Jean E. H. Findlay. New York, Scribner's, 1918. 241 pp. app.

Belgian socialist visits Petrograd, May 18–June 25, 1917, and observes the Lenin-Kerensky struggle for power by going behind the scenes through doors opened to him by Russian associates. He also comments on the war front and the activities of the Petrograd Soviet.

672.   Root, Elihu. *America's message to the Russian people. Addresses by the members of the special diplomatic mission of the United States to Russia in the year 1917.* Boston, Marshall Jones, 1918. pp. 13–154.

Ambassador extraordinary and head of a special diplomatic mission sent by President Woodrow Wilson in May, 1917, Root expresses to the people of Russia the friendship and sympathy of the United States.

673.   Poole, Ernest. *"The dark people": Russia's crisis.* New York, Macmillan, 1919. 226 pp. illus.

Correspondent from the United States surveys the peasant and his emerging consciousness in July, 1917. He provides excellent photographs of street scenes and revolutionists.

674.   Poole, Ernest. *The village: Russian impressions.* New York, Macmillan, 1919. 234 pp.

Poole's (see no. 673) account, partly semi-fictional, is of Tarasov, his interpreter, who accompanies him into the rural areas in 1917. Poole writes with deep sympathy about the peasant and his way of life by means of long stories and conversations in which the participants relate themselves to the Revolution.

675.   Stebbing, E. P. *From Czar to Bolshevik.* London, John Lane, 1918. 313 pp. illus. index.

British businessman observes Russian failures and German successes, July 16–November 8, 1917. Visiting Petrograd, Moscow, and the area around Archangel, the writer concludes that revolution is a rejuvenating force.

676.   Wightman, Orrin Sage. *The diary of an American physician in the Russian Revolution, 1917.* New York, Brooklyn Daily Eagle, 1928. pp. 1–178. illus.

Associated with Colonel William Boyce Thompson, American medical doctor journeys from Petrograd to Odessa, July 26–October 13, 1917, on a tour of inspection. While in Odessa, he witnesses the coming of the Revolution.

677. Ross, Edward Alsworth. *Russia in upheaval.* New York, Century, 1919. 349 pp. illus. index.

Wisconsin University professor of sociology travels from Petrograd through Siberia, autumn, 1917. Claims "scientific objectivity" as his guiding star and concludes that Russians are doing as he would under similar circumstances.

678. Riis, Sergius Martin. *Yankee Komisar.* New York, Speller, 1935. 236 pp.

Naval attaché, American embassy, describes escape journey from Petrograd to Odessa, November, 1917. He is highly critical of the Bolsheviki and the havoc they are wreaking on the country.

679. Bauermeister, (Lieutenant) Alexander. *Spies break through. Memoirs of a German Secret Service officer.* Translated from the German by Hector C. Bywater. London, Constable, 1934. 185 pp. illus. port.

Espionage agent makes some contacts with the Bolsheviki while in underground activities in 1917–18.

680. Beury, Charles E. *Russia after the Revolution.* Philadelphia, George W. Jacobs, 1918. 138 pp. illus. map. port.

A short account of an area usually neglected—conditions in southeast European Russia—by the Commissioner for the American Committee for Armenian and Syrian Relief, July, 1917–early 1918.

681. Brown, William Adams. *The groping giant. Revolutionary Russia as seen by an American democrat.* New Haven, Yale University Press, 1920. 199 pp. index.

American Young Men's Christian Association secretary and later a member of the American Committee on Public Information organizes his account of a journey to Moscow by way of Siberia around an analysis of the people, the Bolsheviki, and the intelligentsia.

682.   * Daniel, W. *Russia, 1918. Bolshevism in practice.* Stockport, privately printed, 1919.

British businessman's journey in 1917–18. See Grierson, *Books on Soviet Russia* (no. 1438).

683.   Kehler, Henning. *The red garden.* Translated from the Danish by F. Toksvig. New York, Knopf, 1922. 204 pp.

Member of the Danish Legation in Petrograd, with no love for the Bolsheviki, describes the tragedy and chaos in 1917, from which he fled through Siberia.

684.   Oudendyk, William J. *Ways and by-ways in diplomacy.* London, Peters Davies, 1939. pp. 131–47, 212–316. port.

Dutch diplomat describes his life in Moscow during 1917–18. Pro-Trotsky, he is extremely critical of Lenin and Stalin.

685.   Power, Rhoda. *Under the Bolshevik reign of terror.* New York, McBride, Nast, 1919. 279 pp.

British teacher living in Rostov-on-Don, learning the Russian language and teaching English, from just before the March Revolution until early 1918, describes how the transition was made from control by the provisional government to control by the Bolsheviki and how foreign intervention began.

686.   Woody, Thomas. *New minds: new men? The emergence of the Soviet citizen.* New York, Macmillan, 1932. 482 pp. illus. map. biblio. index.

Professor of educational history sets out to discover the kind of mind emerging between 1917 and 1930. In 1917–18, 1928, and 1929–30 he visited hundreds of schools of every description.

687. Crosley, Pauline S. *Intimate letters from Petrograd.* New York, Dutton, 1920. 305 pp. app.

The wife of an American embassy attaché, April, 1917–April, 1918, observes the October Revolution and the consolidation of power by the Bolsheviki. She includes an appendix containing samples of enemy propaganda and notes from conferences of workers' and soldiers' deputies.

688. Masaryk, Thomas Garrigue. *The making of a state. Memories and observations, 1914–1918.* London, Allen & Unwin, 1927. pp. 132–91. An English version arranged with an introduction by Henry Wickham Steed.

Founder and president of Czechoslovakia philosophizes about his treatment at the hands of the Russians in 1917–18 and describes the activities of the Czech soldiers in Russia and Siberia.

689. Wild, Max. *Secret service on the Russian front.* Translated from the German by Anthony Haigh. New York, Putnam, 1932. pp. 86–324. map.

Russian-speaking espionage agent attached to the German Eighth Army headquarters is captured, interned in Siberia, and later exchanged. Here he describes his activities, May, 1917–May, 1918.

690. Beatty, Bessie. *The red heart of Russia.* New York, Century, 1918. 480 pp. illus.

San Francisco Bulletin war correspondent journeys from Vladivostok to Petrograd, June, 1917–January, 1918. She describes the events in the city in a very impressionistic manner—women in the revolution, the battalion of death, blasting at the established order, Christmas, 1917, etc. Her account is considered by many critics to rank next to Reed's *Ten Days that shook the world* (see no. 659) in the bibliography of foreign observers' descriptions of 1917.

691. Hill, George Alexander. *Go spy the land. Being the adventures of I. K. 8 of the British Secret Service.* London, Cassell, 1932. pp. 276–361. map. port. index.

British businessman and espionage agent journeys to Petrograd, July, 1917–November, 1918, where he carries out the implications of the book's title.

692.   Bryant, Louise (Mrs. John Reed). *Six red months in Russia. An observer's account of Russia before and during the proletarian dictatorship.* London, Heinemann, 1919. 299 pp. illus.

American correspondent arrives in August, 1917, and departs in January, 1918. She provides many photographs of her contacts with important Bolsheviki and discounts tales of terror and rape.

693.   Sayler, Oliver Martin. *Russia. White or Red.* Boston, Little, Brown, 1919. 303 pp. illus. index.

Drama editor of the *Indianapolis News* journeys to Moscow over the Trans-Siberian Railway from Vladivostok just before October, 1917, and leaves in mid-1918. Manages to penetrate the Kremlin to see the Bolsheviki take power. Account includes the curious Samara proclamation on the "private possession of women," which recommends the opposite.

694.   Sayler, Oliver Martin. *The Russian theater.* New York, Brentano, 1922. 296 pp. illus. index.

Sayler (see no. 693) studies the effects of three years of war and six months of revolution on the Russian theater. He describes the progressive methods and experimentation going on in Petrograd and Moscow.

695.   Ward, (Colonel) John. *With the "Die Hards" in Siberia.* London, Cassell, 1920. 269 pp. illus. port. index.

Memoirs of a British officer in eastern Siberia, 1917–18, who was a sympathizer and supporter of Admiral Kolchak. He claims that American neutrality of attitude permitted the Bolsheviki to survive.

696.   Sisson, Edgar Grant. *One hundred red days. A personal chronicle of the Bolshevik Revolution.* New Haven, Yale University Press, 1931. 430 pp. illus. port. app. index.

Special representative of President Woodrow Wilson recommends non-recognition of the Bolsheviki after their seizure of power, November 25, 1917–March 4, 1918. He includes documents that may have been forged and revolutionary posters. His account is an interesting but often untrustworthy source.

697. Marchand, René. *Why I side with the Social Revolution.* Translated from the French by Eden and Cedar Paul. London, British Socialist Party, 1919. 64 pp.

After experiences during revolution and intervention, 1917–19, Marchand concludes that the Bolshevik solution is the only one.

698. Pollock, (Sir) John. *The Bolshevik adventure.* London, Constable, 1919. 276 pp. index.

In Petrograd during the March and October Revolutions, British worker in the Russian Red Cross travels widely until 1919, establishing contacts with the still idealistic grass-roots revolutionists. See nos. 631 and 635.

699. Price, Morgan Philips. *My reminiscences of the Russian Revolution.* London, Allen & Unwin, 1921. 388 pp. illus. app. index.

Left-wing sympathizer (see no. 609) with numerous contacts describes agrarian conditions, March, 1917–July, 1919. He includes an appendix with the Declaration of Rights of the Working and Exploited Peoples, a chart of the Soviet system, and a map of agrarian Russia.

700. Brun, Alf Harald. *Troublous times. Experiences in Bolshevik Russia and Turkestan.* London, Constable, 1931. 238 pp. illus. port. index.

Danish Red Cross officer responsible for Austrian prisoners of war in Turkestan, October, 1917–July, 1919, describes the impact of the Revolution in areas not held by Moscow.

701. Becvar, Gustav. *The lost legion. A Czechoslovakian epic.* London, Stanley Paul, 1939. 249 pp. illus. port. index.

Czech soldier describes the historic trek of the army as it moves across Siberia, with its contacts with the Russians and its encounters with the forces of intervention, 1917–20.

702.   Dukes, (Sir) Paul. *Red dusk and the morrow. Adventures and investigations in red Russia.* Garden City, New York, Doubleday, Page, 1922. 322 pp. illus. port.

British foreign agent, Young Men's Christian Association worker and then chief of the British Secret Intelligence writes a dashing account of adventures, 1917–20. He includes an excellent discussion on the Red Army. See no. 545.

703.   Williams, Albert Rhys. *Through the Russian Revolution.* New York, Boni and Liveright, 1921. 286 pp. app.

Correspondent for *Outlook* and Chautaqua lecturer, Williams spoke the Russian language, knew many of the Russian leaders from Lenin to Litvinov, and deeply sympathized with the ideals of "The workers and peasants of Russia who fell in defense of the Revolution" (the dedication of this book). Here he describes events in the period from 1917 to 1920; see especially his account of a Red funeral at Vladivostok.

704.   * Englishwoman. *From a Russian diary, 1917–1920.* London, John Murray, 1921. 263 pp. index.

Grierson (see no. 1438) describes this book as an irregularly kept diary from November 14, 1917, to March 12, 1920, and considers it to be extremely unreliable and full of rumors.

705.   Gibson, William James. *Wild career. My crowded years of adventure in Russia and the Near East.* London, Harrap, 1935. 287 pp. port.

Unusual account of adventure in European Russia by a Canadian, born and reared in St. Petersburg, who serves in the Russian army in World War I and becomes a commissar under the Soviets. His description of the seizure of power by the Bolsheviki in 1917 is very informative.

706. Douillet, Joseph. *Moscow unmasked: a record of nine years' work and observation in Soviet Russia.* Translated from the Russian by A. W. King. London, Pilot, 1930. 223 pp. illus.

Belgian consul and relief worker, Russian-speaking, is in south Russia, 1917–26. He describes the image that the Soviet system projects and then illustrates how it really works; in conclusion he predicts a "reign of blood" by the Soviet secret police.

707. Haines, Anna J. *Health work in Soviet Russia.* New York, Vanguard, 1928. 177 pp.

American Friends Service Committee worker with some knowledge of the Russian language contrasts new and old medical programs after three journeys, 1917–27. This account tends to be more impressionistic than statistical, although some statistics are included.

708. Ameel, Joseph. *Red Hell. Twenty years in Soviet Russia.* London, Hale, 1941. 316 pp. illus. port.

Russian-born Belgian engaged in timber trade in the Soviet Union, 1917–30, and a prisoner in Stalin slave camps, 1930–37. He describes the Russian timber trade in considerable detail and provides an equal amount of information about the camps in which he was confined.

709. Davis, Jerome. *Behind Soviet power. Stalin and the Russians.* New York, Readers' Press, 1946. 120 pp. illus. app.

Between 1917 and 1945 Davis made almost yearly journeys to the Soviet Union and apparently never lost faith in the intentions of the Communist party to create a world approximating the ideal: "From each according to his ability; to each according to his needs." In *Behind Soviet power* the American sociologist paints a rosy picture of the future and provides what he considers to be a true account of the purge trials.

710. Dunsterville, (Major-General) Lionel Charles. *The adventures of Dunsterforce.* London, Arnold, 1920. pp. 194–317. illus. map. port. index.

Officer in the British army aiding the forces defending Baku against the Bolsheviki in 1918 describes the operations and stresses the importance of the Baku oil fields to Britain and to Russia.

711.   Hindus, Maurice Gerschon. *The Russian peasant and the Revolution*. New York, Holt, 1920. 323 pp. biblio.

Russian-born American journalist of peasant ancestry studies Russia and its people at first hand during many journeys from the United States to the Soviet Union, 1918–61. His books are an especially valuable source for understanding the collectivization of agriculture and its impact on the lives of the peasants. In this work he makes his first visit to his former home in the Ukraine in 1918 and examines the peasant reactions to the promises of the revolutionists. He concludes that revolution and change were needed but came at the wrong time and too brutally.

712.   Steele, Dan. *Snow trenches*. Chicago, McClurg, 1931. pp. 1–361. map. port.

Soldier and businessman writes a description of the operations of the American Expeditionary Force in Archangel, 1918.

713.   French, (Lieutenant Colonel) F. J. F. *From Whitehall to the Caspian*. London, Oldhams Press, 1920, pp. 38–255. illus. map.

Officer describes British efforts in 1918–19 to save the Caspian Sea area from the Turks and their allies after the collapse of Russia's central government during the 1917 revolutions.

714.   Ironside, William Edmund. *Archangel, 1918–1919*. London, Constable, 1953. 201 pp. illus. map. port. app. index.

British general's account of the international army in north Russia and later the British Relief Force, in which strong criticism is directed at the Bolsheviki and their operations.

715.   Terpenning, Walter A. *To Russia and return*. Privately printed, n.d., 120 pp. illus.

Young Men's Christian Association secretary describes a year spent in three villages near Lake Onega, 1918–19. He defends the peasants against their critics, who have often described them as sodden and depraved.

716.   Varney, John Cushing. *Sketches of Soviet Russia; whole cloth and patches.* New York, Nicholas Brown, 1920. 288 pp.

Working in the upper Volga River area, April, 1918–March, 1919, American Young Men's Christian Association representative sees Russia and its problems as a serious challenge to the West.

717.   Rawlinson, (Lieutenant Colonel) Alfred. *Adventures in the Near East, 1918–1922.* London, Andrew Melrose, 1923. pp. 63–106, 123–205. illus. port.

British officer describes the operations of the military against the Bolsheviki in the Caspian and Transcaucasian areas, May, 1918–August, 1919.

718.   Maynard, Charles Clarkson Martin. *The Murmansk adventure.* London, Hodder & Stoughton, 1928. 311 pp. illus. map. port. app.

Commander-in-chief of allied forces in northwest Russia describes the operations of his army and gives British reasons for intervention in the affairs of the Bolsheviki, May, 1918–September, 1919.

719.   Bailey, Frederick Marshman. *Mission to Tashkent.* London, Jonathan Cape, 1946. 294 pp. illus. map. index.

British officer in the Indian army describes his journey into Russian Transcaspia, June, 1918–January, 1919, to prevent Germany from getting oil and cotton during her blockade by the Allied forces. Bailey provides an excellent description of the emerging power of the local Bolsheviki, by whom he is arrested and imprisoned and from whom he finally escapes by a series of daring strategems.

720.   Cudahy, John. *Archangel. The American war with Russia.* Chicago, McClurg, 1924. 216 pp. illus. map.

Member of the American Expeditionary Force comments on operations, August, 1918–June, 1919. Cudahy sees no meaning or purpose in the expedition and considers 2,500 casualties as far too high a cost for the benefits derived.

721.   Moore, Frederick F. *Siberia today.* New York, Appleton, 1919. 333 pp. illus.

American correspondent with the American Expeditionary Force in eastern Siberia, September, 1918–February, 1919, is very critical of the Bolsheviki, ending his account with the observation: "We must understand Asia—or our children's children will wash the pots in Asiatic sculleries."

722.   Albertson, Ralph. *Fighting without a war; An account of military intervention in North Russia.* New York, Harcourt, Brace & Howe, 1920. 138 pp. illus. map.

Young Men's Christian Association secretary with the United States Army in Murmansk, November, 1918–August, 1919, criticizes the British military and emphasizes the futility of guarding without fighting. He condemns the Bolsheviki but claims the Russian common people loved the Americans.

723.   Ackerman, Carl W. *Trailing the Bolsheviki: Twelve thousand miles with the Allies in Siberia.* New York, Scribner's, 1919. 280 pp. illus. app.

Anti-Bolshevik reporter on the *New York Times,* accredited to the Czechoslovakian army in Siberia, December, 1918–March, 1919, describes the civil war, the birth of new governments in Siberia, and the fate of Nicholas II.

724.   Aten, Marion, and Arthur Orrmont. *Last train over Rostov bridge.* New York, Julian Messner, 1961. 340 pp. index.

Total recall of events and conversations forty years after the events in 1918–20, by an American in the Royal Air Force.

725. Kindall, Sylvian G. *American soldiers in Siberia.* New York, Richard R. Smith, 1945. 251 pp.

An American soldier's observations of the conflict between the Bolsheviki and the Japanese in eastern Siberia, 1918–20, in which strong criticism is leveled against both parties.

726. Hill, George Alexander. *Dreaded hour.* London, Cassell, 1936. 272 pp. illus. map. port. index.

British secret service account of activities for Russia before 1917 and against her after the Revolution, 1918–22. Very impressionistic without many chronological moorings.

727. Blacker, (Captain) Latham Valentine Stewart. *On secret patrol in high Asia.* London, John Murray, 1922. 294 pp. illus. map. index.

British secret service agent in Turkestan, 1919, describes his adventures but provides few dates.

728. Dwinger, Edwin Erich. *Between white and red.* Translated from the German by Marion Saunders. New York, Scribner's, 1932. 492 pp. map.

Further adventures of a German prisoner of war (see no. 633) who joins Admiral Kolchak to fight the Bolsheviki in 1919.

729. Pridham, (Sir) Francis. *Close of a dynasty.* London, Wingate, 1959. pp. 50–83. illus.

Vice-Admiral commanding H. M. S. "Marlborough" describes the evacuation of Dowager Empress Marie from Sebastopol in 1919 and, by emphasizing how royalty looks after its servants, attempts to offset the Bolshevik image of the royal family.

730. Ransome, Arthur. *Russia in 1919.* New York, Huebsch, 1919. 232 pp.

Manchester Guardian correspondent and Russian-speaking lecturer describes Petrograd and Moscow in February–March, 1919. He interviews Lenin and comments on the increasing control by the Bolsheviki.

731.   Bullitt, William Christian. *The Bullitt mission to Russia: Testimony before the Committee on Foreign Relations, U.S. Senate, of William C. Bullitt.* New York, Huebsch, 1919. 151 pp.

President Woodrow Wilson's personal delegate is sent to Petrograd in March, 1919, where he counsels with Lenin and returns to the Paris Peace Conference with a plan for peace approved by the Bolsheviki. Here he describes his mission and its betrayal. Included are sympathetic testimonies of Captain W. W. Pettit, U.S. Army and member of the Commission, and Joseph Lincoln Steffens, an American journalist accompanying Bullitt.

732.   Channing, C. G. F. (pseudonym of Christian C. Gross). *Siberia's untouched treasure, its future role in the world.* New York, Putnam, 1923. pp. 99–307. illus. map. port. app. index.

Lieutenant in the American Expeditionary Force assigned to keep an eye on Japanese activities, March–October, 1919, describes the attitudes of Americans toward the land and peoples of Siberia as they help rebuild the Trans-Siberian Railway. He mentions that four hundred of the soldiers brought home Russian wives.

733.   Soutar, Andrew. *With Ironside in North Russia.* London, Hutchinson, 1940. 250 pp. illus. port.

London *Times* correspondent with the British forces around Murmansk, April–October, 1919, recalls his experiences two decades later during the Russo-Finnish war of 1940. It appears that his comments may have been influenced by his attitude toward the Russians in their dealings with the Finns.

734.   * Singleton-Gates, G. R. *Bolos and Barishynas, being an account of the doings of the Sadleir-Jackson Brigade, and*

Altham Flotilla, on North Dvina during the summer, 1919. Aldershot, private circulation, 1920. 194 pp. illus.

735. Goode, William T. *Bolshevism at work.* London, Allen & Unwin, 1920. 142 pp.

Manchester Guardian journalist and scholar interviews Lenin, July–August, 1919, and records neutral to favorable impressions of Bolshevik handling of labor, transport, education, etc.

736. McBride, Isaac. *"Barbarous Soviet Russia."* New York, Thomas Seltzer, 1920. 155 pp. illus. app.

Reporter from the United States journeys to Moscow and Petrograd, September–October, 1919, and finds "nothing but the utmost kindness and goodwill toward the whole world." He claims that the Whites terrorized the Reds but that the Reds treated their prisoners with kindness and educated them.

737. Malone, (Colonel) Cecil L'Estrange. *The Russian republic.* London, Allen & Unwin, 1920. 135 pp. map. app.

After negotiating with the Bolsheviki, September 29–October 20, 1919, British officer predicts that Russia will be the greatest military power in Europe by the end of a generation.

738. * Schwartz, Alexander. *The voice of Russia.* New York, Dutton, 1920. illus.

739. Sutton, Francis Arthur. *One-Arm Sutton.* New York, Viking, 1933. pp. 47–277. map. port.

British businessman trading near the border between Russia and Manchuria in 1919–20, describes the increasing difficulties faced when negotiating with the Bolsheviki.

740. Hodges, (Major) Phelps. *Britmis. A great adventure of the war. Being an account of Allied intervention in Siberia*

and of escape across the Gobi to Peking. London, Jonathan Cape, 1931. pp. 17–231. illus. map. port. index.

Member of the British Political Mission describes his escape from Vladivostok to the Ural Mountains, south across the Gobi desert into China, January, 1919–May, 1920. His account includes details on all the war conditions he encountered.

741.   Vining, (Major) L. E. *Held by the Bolsheviks. The diary of a British officer in Russia, 1919–1920.* London, St. Catherine's Press, 1924. 280 pp. illus. port.

Vining describes his service with the Whites and subsequent capture and imprisonment by the Reds, May, 1919–October, 1920. His account of his treatment by the Bolsheviki may be compared to the gentle handling accorded captured British aviators by the Nazis in the early part of World War II.

742.   Gora, Dirk (pseudonym of Diedrich Navall). *Russian dance of death.* Claremont, Calif., Key Books, 1930. 186 pp.

Russian-speaking member of Dutch Mennonite colony along the Dnieper River describes the depredations of the Makno anarchists, September 15, 1919–March 5, 1920. He states that as a result of their treatment during this period, eventually 22,000 of the colony moved to Canada.

743.   Roberts, Carl Eric Bechhofer. *In Deniken's Russia and the Caucasus, 1919–1920. Being the record of a journey to South Russia, the Crimea, Armenia, Georgia, and Baku in 1919 and 1920.* London, Collins, 1921. 324 pp. map.

Roberts (see no. 617) provides here a vivid description of the demoralization of small peoples before the onslaught of the Bolsheviki, winter, 1919–spring, 1920. See especially "The Green guards" and his account of the ravaging of Baku by both Whites and Reds.

744.   Hunt, Frazier. "I capture Vladivostok." In Eugene Lyons, editor, *We cover the world.* New York, Harcourt, Brace, 1937. pp. 77–89.

Chicago *Tribune* war correspondent describes activities of the Siberian partisans near Vladivostok, December, 1919–January, 1920.

745. Rubin, Jacob H. *Moscow mirage.* London, Bles, 1935. 320 pp.

Russian-born Jewish Social Democrat from the United States journeys to Odessa to found and organize the Russian-American Chamber of Commerce in 1919. He describes the hard work of the common man and his struggles against the cynicism of the officials, 1919–21.

746. Berkman, Alexander. *The Bolshevik myth. (Diary, 1920–1922).* New York, Boni & Liveright, 1925. 319 pp.

Russian-American anarchist occupying administrative posts, December, 1919–September, 1922, registers his protest against increasing centralization and is finally deported from the country. He includes comments on many high-placed Bolsheviki with whom he was well acquainted.

747. Rubin, Jacob H., and Victor Rubin. *I live to tell. The Russian adventures of an American socialist.* Indianapolis, Bobbs-Merrill, 1934. 330 pp. illus. port.

Rubin (see no. 745) comments on his disillusionment with communism in practice in Russia after ten years in Odessa, 1919–29.

748. Serge, Victor (pseudonym of Victor Lvovich Kibalchich). *Russia twenty years after.* Translated from the French by Max Shachtman. New York, Hillman-Curl, 1937. 298 pp.

Belgian-born son of Russian *emigrés,* in Petrograd shortly after the Revolution, becomes a member of the Comintern and is ousted with Trotsky. Analyzes communism under such headings as "The cult of the leader," "Managed science, literature, and pedagogy," "The system," "Condition of man and mind," etc.

749. Clarke, John S. *Pen pictures of Russia under the "Red Terror." (Reminiscences of a surreptitious journey to*

Russia to attend the Second Congress of the Third International). Glasgow, National Workers Committee, 1921. 327 pp. illus.

British socialist views the Bolsheviki and the system they are developing with favor in Moscow visit in 1920.

750.   Guest, Leslie Haden. *The struggle for power in Europe, 1917–1921. An outline. Economic and political survey of the Central States and Russia.* London, Hodder & Stoughton, 1921. pp. 38–108.

Comments by the physician and secretary to the British Labour Delegation (see no. 759) in 1920. He examines the health conditions as a background to understanding the famine and includes an interview with Lenin.

751.   Hanssen, Helmer Julius. *Voyages of a modern Viking.* London, George Routledge, 1936. pp. 145–94. illus. map.

Norwegian explorer describes Chukchi way of life after a journey to northeast Siberia in 1920.

752.   Harding, Sidnie Milana (Mrs. J. P.). *The underworld of state.* London, Allen & Unwin, 1925. pp. 39–199. port.

Correspondent of "Woodrow Wilson's newspaper," the New York *World,* journeys to Petrograd and Moscow in 1920, where she is denounced as head of the British spy system by Marguerite Harrison (see no. 769). Mrs. Harding compares the better Soviet conditions with the miserable London Euston area.

753.   Russell, Bertrand. *The practice and theory of Bolshevism.* London, Allen & Unwin, 1921. 188 pp.

English philosopher, mathematician, and pacifist journeys to Petrograd and south Russia with the British Labour Delegation in 1920 (see no. 759) where he sees communism as necessary to world and equates it as equal to the French Revolution plus the teachings of Mohammed. However, he does not hesitate to criticize the Bolsheviki where they have failed to live up to their ideals.

754. Wells, Herbert George. *Russia in the shadows.* New York, Doran, 1921. 179 pp. illus.

Famous British novelist and critic of society visits Moscow and Petrograd in 1920 and draws a dismal verbal picture of the existing situation under the Bolsheviki. Along with visits with important leaders, he interviews Lenin and learns that the revolutionists have not been totally destructive in their dealing with evidences of the past but have preserved nearly all the great national treasures.

755. Ransome, Arthur. *The crisis in Russia.* New York, Huebsch, 1921. 201 pp. index.

On his second journey (see no 730) British reporter describes how foreign intervention affected the people and the Communist party.

756. McCullagh, Francis. *A prisoner of the reds. The story of a British officer captured in Siberia.* London, John Murray, 1921. 310 pp. illus. app. index.

Pseudo-journalist and spy describes his life from January to April, 1920, expresses the belief that revelation of the "truth about Communism" will destroy it, and indicates his intention of becoming the revelator.

757. Lansbury, George. *What I saw in Russia.* New York, Boni & Liveright, 1920. 166 pp. app.

English pacifist correspondent of the *Daily Herald* journeys to Moscow and Petrograd in February, 1920, and observes: "I see the Socialists of Russia as a band of men and women striving to build the New Jerusalem. . . . "

758. Snowden, (Mrs.) Ethel A. *Through Bolshevik Russia.* London, Cassell, 1920. 188 pp.

Member of the British Labour Delegation to Russia in 1920 (see no. 759) expresses opposition to the Bolshevik seizure of power because she feels that the world and humanity need "Russian" dreams.

759.   British Labour Delegation to Russia. *Report.* London,
Trades Unions Congress Labour Party, 1921. 31 pp. app.

Two women and seven men journey from Petrograd to the Caspian
Sea, May–June, 1920, and find no evidence of the conditions
usually described by the "perverted" capitalist press.

760.   Cameron, (Captain) Evan Percival. *Goodbye Russia: Adventures of H. M. Transport Rio Negro.* London, Hodder
& Stoughton, 1934. 244 pp. illus. map. port. biblio.

British merchant marine captain describes the sufferings of Russian refugees on the Black Sea in 1920 during the evacuation from
Odessa.

761.   Buxton, Charles Roden. *In a Russian village.* London,
Labour Publishing Co., 1922. 96 pp.

British worker takes an unauthorized journey to the Volga River
area in 1920 and observes that the peasants favor the Revolution
but not the Communist party. He also brings out the sharp
cleavage that divides the needs and wants of rural and urban areas.

762.   Pankhurst, (Mrs.) Estelle Sylvia. *Soviet Russia as I saw
it.* London, The "Workers' Dreadnought," 1921. 195 pp.

During the summer of 1920 British suffragette journeys from
Murmansk to Petrograd and Moscow, where she sees a peace-
loving Russia in a war-torn, war-loving world. Her comparisons of
conditions in Russia with those of depression-ridden England are
all to Russia's advantage.

763.   Brailsford, Henry Noel. *The Russian workers' republic.*
New York, Harper, 1921. 274 pp.

American left-wing sympathizer with Soviet aims describes the
considerate and kind treatment he received on his journey to
Petrograd, Moscow, and Minsk in the autumn of 1920 and claims
he talked freely (through an interpreter) with those in power and
those in opposition to the Bolsheviki.

764. Sheridan, Clare Consuelo (Frewen). *Mayfair to Moscow;
Clare Sheridan's diary*. New York, Boni & Liveright, 1921.
239 pp. illus.

Winston Churchill's cousin sculpts Bolsheviki (Trotsky, Lenin,
Krassin) during September–November, 1920, sojourn in Moscow.
The home life of the Soviet leaders who lived in the Kremlin is
carefully described from data she accumulates during the sittings.

765. Baldwin, Oliver. *Six prisons and two revolutions. Adventures in Trans-Caucasia and Anatolia, 1920–1921*. London,
Hodder & Stoughton, 1925. 271 pp. illus. map. port.

Sometime lieutenant colonel in the Armenian army, a British Lord
Byron type of mercenary, describes the resistance to the Bolsheviki
by Armenians.

766. Keun, Odette. *In the land of the Golden Fleece: through
independent Menshevist Georgia*. Translated from the
French by Helen Jessiman. London, John Lane, 1924.
270 pp. map.

French Menshevik sympathetically records attempt of the Georgians to secure independence from Moscow's domination, 1920–21.

767. Keun, Odette. *My adventures in Bolshevik Russia*. Translated from the French by the author. New York, Dodd,
Mead, 1923. 320 pp. port.

After being thrown out of Georgia (see no. 766) by the triumphant
Bolsheviki, the author is deported from Constantinople to southern
Russia by the British, who classify her as a Communist agitator.
Here she describes conditions as they existed in 1920–21.

768. Lied, Jonas. *Sidelights on the economic situation in Russia*.
Moscow, Kushnerev, 1922. 148 pp. map. app.

Lied (see nos. 560 and 561) provides a valuable survey of the
Soviet Union just before the New Economic Policy began, 1920–21.

In the appendix he includes railway maps, the law for domestic help, and the labor code.

769. Harrison, Marguerite E. *Marooned in Moscow. The story of an American woman imprisoned in Russia.* New York, Doran, 1921. 316 pp. port. app.

Baltimore Sun correspondent penetrates Russia without a visa, is permitted to remain, then is imprisoned, February, 1920–July, 1921. She provides a detailed description of Moscow and the countryside along with her mild treatment in prison. See Harding, no. 752, for details of Harrison's activities as a Soviet spy.

770. Miller, Orie O. "The first essay into Russia." In Hiebert and Miller, editors, *Feeding the hungry,* pp. 92–99, 387–389. (See no. 1443.)

American industrialist journeys to the Ukraine and the Crimea, autumn, 1920–spring, 1921, setting up the organization of Mennonite famine relief.

771. Goldman, Emma. *My disillusionment in Russia.* Garden City New York, Doubleday, Page, 1923. 242 pp. *My further disillusionment in Russia.* Garden City, New York, Doubleday, Page, 1924. 178 pp. [These two books are really one; the second includes the missing twelve chapters from the first.]

German-American socialist, Russian-speaking, is deported from the United States to Bolshevik Russia, where she journeys south from Petrograd to the Black Sea, September, 1920–December, 1921. Observes that "in reality the Russian people have gained nothing from the Bolshevist experiment" because monarchical absolutism has been replaced by party absolutism. She provides an informative description of the death and funeral of Peter Kropotkin.

772. Blair, Dorian. *Russian hazard. The adventures of a British secret service agent in Russia.* C. H. Dand, editor. London, Hale, 1937. pp. 13–288. illus. port.

Blair claims to have been part of a plot to murder Lenin, but his account is so impressionistic that it is very difficult to pin down the facts to any specific dates. The events he describes probably occurred between 1920 and 1922.

773. Farbman, Michael S. *Bolshevism in retreat.* London, Collins, 1923. 312 pp.

Left-wing *Manchester Guardian* correspondent in Moscow, 1920–22, claims to recognize the beginning of Bolshevism's decline in the New Economic Policy.

774. Bergman, Sten. *Through Kamchatka by dog-sled and skis. A vivid description of adventurous journeys among the interesting and almost unknown peoples of the most inaccessible parts of this remote Siberian peninsula.* Translated from the Swedish by Frederick White. London, Seeley, Service, 1927. pp. 7–284. illus. map. port. index.

Leader of Swedish Geographical Society expedition to study the zoology, botany, and ethnology of Kamchatka, provides a popular account of two journeys undertaken between June 14, 1920 and April 7, 1921.

775. Wilson, Lucy Williams. *The new schools in new Russia.* New York, Vanguard, 1928. 216 pp. index.

American teacher, sympathetic to Soviet experiments in education, visits Moscow and Petrograd (Leningrad) twice in the 1920's. She concludes that the Soviet Union is not an educational utopia but a laboratory.

776. Burnham, John Bird. *The rim of mystery. A hunter's wanderings in unknown Siberian Asia.* New York, Putnam, 1929. 281 pp. illus. map.

American hunter illuminates his account of a journey to the Chukotsk Peninsula in 1921 with excellent photographs which he claims establish the relationship between the mountain sheep of Alaska and Siberia. His description of the peoples' way of life is informative and inclusive.

777. McKay, Claude. *A long way from home.* New York, Lee Furman, 1937. pp. 153–225.

American Negro poet visiting Petrograd and Moscow in 1921 describes the Soviet Union in verse as the New Jerusalem.

778.   Roberts, Carl Eric Bechhofer. *Through starving Russia. Being the record of a journey to Moscow and the Volga provinces in August and September 1921.* London, Methuen, 1921. 165 pp. illus.

To Roberts (see nos. 617 and 743) the horror far exceeds the most sensational reports; he estimates that 35,000,000 people have only one month's supply of food. He includes poignant photographs of the starving population and asserts that the Bolsheviki reverted to capitalism in order to save face.

779.   Gibbs, (Sir) Philip Hamilton. *Since then. The disturbing story of the world at peace.* New York, Harper, 1930. pp. 373–404. port.

European Russia in the autumn of 1921 is observed by British novelist engaged in famine relief conducted under the auspices of the American Relief Administration. Gibbs sees the New Economic Policy as a definite improvement and that "only for those of the Old Regime was it quite intolerable." He sees the young as those who can hope for, and eventually enjoy, a better future.

780.   Slagel, A. W. "The Novorossisk trip"; "Visualizing famine conditions and feeding operations"; "Comrade Titov." In Hiebert and Miller, editors, *Feeding the hungry,* pp. 111–16, 231–55, 334–37. (See no. 1443.)

College professor volunteer describes the actual feeding operations of the Mennonites in the Ukraine, 1921–23.

781.   Golder, Frank A., and Lincoln Hutchinson. *On the trail of the Russian famine.* Stanford, California, Stanford University Press, 1927. 319 pp. illus. map.

Special investigator for the American Relief Administration, who is required to check on requests for aid, describes conditions in the Volga River area and south Russia, August, 1921–March, 1923. His information is illustrated with photographs showing the ravages of the famine on man and beast.

782. Strong, Anna Louise. *The first time in history; two years of Russia's new life (August, 1921, to December, 1923)*. New York, Boni & Liveright, 1924. 249 pp.

The author, who later lived in Russia after her gradual conversion to communism (see no. 792), here describes the operation of the New Economic Policy, attempting to show the good and bad by discussing "The war with alcohol," "How Russia is different," "Do the Jews rule Russia?", etc., In the preface to her account she is complimented by Leon Trotsky for her fair picture.

783. Mackenzie, Frederick Arthur. *Russia before dawn*. London, Fisher Unwin, 1923. 282 pp. illus. map. index.

British journalist (see no. 506) journeys to "New Russia" and comments on the New Economic Policy, September, 1921–January, 1923. On every side he sees hope return with capitalism, symbolized by the rebuilding of the great fair at Nizhni-Novgorod.

784. Duncan, Irma, and Allan Ross MacDougall. *Isadora Duncan's Russian days and her last years in France*. New York, Covici-Friede, 1929. pp. 1–280.

Between 1921 and 1924 American dancer lives in Russia, teaching dancing and adding her share to the cultural uplift of the Bolshevik system. Here she describes her tours of the cities and the difficulties she encountered in dealing with the bureaucracy.

785. Hullinger, Edwin Ware. *The reforging of Russia*. New York, Dutton, 1925. 390 pp. app.

United Press staff correspondent in Russia sketches way of life at the beginning of the New Economic Policy, 1921–24. Comments on his personal recollections of Lenin.

786.   Miller, Alvin J. "The door opens for relief work in Russia." In Hiebert and Miller, editors, *Feeding the hungry*. pp. 116–203, 312–22. (See no. 1443.)

American psychology professor and director of American Mennonite Relief describes his work in Moscow and the Ukraine, and in Siberia, 1921–26.

787.   Scheffer, Paul. *Seven years in Soviet Russia. With a retrospect*. Translated from the German by Arthur Livingston. New York, Putnam, 1931. 280 pp.

German correspondent in Moscow, 1921–28, describes the New Economic Policy's impact, the Stalin-Trotsky struggle for control, the activities of the Comintern, and the arts under communism.

788.   Hammer, Armand. *The quest of the Romanoff treasure*. New York, Paisley Press, 1936. 234 pp. illus. app.

Representative of Ford Motor Company and thirty-eight other businesses signs a contract insuring him a concession to do business under the New Economic Policy. Here he describes foreign business operations, 1921–30, concluding that the Soviet system will succeed.

789.   Mackenzie, Frederick Arthur. *The Russian crucifixion. The full story of the persecution of religion under Bolshevism*. London, Jarrolds, 1930. 140 pp. illus.

Journalist (see nos. 506 and 783) in Moscow, 1921–30, provides excellent photographs of the antireligious activities carried on by the Bolsheviki along with numerous quotations from the persecuted.

790.   Duranty, Walter. *Duranty reports Russia*. Gustavus Tuckerman, Jr., compiler. New York, Viking, 1934. 351 pp. app. index.

Duranty's articles and dispatches published in the *New York Times* are chronologically arranged, along with "A personal note on Walter Duranty" by Alexander Woollcott. See no. 791.

791. Duranty, Walter. *I write as I please*. Cleveland, World Publishing Co., 1942. 342 pp. index.

Russian-speaking dean of foreign correspondents in Moscow describes his gradual disillusionment with Soviet theory and practice from 1921 to 1933. See no. 790.

792. Strong, Anna Louise. *I change worlds; The remaking of an American*. New York, Holt, 1935. 422 pp.

Here the author (see no. 782) describes her life in Russia in the twenties and thirties (1921–34) and is especially informative about the origins of the *Moscow Daily News,* published in the English language for engineers and fellow travelers in the U.S.S.R.

793. Bloor, (Mrs.) Ella Reeve. *We are many. An autobiography*. New York, International Publishers, 1940. pp. 167–319. port.

Famous American communist—"Mother Bloor"—who helped to found the Communist party in the United States, journeys to Moscow, March–May, 1921, where she witnesses the beginnings of the New Economic Policy and hears the workers sing for joy. Sixteen years later, she makes another journey, September–November, 1937, to celebrate the October Revolution. She makes no mention of the purges.

794. Borders, Karl. *Village life under the Soviets*. New York, Vanguard Press, 1927. 191 pp.

American Quaker, involved in relief work in 1922 and in agricultural reconstruction, 1925–27, describes the conditions of the peasants from emancipation in the nineteenth century through the New Economic Policy, implying that their situation has improved greatly.

795. Bryant, Louise (Mrs. John Reed). *Mirrors of Moscow*. New York, Thomas Seltzer, 1923. 209 pp. illus.

American journalist (see no. 692) describes the Soviet scene in 1922 and provides some very informative details about the leadership of the country—but at no time does she mention Stalin!

796.   Fischer, Bertha Markoosha. *My lives in Russia*. New York, Harper, 1944. 269 pp.

Born in Russia and educated at a Swiss conservatory of music, she came to the United States in 1915 to work with the Red Cross. Journeying to Moscow in 1922, she married Louis Fischer, *Nation* correspondent. She describes Moscow as a grim place at this time, just before the New Economic Policy brought a measure of prosperity. In 1927, after being out of the country for five years, she returned to Moscow and remained there until 1939. She comments in detail on these years of change, especially on the *Moscow Daily News*, which she castigates as a purveyor of the party line to foreigners.

797.   Harrison, Marguerite E. *Red bear or yellow dragon*. New York, Doran, 1924. pp. 85–130, 173–284. illus.

Baltimore Sun correspondent (see no. 769) comments on Russian law and justice after her journey to eastern Siberia to check Sino-Russian friction along mutual boundaries in 1922.

798.   Reswick, William. *I dreamt revolution*. Chicago, Regnery, 1952. 328 pp. illus. port.

Russian-born American, Russian-speaking Associated Press war correspondent during the purge years, describes his service with the American Relief Administration in 1922 and Stalin's climb to power, 1923–34. Reswick claims to have been the first correspondent to report Lenin's death.

799.   Payne, Muriel A. *Plague, pestilence and famine*. London, Nisbet, 1923. 146 pp.

British nurse serving with the Quaker famine relief teams, March–August, 1922, around Moscow pities the genuine communists, whom she considers to have been tarred with the brush of violent men.

800.   Hiebert, Peter C. "Report of the Chairman's trip to the field of operations." In Hiebert and Miller, editors, *Feeding the hungry*, pp. 75–81. (See no. 1443.)

Pastor-teacher of Tabor College appointed as special representative to survey famine relief work of Mennonite Executive Committee journeys through the Ukraine in March–July, 1922.

801. Ashton, James M. *Icebound. A trader's adventures in the Siberian Arctic.* New York, Putnam, 1928. 235 pp. illus. map. port.

Representative of Tacoma, Washington, trading company outlines the prospects for future trade with Russia after a journey into the Siberian Arctic, June–September, 1922.

802. Fox, Ralph. *People of the steppes.* London, Constable, 1925. 244 pp. illus. map. app.

Member of a British mission to relieve famine conditions in 1922–23 journeys to the Transcaspian steppes to buy and train horses. He is very informative on the impact of Communism on the Kazakh way of life.

803. Halliburton, Richard. *Richard Halliburton. His story of his life's adventure. As told in letters to his Mother and Father.* Indianapolis, Bobbs-Merrill, 1940. pp. 199–202, 358–62. illus.

Richard Halliburton was born in 1900, began his adventures and travels in 1921 and disappeared at sea in 1939. Here he briefly describes his visit to Vladivostok, in 1922–23 (see no. 804) and to Leningrad, Moscow, Sverdlovsk, and the Caucasus in 1934 (see no. 1060).

804. Halliburton, Richard. *The royal road to romance.* Indianapolis, Bobbs-Merrill, 1925. pp. 361–69. illus.

Vladivostok in late December and early January, 1922–23, is described by Halliburton who tells how he defies Soviet restrictions and secures a visa to the harbor city by subterfuge. See nos. 803 and 1060.

805. Krehbiel, C. E. "Clothing distribution in Russia." In Hiebert and Miller, editors, *Feeding the hungry,* pp. 260–76, 338–40. (See no. 1443.)

Secretary of General Mennonite Conference describes clothing distribution during famine relief, 1922–23.

806.   Eastman, Max. *Love and revolution; my journey through an epoch.* New York, Random House, 1964. pp. 311–436. illus. port.

Max Eastman has moved all the way from an admirer of communism and its ideals to that of roving editor at the *Reader's Digest.* An American of catholic tastes, he went to Russia in 1922 when it was still possible to talk freely to anyone, and he records some of his interesting and informative conversations before he departed in 1924. By that time he was becoming aware that communism demanded more than a casual allegiance, and he describes in detail his changing relationship.

807.   Smith, Jessica. *Women in the Soviet Union.* New York, Vanguard Press, 1928. 216 pp.

Member of the American Friends Service Committee relief team, 1922–24, returns for another visit, 1926–28. She describes the introduction of new marriage laws, housing, and child care as a great advance over Russia's former practices in these areas.

808.   Fry, Anna Ruth. *Three visits to Russia (1922–1925).* London, Merlin Press, 1960. 56 pp.

Honorary general secretary of Friends' War Victims Relief describes her part in aiding the victims of famine.

809.   Chamberlin, William Henry. *Soviet Russia. A living record and a history.* New York, Chautauqua Press, 1930. 425 pp. illus. map. biblio. index.

Christian Science Monitor correspondent, Russian-speaking, in Moscow, 1922–32, Chamberlin is one of the most informative of the many Americans who served in the same capacity after 1917. *Soviet Russia* is a solid account in which current conditions and historical backgrounds are interrelated. He is especially valuable in the areas of youth and intelligentsia. See no. 810.

810. Chamberlin, William Henry. *The confessions of an individualist.* New York, Macmillan, 1940. pp. 63–201.

Chamberlin came back from his assignment in Moscow a much concerned and highly vocal critic of the Soviet system. Here he describes his journey to "Paradise," disillusionment, and "retreat from Moscow." He is excellent, especially on the early purge trials. See no. 809.

811. Chiang Kai-shek. *Soviet Russia in China. A summing-up at seventy.* New York, Farrar, Straus & Cudahy, 1957. pp. 19–25.

Sent to Moscow for three months in 1923 by Dr. Sun Yat-sen to study military organization, Chiang Kai-shek saw the Communist party and its international ambitions as a threat to China's independence.

812. Davidson, Jo. *Between sittings: an informal autobiography.* New York, Dial Press, 1951. pp. 178–84, 303–8. port.

American sculptor compares the friendly atmosphere in 1923 in Moscow when he did the busts of Radek, Kalinin, and others (Lenin was too ill to sit) with a visit in 1937, when fear arising out of the purges was in the air, and Stalin was not available for a sitting.

813. Eaton, Richard. *Under the red flag.* New York, Brentano, 1924. 262 pp. illus.

American correspondent records conversations with fellow prisoners in Moscow, 1923. Predicts Europe will be dominated by Russia within fifty years.

814. McCullagh, Francis. *The Bolshevik persecution of Christianity.* London, John Murray, 1924. 329 pp. illus. app. index.

Roman Catholic journalist is present in Moscow in 1923 to cover the anti-religious trials of Russian Orthodox leaders. He provides full details of Patriarch Tikhon's fall and of Roman Catholic Archbishop Cieplak's trial.

815.   Marx, Magdeleine. *The romance of new Russia.* Translated from the French by Anita Grannis. New York, Thomas Seltzer, 1924. 225 pp.

French novelist with a smattering of Russian makes a journey in 1923 "to adore" Russia as one adores a lover. She considers the Soviet Union the "second day" of a two-day existence of the world. Very impressionistic with few statistics.

816.   Spencer, Franz. *Battles of a bystander.* New York, Liveright, 1941. pp. 165–204.

German bureaucrat in Petrograd and Moscow, 1923–24, prepares a peculiar mélange of observations.

817.   Yarmolinsky, Avraham. *The Jews and other minor nationalities under the Soviets.* Jerome Davis, editor. New York, Vanguard Press, 1929. 182 pp. biblio.

Russian-born American (naturalized in 1922), writer on Russian topics and contributor to periodicals, returns to Moscow and its rural surroundings, 1923–24. Sees Russia under Soviet leadership as the hope of the Jews but questions the emphasis on what he refers to as Jewish nationality.

818.   Bury, Herbert. *Russia from within: personal experiences of many years, and especially since 1923. With opinions and convictions formed in consequence.* London, Churchman Publishing Co., 1927. 226 pp. illus. index.

Anglican assistant bishop of London journeys to Moscow and European Russia to visit former associates (see no. 598) and to study religious conditions under the Soviets, 1923–27. He reports the situation to be generally favorable to the church, but in comparing the old and the new Russia (before and after 1917) he remarks: "There could hardly be a greater [contrast]!"

819. Seldes, George. *You can't print that! The truth behind the news, 1918–1928.* Garden City, New York, Garden City Publishing Co., 1929. pp. 153–245. illus.

Correspondent for the Chicago *Tribune* describes how terror rules under the New Economic Policy, 1923–28. He underscores his critical attitude with the remark: "So if you want to hear about the regeneration of Russia under the Bolsheviks you will have to read elsewhere."

820. Wicksteed, Alexander. *My Russian neighbors. Recollections of ten years in Soviet Russia.* New York, Whittlesey House, 1934. 218 pp.

British English-language teacher and friend of Russia in Moscow, 1923–33, describes way of life with emphasis on the non-political, such as shops, housing, transportation, amusements, and, of course, education.

821. Conway, (Sir) William Martin. *Art treasures in Soviet Russia.* London, Arnold, 1925. 278 pp. illus. index.

British Member of Parliament and art expert journeys to Leningrad and Moscow in 1924 to survey Soviet art museums. Makes no political comment.

822. Farbman, Michael S. *After Lenin. The new phase in Russia.* London, Parsons, 1924. 280 pp.

Farbman (see no. 773) returns to Moscow in 1924 and comes to the conclusion that Russia is moving back to Asia as the paradox mounts between idealism and practice.

823. Karlgren, Anton. *Bolshevist Russia.* Translated from the Swedish by Anna Barwell. New York, Macmillan, 1927. 311 pp. illus.

Swedish professor at the University of Copenhagen, many times a traveler to Russia, visits Moscow in 1924 and makes a detailed and critical examination of proletarian power, industry under the New Economic Policy, the condition of the peasants, etc.

824.   Lawton, Lancelot. *The Russian Revolution (1917–1926)*. London, Macmillan, 1927. 499 pp. illus. index.

Correspondent of the London *Daily Chronicle,* a prewar visitor, returns to Moscow in 1924 to analyze the impact of the Revolution on institutions, people, and the full spectrum of daily life.

825.   Pollitt, Harry. *Serving my time. An apprenticeship to politics.* London, Lawrence & Wishart, 1940. pp. 189–94. port.

Attending the Red International of Labour Unions in 1924, British workingman and communist learns that Lenin has died and provides a moving description of his funeral.

826.   Sarolea, Charles. *Impressions of Soviet Russia.* London, Nash & Grayson, 1924. 276 pp.

Edinburgh professor of French literature journeys to Moscow and Leningrad in 1924 and predicts that the Russians will reject all forms of collectivism. Grierson (see no. 1438) has this to say of Sarolea: "Remarkable for confidence and incorrectness of political prophecies."

827.   Sheridan, Clare Consuelo (Frewen). *Across Europe with Satanella.* New York, Dodd, Mead, 1925. pp. 65–211. illus. port.

Sheridan (see no. 764) and her brother travel through the Crimea and the Ukraine by motorcycle (Satanella) in 1924. Her comments are not especially profound but are interesting because of the situations into which their mode of transportation leads them.

828.   Roosevelt, Kermit. "On the Trans-Siberian, 1923–1924." In Mrs. Theodore Roosevelt, Sr., Mrs. Kermit Roosevelt, Richard Derby, and Kermit Roosevelt, *Cleared for strange ports.* New York, Scribner's, 1927. pp. 87–114. illus.

Journey from Manchuria west to Moscow in February, 1924, by son of Theodore Roosevelt in which he describes Soviet Russia mourning Lenin's death. Observes that friendly train officials made the trip "interesting—but glad its over!"

829. Wald, Lillian D. *Windows on Henry Street*. Boston, Little, Brown, 1934. pp. 251–84. illus.

New York settlement worker, sympathetic to the Russian experiment, is in Moscow at the time of Lenin's funeral in 1924. Along with a description of Moscow in mourning she provides useful information on children's homes and public health facilities, emphasizing that prevention rather than cure is basic to the purposes of the system.

830. British Trade Union Delegation to Russia and Caucasus. *Russia*. London, Trades Unions Congress General Council, 1925. 234 pp. illus. map. biblio. index.

Group, accompanied by Russian-speaking advisers, attends the Sixth Congress of All-Russian Trade Unions in November, 1924, to observe the impact of communism on Russian institutions and the people and to stimulate trade between the Soviet Union and Britain. The report includes a special section on the Baku oil fields.

831. Krist, Gustav. *Alone through the forbidden land. Journeys in disguise through Soviet Central Asia*. Translated from the German by E. O. Lorimer. London, Readers' Union, 1938. 257 pp. illus. map. app. index.

Austrian soldier-adventurer (see no. 656) tells of his journey through Transcaspia and provides details about the customs of the Islamic inhabitants and their reaction to the impact of Bolshevism. Has a fictional air about it, especially the conversations. The photographs are excellent and unusual.

832. Kindermann, Karl. *In the toils of the O.G.P.U.* Translated from the German by Gerald Griffin. London, Hurst & Blackett, 1933. 312 pp. illus. port. index.

German student with some Russian language training, joins the Communist party in order to get a visa to Siberia. Denounced as a spy, he is confined in the Lubianka prison from October, 1924, to October, 1926. Much of his account describes the preparations for his trial, in which he claims to have been offered a large sum of money to plead guilty to a prepared confession.

833.   Unger, (Dr.) Heinz, written in collaboration with Naomi Walford. *Hammer, sickle and baton. The Soviet memoirs of a musician.* London, Cresset Press, 1939. 275 pp.

German conductor is invited to Kiev, Kharkov, and Odessa during the years 1924–37 to lead orchestras. He describes the way of life of the intellectuals and records the opposition he encountered from the bureaucracy. Observes: "Highest hopes followed by the deepest disappointment." See no. 834.

834.   Unger, (Dr.) Heinz. "Music." In Griffith, editor, *Playtime in Russia,* pp. 119–35. (See no. 1439).

German conductor (see no. 833) observes that Russians are not gifted organizers.

835.   Acheson, Judy. *Young America looks at Russia.* New York, Frederick Stokes, 1932. 253 pp. illus. port.

Teen-age daughter of Near East Relief worker describes famine area in 1925 along the north Black Sea coast to the Caucasus. She does not hesitate to point out the handicaps of communism but puts her hope in the Russian youth.

836.   Alec-Tweedie, (Mrs.) Ethel Brilliana. *An adventurous journey (Russia-Siberia-China).* London, Hutchinson, 1926. pp. 1–81. illus. map. port.

Professional traveler and writer journeys east on the Trans-Siberian Railway into Manchuria "out of Hell". She says of her visit to Lenin's tomb: "Here in Moscow lay a plebeian, bandy-legged little man with twenty-four soldiers with bowed heads to guard him in his glass case. This is Russia's God."

837.   Béraud, Henri. *The truth about Moscow as seen by a French visitor.* Translated from the French by John Peile. London, Faber & Gwyer, 1926. 261 pp.

Correspondent supplies what he considers to be the facts in 1925, with emphasis on the worst features in Leningrad and Moscow, including "sights not shown to western comrades." He says he went to Russia a sympathizer but returned a critic.

838. Duggan, Stephen. *A professor at large.* New York, Macmillan, 1943. pp. 191–229. port.

Comparison of conditions in 1925 and 1934, especially in education, by American professor and director of international education. He crosses Siberia to Moscow in 1925 and nine years later arranges for several hundred American and British students to attend Moscow University summer session. The students go to Moscow, but the summer session never materializes.

839. Hindus, Maurice Gerschon. *Broken earth.* New York, Cape & Smith, 1931. 285 pp.

Hindus (see no. 711) comments on the peasant reaction to impending collectivization of their lands after his journey to the interior of European Russia in 1925.

840. Ikbal, Ali Shah Sirdar. *Westward to Mecca. A journey of adventure through Afghanistan, Bolshevik Asia, Persia, Iraq and Hijaz to the cradle of Islam.* London, Witherby, 1928. pp. 126–64. illus.

Indian mullah buys and sells in order to pay his expenses to the holy city of his faith. He describes his persecution by the Communist bureaucrats who refer to him as a "priest and peddler." Some of his political comments emphasize the Russian threat to the British Empire in 1925.

841. Nansen, Fridtjof. *Through the Caucasus to the Volga.* Translated from the Norwegian by G. C. Wheeler. New York, Norton, 1931. 252 pp. illus. port. index.

As member of the League of Nations commission to discover a resettlement area for displaced Armenians, Nansen (see no. 583) travels through the Russian lands bordering the Black Sea. His descriptions of the people and their customs are useful and informative.

842.   Nearing, Scott. *Education in Soviet Russia.* New York, International Publishers, 1926. 159 pp. index.

American left-wing sociologist journeys to Leningrad and Moscow in 1925 to get information on the Russian experiment not available in the United States. On the whole, his comments on education in the Soviet Union are complimentary, although he does indicate some drawbacks in the relationship between ideals and practices.

843.   Scott, A. MacCallum. *Beyond the Baltic.* London, Thornton Butterworth, 1925, pp. 55–137. illus. map. index.

British novelist makes a brief journey to Leningrad and Moscow in 1925 and, although critical, makes amusing comments on change and its hazards.

844.   Wilson, Helen Calista, and Elsie Reed Mitchell. *Vagabonding at fifty. From Siberia to Turkestan.* New York, Coward-McCann, 1929. 335 pp. illus. map.

Two American women, members of a radical group working in a chemical plant, Kuzbas, on the Tom River in 1925, set out for a vacation with their dog Ferghana and, by hitchhiking and traveling on the Trans-Siberian Railway, see the way the people live all the way to Vladivostok.

845.   British Women Trade Unionists. *Soviet Russia: An investigation by Women Trade Unionists—April to July, 1925.* London, Coates, 1925. 88 pp. illus.

As they journey from Moscow to the Caucasus, delegates to the Trade Union Congress ask no questions about the means used by the Bolsheviki but concern themselves only if the end has been achieved. See the Soviet system full of hope and accepted by the majority of the people.

846. Porter, Anna. *A Moscow diary*. Chicago, Charles H. Kerr, 1926. 153 pp.

Enthralled American school teacher describes Moscow between July and November, 1925, as she views the life of the people and culminates her experience by marching in the October parade past Trotsky standing on Lenin's tomb.

847. Keynes, John Maynard. *A short view of Russia*. London, Woolf, 1925. pp 11–28.

British economist visits Moscow in September, 1925, and concludes that Leninism is becoming a cult, a combination of religion and business. He views Marx and Lenin as writers of obsolete textbooks but sees communism succeeding as a moral force.

848. Nearing, Scott, and Jack Hardy. *The economic organization of the Soviet Union*. New York, Vanguard Press, 1927. 245 pp.

Using his experiences from a journey in 1925 (see no. 842), Nearing attempts to offset anticommunist attitudes in the United States.

849. Siebert, Theodor. *Red Russia*. Translated from the German by Eden and Cedar Paul. London, Allen & Unwin, 1932. 408 pp. app.

Russian-speaking journalist travels from Leningrad through Moscow to Siberia, 1925–29, on a mission to secure permission for German newspapermen to work in the Union of Soviet Socialist Republics. He claims to have presented the first comprehensive account of the permanent features of Bolshevism.

850. Lansbury, Violet. *An Englishwoman in the U.S.S.R.* London, Putnam, 1940. pp. 18–325.

Daughter of George Lansbury (see no. 757) marries a Russian and helps to earn their living as a translator in Moscow, 1925–28.

She expresses her confidence in the future of communism with the following words: "My sons are living in a land that will ever strive to live in peace and prosperity, in a land which offers golden opportunities to the growing generation."

851.   Lansbury, George. *My life*. London, Constable, 1928. pp. 223–64. port.

Comparison of conditions in 1926, on a journey to Moscow and Leningrad, with those in 1920 (see no. 757). Lansbury concludes that generally the Russian is better off.

852.   Nearing, Scott. *Glimpses of the Soviet Republic*. New York, Social Science Publishers, 1926. pp. 1–32.

Impressions from a 1926 journey (see nos. 842 and 848) in which Nearing remarks that leaving the Soviet Union is "like going from a bright spring day to a cellar."

853.   Toller, Ernest. *Which world—which way? Travel pictures from Russia and America*. Translated from the German by H. Ould. London, Low, Marston, 1931. pp. 75–176. illus. port.

German antiwar radical and communist compares the United States and the Union of Soviet Socialist Republics in 1926, with definite leanings in the direction of the Soviet system.

854.   Viollis, Andrée (pseudonym of Ardenne de Tizac). *A girl in Soviet Russia*. Translated from the French by Homer White. New York, Crowell, 1929. 347 pp. map.

Russian-speaking French correspondent journeys from the Baltic to the Black Sea in 1926 and observes that the Russian youth appear to favor the "barrack state" system. She also provides a terrifying description of the homeless children roaming the countryside and scavenging in the cities.

855.   Oxnam, Garfield Bromley. *Russian impressions*. Los Angeles, privately printed, 1927. 96 pp. illus.

Pastor of the Los Angeles Church of All Nations journeys to Leningrad, Moscow, Nizhni-Novgorod, and Kazan in the summer of 1926. In his brief account he emphasizes the vast differences that exist between the ideal and its practice in communism.

856. Mears, John Henry, and (Captain) Charles B. D. Collyer. *Racing the moon (and winning). Being the story of the swiftest journey ever made, a circumnavigation of the globe by airplane and steamship in 23 days, 15 hours, 21 minutes and 3 seconds by two men and a dog.* New York, Rae D. Henkle, 1928. pp. 118–52. illus. port.

Americans journey across Siberia from Moscow to Vladivostok on the Trans-Siberian Railway, July–August, 1926, and record as one of their chief impressions the lack of joy in the faces of the people along with the absence of laughter.

857. McWilliams, Ronald Fairbairn and Margaret S. *Russia in nineteen twenty-six.* New York, Dutton, 1927. 128 pp.

Canadian tourists in Leningrad, Moscow, and Kiev, August, 1926, place the emphasis on family relations and education. They conclude that (1) the old regime is dead and gone forever, (2) the land will not be restored to private ownership, and (3) the Bolsheviki must be credited with genuine reform. Mrs. McWilliams wrote most of the account.

858. Slocombe, George Edward. *The tumult and the shouting. The memoirs of George Slocombe.* London, Heinemann, 1936. pp. 248–66. illus. port.

American journalist accompanies Chase National Bank group to Russia in August, 1926, to arrange for Bolshevik purchases in the United States. He portrays the emergence of the Stalin generation as the appearance of a band of hard and tough opportunists.

859. Wood, Junius B. *Incredible Siberia.* New York, Dial Press, 1928. 261 pp. illus.

Russian-speaking correspondent of Chicago *Daily News* reports on his journey across Siberia in 1926. Excellent photographs tend to emphasize bad features in a socialist land where private and state cars still run on the Trans-Siberian Railway.

860.   Freeman, Joseph. *An American testament. A narrative of rebels and romantics.* New York, Farrar & Rinehart, 1936. pp. 408–631. index.

American communist, Russian-born, visits the Soviet Union in 1926–27 and observes the operation of the proletarian republic. His description is rhapsodic, and he finds little to criticize as he examines all areas of life. Among his comments are those on Eisenstein and, in the chapter on "The Party," on John Reed and his meaning to America.

861.   Ciliga, Anton. *The Russian enigma.* Translated from the French by Fernand G. Renier and Anne Cliff. London, The Labour Book Service, 1940. 304 pp.

Russian-speaking Yugoslav communist journeys to European Russia in 1926. In the following decade he becomes disillusioned and finally even critical of Lenin. He observes that all means are "not permissible in the service of revolution." Arrested and imprisoned in 1930, he describes his treatment and exposes police techniques used on political prisoners.

862.   American Trade Union Delegation to the Soviet Union. *Russia after ten years.* New York, International Publishers, 1927. 96 pp. illus. map.

Journey in 1927 by five union officials and twelve non-union experts on the family, etc. Visits are made to Baku and Sverdlovsk as well as Moscow and Leningrad. More material may be found in Stuart Chase, Robert Dunn, and Rexford G. Tugwell, *Soviet Russia in the second decade. A joint survey by the technical staff of the first American Trade Union Delegation.* New York, John Day, 1928. 364 pp. index.

863.   Baldwin, Roger N. *Liberty under the Soviets.* New York, Vanguard Press, 1928. 272 pp.

After one month in Moscow and a month working in villages in Georgia and the Ukraine, 1927, founder of the American Civil Liberties Union compares political control and social liberty, justifying repression by saying that liberty must be based on economic power.

864. Counts, George Sylvester. *The Soviet challenge to America*. New York, John Day, 1931. 339 pp. biblio. index.

Professor of education at Columbia University makes two journeys to European Russia, in 1927 and in 1929. Impressed by the accomplishments, Counts suggests that the United States should try to match the Soviet Union with a plan instead of with criticism. The beginning of the Five Year Plan in 1929 leads him to see the Communist party as a useful prod to production. See no. 920 for additional data on the journey in 1929.

865. Flanagan, Hallie. *Shifting scenes of the modern European theater*. New York, Coward-McCann, 1928. pp. 81–178. illus.

Vassar College director of experimental theater, on a Guggenheim Fellowship, spends a few months in Leningrad and Moscow in 1927, where she concludes that the Russian theater is great because it is dedicated to the ideals and practices of Stanislavsky and Meyerhold.

866. London, Geo. *Red Russia after ten years*. Translated from the French by G. E. R. Gedye. London, Methuen, 1928. 182 pp.

Paris Journal correspondent journeys to Leningrad, Moscow, and Nizhni-Novgorod to, as he puts it, really see communism in action. He presents his account of 1927 by examining many aspects of the Russian scene, including a chapter on anti-Semitism.

867. Thompson, Dorothy. *The new Russia*. New York, Holt, 1928. 317 pp. illus. map. index.

New York *Evening Post* correspondent comments on her first impressions of the Soviet Union during 1927 journey to Moscow. In addition to details on the Communist party activities, the Red Army, sex mores, the Soviet man, etc., she provides useful information on the life and activities of foreign correspondents and journalists stationed in Moscow.

868.   Utley, Freda. *The dream we lost.* New York, John Day, 1940. 361 pp. index.

British Communist party member describes her gradual disillusionment after visits to Moscow in 1927 and between 1930 and 1936, when she lived with her Russian husband. She finally comes to the conclusion that only through Hitler and German Nazism can Europe be saved from communism.

869.   Williams, Albert Rhys. *The Russian land.* New York, New Republic, 1927. 294 pp.

Here Williams (see no. 703) composes a song of praise of communist blessings and their acceptance by the Russian people. He includes verses on peasant life, the Young Pioneers, a former member of the nobility, and village justice.

870.   Lattimore, (Mrs.) Eleanor Holgate. *Turkestan reunion.* New York, John Day, 1934. pp. 1–84. map.

In 1927 Owen Lattimore made a long journey through China and Mongolia into Chinese Turkestan to study the land, its people, and their customs. Mrs. Lattimore joined her husband by coming across Siberia to Novosibirsk, then through Kazakhstan, in February, 1927. Along with the details of her journey she provides information on the Transcaspian peoples.

871.   Lee, Ivy Ledbetter. *Present day Russia.* New York, Macmillan, 1928. 204 pp. app.

American correspondent and European manager of a coal and railway corporation spends ten days in Moscow in May, 1927, and arrives at three conclusions about the Soviet system: (1) the regime is here to stay; (2) the situation is changing daily; and (3) the present tendency is away from socialism in the direction of capitalism.

872. Rosenberg, James N. *On the steppes. A Russian diary.* New York, Knopf, 1927. 215 pp.

In May, 1927, the American member of the Jewish Joint Distribution Committee makes a journey to review the results of four hundred thousand dollars' worth of aid to Ukrainian peasants.

873. Noé, Adolf Carl. *Golden days of Soviet Russia.* Chicago, Rockwell, 1931. 181 pp. illus.

Mining geologist, member of an American commission to examine old mines and plan new ones, journeys from Leningrad to Kharkov, May–September, 1927, and returns with a comment on how well the Russians treat the Americans.

874. Brailsford, Henry Noel. *How the Soviets work.* New York, Vanguard Press, 1927. 169 pp.

Sympathetic account of the relationship between government and the Communist party of the Soviet Union by the editor of the *New Leader* (see no 763) after 1927 journey to European Russia.

875. Brown, William John. *Three months in Russia.* London, Labour Publishing Co., 1928. pp. 11–189. port.

Labour party member journeys to Moscow and Leningrad during the summer of 1927. He finds the Russians to be simple and direct and inclined to introspection, with a dislike of religion but almost worshipping Lenin, and with a strong streak of callousness. He concludes that it was historical circumstances, not the actions and leadership of the Bolsheviki, that made the Revolution.

876. Buxton, (Mrs.) Dorothy Francis. *The challenge of Bolshevism. A new social ideal.* London, Allen & Unwin, 1928. 95 pp.

Sympathetic and well-informed British Quaker spends twenty-four days in Leningrad and Moscow, in small towns and one village near the capital, in the summer of 1927. She describes the Bolshevik ethic as "a sense of new moral advance," with the people benefitting as the bourgeoisie disappears. For her, the communist good will toward the majority more than compensates for any ill will directed against the minority.

877.   Dykstra, Gerald Oscar. *A belated rebuttal with Russia.* Allegan, Michigan, Allegan Press, 1928. 196 pp. illus.

Taking a Grand Tour after college graduation, during the summer of 1927, American observes that the Soviet Union is on the way to perfection, and the United States should recognize her.

878.   Newman, E. M. *Seeing Russia.* New York, Funk & Wagnalls, 1928. 382 pp. illus. map. biblio. index.

Chautauqua lecturer takes one of the usual tours (Leningrad, Moscow, and Kiev) during the summer of 1927 and presents an illustrated account (300 pictures) that he claims approaches objectivity.

879.   Dreiser, Theodore. *Dreiser looks at Russia.* New York, Liveright, 1928. 264 pp.

American novelist journeys through European Russia and the Caucasus, October–December, 1927, where he sees Russia as "slow, backward, inclined to meditate too much" but "with signs of things that must surely tend to shake and wake them out of this lethargy."

880.   Vidor, John. *Spying in Russia.* London, Long, 1929. 284 pp. illus. port.

British communist journeys to Leningrad, Moscow, and central Asia in November, 1927, as a guest of the Soviet Union to attend the annual October celebrations but returns disillusioned and very critical.

881. Greenwall, Harry James. *Mirrors of Moscow*. London, Harrap, 1929. 244 pp. illus. app. index.

Attempt to reflect the life of the people apart from politics by British journalist in 1927–28. He uses excellent illustrations and includes an appendix on Trotsky's story of his exile.

882. Istrati, Panaït. *Russia unveiled*. Translated from the French by R. J. S. Curtis. London, Allen & Unwin, 1931. 262 pp. index.

A left-wing Russian-speaking Rumanian tells of his bitter disillusionment after a year in Moscow, 1927–28, to study Soviet institutions. Observes: "Soviet system was, in practice, both oppressive and unworkable."

883. White, William C. *These Russians*. New York, Scribner's, 1931. 376 pp.

Attempt by Russian-speaking American correspondent, 1927–30, to describe Russians as people. He tries to avoid sweeping generalizations such as "the land of paradoxes," "the great menace," etc., by devoting a chapter to one occupation, such as, housewife, professor, barber, and others.

884. Barbusse, Henri. *One looks at Russia*. Translated from the French by Warre B. Wells. London, Dent, 1931. 206 pp.

Communist delegate from France to the Sixth International Congress of Writers in 1928 records favorable impressions of his journey from Moscow south to the Crimea.

885. Dewey, John. *Impressions of Soviet Russia and the revolutionary world. Mexico-China-Turkey*. New York, New Republic, 1929, pp. 3–133.

American philosopher-educator takes a brief journey to Leningrad and Moscow in 1928 and sees a new world in the process of creation by the efforts of a buoyant, energetic, and naïve "strangely young folk."

886.   Dillon, Emile Joseph. *Russia today and yesterday.* London, Dent, 1929. 325 pp.

When the Revolution came to Russia, Dillon (see nos. 386 and 428) lost all his possessions and was forced to leave the country penniless. In 1928, an elderly man, he returns to Moscow and Leningrad to view without rancor the great changes in the institutions and the peoples' way of life. His report is especially valuable because of his comparisons between past (before 1917) and present.

887.   Dos Passos, John R. *In all countries.* New York, Harcourt, Brace, 1934. pp. 9–72.

American novelist and traveler, touring from Leningrad to the Caspian Sea area in 1928, is critical and impressionistic on the rural way of life.

888.   Du Bois, William Edward Burghardt. *Dusk of dawn. An essay toward an autobiography of a race concept.* New York, Harcourt, Brace, 1940. pp. 287–91.

Negro cofounder of the National Association for the Advancement of Colored People and a communist sympathizer spends two months in European Russia (Leningrad south to Odessa) in 1928 and comes away saying that Russia offers much hope for the future under the leadership of the Communist party.

889.   Freuchen, Peter. *It's all adventure.* London, Heinemann, 1938. pp. 98–144. port.

Danish explorer attends a conference in Leningrad to plan for the use of dirigibles to explore the Arctic in 1928. His account is a humorous critique of his experiences in the Russian capital and the White Sea area.

890.   Haldane, Charlotte Franken. *Truth will out.* New York, Vanguard Press, 1950. pp. 41–51, 190–327. index.

Twice, British free-lance writer and later war correspondent journeys to Leningrad and Moscow. In 1928, in sympathy with the aims of the communists, she describes the increasing emphasis on science and technology, especially in engineering. In 1941 she comments on the triumph of Lysenko and the hysteria accompanying the German invasion.

891. Kallen, Horace M. *Frontiers of hope.* New York, Liveright, 1929. pp. 271–433.

American specialist in comparative education views the Soviet experiment during a stay in Moscow in 1928. He observes that Russia under communism is perhaps the last hope for the Jews.

892. McCormick, Anne O'Hare. *The hammer and the scythe. Communist Russia enters the second decade.* New York, Knopf, 1929. 295 pp. index.

Correspondent with the *New York Times* analyzes and compares Soviet life with the West after a journey to European Russia, including a trip down the Volga River, in 1928. One of the most useful sections she includes is on the women and children, their lives and their advantages.

893. Huld, Palle. *A Boy Scout around the world.* Translated from the Danish by Eleanor Hard. New York, Junior Literary Guild, 1929. pp. 148–72. illus.

Young Danish boy journeys across Siberia to Moscow on a trip won as a prize in April, 1928.

894. Shaw, Elizabeth. *Painted maps.* New York, MacVeagh, 1931. pp. 159–213. illus.

American tourist describes the friendly people she meets and the stupid functionaries who thwart her plans on a journey in the summer of 1928. She refers to Leningrad as the "city of the dead," visits Moscow, where she sees the unfinished Lenin mausoleum, and then travels to the Crimea down the Volga River.

895. Zelitch, Judah. *Soviet administration of criminal law.* Philadelphia, University of Pennsylvania Press, 1931. 405 pp. index.

Law student, writing his thesis for a Master of Arts degree, attends
court trials in Moscow in the summer of 1928.

896.   Strong, Anna Louise. *Red Star in Samarkand.* New York,
        Coward-McCann, 1929. 329 pp. illus. map.

In October, 1928, Anna Louise Strong (see nos. 782 and 792)
traveled through Uzbekistan to Samarkand, where she studied the
impact of communism on Islamic institutions. Her story is a sympathetic account of change, especially on the women.

897.   Ashmead-Bartlett, Ellis. *The riddle of Russia.* London,
        Cassell, 1929. 266 pp. map. index.

British correspondent visits Moscow and Leningrad in November, 1928, and attempts to compare the Soviet Union's way of life
with that of Britain and the West. In addition to tours arranged
by Intourist, he visits prisons and investigates the position of
women in social life.

898.   Glassman, Leo M. "I remember Natasha." In Overseas
        Press Club of America, compiler, *As we see Russia,* pp.
        150–60. (See no. 1458.)

Russian-speaking correspondent of Jewish Telegraphic Agency in
Moscow, 1928–29, describes one soul's torment in the Stalin-
Trotsky struggle.

899.   Winterton, Paul. *A student in Russia.* Manchester, Co-
        operative Union, 1931. pp. 1–80.

Impressions of the peasants during the first Five Year Plan by
British economics student, 1928–29, who describes how suspicions
of his intentions change to friendship as the language is learned
and motives discerned.

900.   Rukeyser, Walter Arnold. *Working for the Soviets. An
        American engineer in Russia.* New York, Covici-Friede,
        1932. 286 pp. illus.

Consulting engineer to the Soviet Asbestos Mining Trust describes life in the Ural Mountains, 1928–30. Speaking German usually but learning some Russian, he accumulates evidence for the verbal and pictorial illustrations of mining methods and conditions in Asbest, thirty-five miles east of Sverdlovsk.

901. Kitchin, George. *Prisoner of the OGPU*. London, Longmans, Green, 1935. 333 pp. illus. map. port. app.

Penal-camp recollections are presented here by Russian-speaking Anglo-Finnish representative of an American company, 1928–32. He tells a stark tale of horror and includes an appendix list of prison camps and a map to the penal-camp area around the White Sea.

902. Lyons, Eugene. *Assignment in Utopia*. New York, Harcourt, Brace, 1937. 648 pp. index.

Born in Russia and naturalized in the United States in 1918, Lyons served as United Press correspondent in Moscow, 1928–34. The story of his love affair with the Soviet Union may be illustrated by two quotations from this account: ". . . . December 31, 1927 . . . I sailed with Billy and our five-year-old daughter, Eugenie, for the land of our dreams." Six years later: "Above all, I had the sense of leaving behind me *a nation* trapped."

For another account of his Moscow assignment see *Moscow Carrousel*. New York, Knopf, 1935. 357 pp. See also 903.

903. Lyons, Eugene. "My six years in Moscow." In Overseas Press Club of America, compiler. *As we see Russia,* pp. 261–73. (See no. 1458.)

Lyons' summary of the Stalin Revolution, 1928–34. See no. 902.

904. Littlepage, John D., and Demaree Bess. *In search of Soviet gold*. New York, Harcourt, Brace, 1937. 310 pp.

Littlepage, an American mining engineer working for the Soviet Gold Trust in Kochkar, Siberia, 1928–37, comments on the operation of the Five Year Plans. He is non-political in his account, emphasizing the results of technical inexperience and industrial sabotage.

905.   Mehnert, (Dr.) Klaus. *Soviet man and his world.* Translated from the German by Maurice Rosenbaum. New York, Praeger, 1962. 292 pp. index.

Born in Russia of a German family doing business and trade there since 1928, Mehnert provides a total analysis of Soviet life from the observations of thirteen journeys, 1928–58. He concludes that Soviet man may criticize the operation of the system he lives in but not its philosophy and theory. He discusses the social framework, the private sphere, the material world, culture, the individual and the state, the world outside and the Soviet man, and the Soviet Union and the West. Required reading for anyone who is seriously interested in life in the Soviet Union.

906.   Edelhertz, Bernard. *The Russian paradox. A first-hand study of life under the Soviets.* New York, Walton Book Co., 1930. 152 pp. illus. index.

American artist and writer encounters what he considers to be incredible paradoxes in Moscow and European Russia in 1929. He pays particular attention to village life and the Jewish colonies, and finally concludes that better times will come when the people demand them.

907.   Farson, Negley. *Seeing red today.* London, Eyre & Spottiswoode, 1930. 275 pp. illus.

Farson (see no. 605) journeys through European Russia in 1929 making a detailed examination of living conditions in town and country. His account includes a rich selection of antireligious, antipolitical, and anti-imperialist posters.

908.   Farson, Negley. *Caucasian journey.* London, Evans, 1951. 152 pp. illus. port. index.

In this account (see nos. 605 and 907) a backward look is cast on a journey taken into the Caucasus mountains in 1929. Farson and Alexander Wicksteed (see no. 820) establish close contacts with the mountain people, and many of their anticommunist sentiments are recorded.

909.   Foss, Kendall. *Black bread and samovars. An account of an unconventional journey through Soviet Russia*. London, Arrowsmith, 1930. 247 pp. illus. port.

American student at Oxford University and companion on holiday journey to Sverdlovsk in 1929. With about $50 a month in their budget, they manage to visit many of the cities of European Russia, finding the people to be friendly and co-operative but the officials surly and obstructive—attitudes that might have been encouraged by the students themselves through their deliberate baiting of the police and other functionaries.

910.   Claudia (pseudonym of Mary Pryor Hack). *Back to our own country. Russia: land of the romantic past and the pregnant future*. London, Stockwell, 1938. 256 pp.

Russian-born Australian, traveling with her brother and sister, describes her adventures in trying to locate relatives in Moscow and the Volga River area in 1929.

911.   Herrington, Lewis Marion. *A doctor diagnoses Russia*. McKees Rocks, Pennsylvania, Herrington, 1930. 127 pp.

Somewhat sympathetic to the Soviet experiment, an American medical doctor becomes strongly critical after 1929 visit to Leningrad, Moscow, and the rural areas. He concludes that too much government protection of the individual destroys initiative.

912.   Tenenbaum, Samuel. *William Heard Kilpatrick. Trail blazer in education*. New York, Harper, 1951. pp. 263–69. port.

American disciple of John Dewey views Soviet progressive education in 1929. He strongly disapproves of using hate as a means and sees Russia's schools as midway between America's best and worst.

913.   Lockhart, John Gilbert. *Babel revisited; a churchman in Soviet Russia.* London, Centenary Press, 1933. 128 pp. illus.

British clergyman on tour in 1929 sees Russia as a rising competitor to British power and communism as a menace to Christianity. He illustrates his account with reproductions of anti-religious posters.

914.   Sorenson, Charles E., and Samuel T. Williamson. *My forty years with Ford.* New York, Norton, 1956. pp. 193–216.

Ford Motor Company official describes his journey to Moscow in 1929 when he accompanied an entire automobile plant shipped from the United States to the Soviet Union.

915.   Strong, Anna Louise. *The road to the grey Pamir.* Boston, Little, Brown, 1931. 289 pp. illus. map.

In 1929 Strong (see nos. 782 and 792) sets out to see Soviet Transcaspia. She writes a detailed account of the impact of communism on a little-known part of the world.

916.   Toynbee, Arnold Joseph. *A journey to China, or things which are seen.* London, Constable, 1931. pp. 194–99, 296–331.

Famous British historian on a journey to the Far East in 1929 has a brief contact with Russia-in-Manchuria and asks the question "What if the Five Year Plan works?"

917.   Hindus, Maurice Gerschon. *Red Bread.* New York, Jonathan Cape and Harrison Smith, 1931. 372 pp. illus.

Here Hindus (see nos. 711 and 839) presents a brilliant and poignant portrait of the peasant under the impact of collectivization in the summer of 1929. At the end of his account he observes: "Meanwhile the Kolkhoz with its turmoil, all its agony, all its romance and all its promises, rolls on."

918. Segal, Louis. *The Soviet Union in reconstruction.* London, Blackfriars Press, 1931. pp. 1–65.

British professor of economics journeys to Moscow in July–August, 1929, to study the first Five Year Plan in operation. His account is illuminated with detailed charts and other analytical materials.

919. Villard, Oswald Garrison. *Russia from a car window.* New York, The Nation, 1929. 78 pp.

American newspaperman and crusader and a member of the American-Russian Chamber of Commerce travels 6,000 miles by train during July–August, 1929. His short account concentrates on the relationship between ideals and their achievement.

920. Counts, George Sylvester. *A Ford crosses Soviet Russia.* Boston, Stratford, 1930. 233 pp. map.

Columbia University professor (see no. 864) journeys through European Russia from Leningrad to the Black Sea, July–October, 1929. He claims to have had complete freedom of movement, unmolested or obstructed by Communist party functionaries or the secret police, and his account emphasizes the contrasts between the urban and the rural scene.

921. Gilliard, Alfred James. *Another innocent abroad. Some impressions of a journey across Siberia to the Far East, related in letters to a Young People's Band.* London, Salvationist Publishers, 1930. pp. 27–49.

On a journey through "a land from which God had fled" in the autumn of 1929, a British Salvationist sergeant writes a few simple observations on how a man of God feels in a land of state atheism.

922. Feiler, Arthur. *The Russian experiment.* Translated from the German by H. S. Stenning. New York, Harcourt, Brace, 1930. 269 pp. index.

Beginning with the "Pathos of Revolution," German author and wife work through industrial and agricultural patterns in 1929–30 journey to Moscow and European Russia. This is a well-written, but not particularly exciting, account.

923.   Hoover, Calvin B. *The economic life of Soviet Russia.* New York, Macmillan, 1931. 347 pp. app. biblio. index.

Unfriendly description written after 1929–30 trip to Moscow and surrounding areas by Duke University professor of economics, who suspects all statistics from the Soviet Union but believes that the system will survive and eventually meet the West's standard of living.

924.   Kingsbury, Susan M., and Mildred Fairchild. *Factory, family and woman in the Soviet Union.* New York, Putnam, 1935. 273 pp. app. biblio. index.

Bryn Mawr professors of social economy journey to Moscow and nearby areas in 1929–30 and in 1932. Their account is detailed and illustrated with tables and statistics—they express confidence in Soviet statistics.

925.   Loder, J. de V. (pseudonym of John de Vere Loder Wakehurst). *Bolshevism in perspective.* London, Allen & Unwin, 1931. 244 pp. illus. map. app. biblio. index.

British writer, accompanied by Russian-speaking companion, travels 15,000 miles from Leningrad and Moscow through Siberia for four months in 1929–30. He presents a reasonably objective account, with comments on all aspects of life, accompanied by historical backgrounds.

926.   Strong, Anna Louise. *The Soviets conquer wheat. The drama of collective farming.* New York, Holt, 1931. 288 pp. illus. app.

After studying the process of rural collectivization in 1929–30, Anna Louise Strong (see nos. 782, 792, 896, and 915) concludes that the benefits to the peasant justify the liquidation of the kulaks and the introduction of mechanized agriculture.

927. Campbell, Thomas Donald. *Russia: Market or menace?* London, Longmans, Green, 1932. 148 pp. map. port.

Large-scale farming expert from the United States comments on the agrarian aspects of the first Five Year Plan after two journeys, January, 1929, and July, 1930. He favors collectivization but does not directly answer the question posed by the title of his account.

928. Muldavin, Albert. *The red fog lifts.* New York, Appleton, 1931. 311 pp.

Bored with American prosperity, businessman who lived in Russia in czarist times secures a letter of introduction from Amtorg and spends 1929–31 in the rural areas of the Ukraine. The account does not claim to be the truth about Russia but "the truth about myself in Russia."

929. Westgarth, John R. *Russian engineer.* London, Denis Archer, 1934. 193 pp. illus. port. app. index.

British consulting engineer to the Gosplan, 1929–31, reports on the unfavorable conditions at Kuzneitsk. A very interesting part of this account describes Westgarth's feud with Bernard Shaw (see no. 980), who defended his favorable impressions of the Soviet Union after a two-week tour in 1931 against Westgarth's exposé after a sojourn of two and one-half years.

930. Chamberlin, William Henry. *Russia's iron age.* Boston, Little, Brown, 1934. 389 pp. illus. index.

A comprehensive analysis of the Soviet Union under the stimulus of the first Five Year Plan, by an American correspondent in Moscow (see no. 809).

931. Beauchamp, Joan. *Agriculture in Soviet Russia.* London, Gollancz, 1931. 126 pp.

British student journeys to the Caucasus in 1930 to live in the villages. Claims to have observed no forced collectivization.

932. Chesterton, (Mrs.) Ada Elizabeth (Jones). *My Russian venture.* Philadelphia, Lippincott, 1931. 283 pp.

British novelist and reporter visits areas around Minsk and Kiev in 1930 to study the kolkhoz. Sympathetic toward the people, she describes the Soviet Union as "a young country for young people" but warns against "the shadow of the robot."

933.   Ferrara, Maria (Sanchez y Ramirez) de. *From Tientsin to Byelo-Ostrow*. Washington, D.C., privately printed, 1931. 95 pp.

Spanish diplomat and wife travel across Siberia from Vladivostok to Leningrad, 1930. Her account is very impressionistic as she compares present-day Russia with the world she knew in imperial times.

934.   Grady, Eve Garrette. *Seeing red. Behind the scenes in Russia today*. New York, Brewer, Warren & Putnam, 1931. 307 pp.

Wife of American engineer in Kharkov exposes the true conditions in 1930. Her account is extremely negative, and she considers the unemployed Americans to be better off than employed Russians. She is especially critical of American tourists, whom she castigates as unpaid communist propagandists.

935.   Knickerbocker, H. R. *The red trade menace. Progress of the Soviet Five Year Plan*. New York, Dodd, Mead, 1931. 277 pp. illus.

In 1930 American businessman and correspondent (New York *Evening Post*) travels 10,000 miles in European Russia during a seven-weeks visit. He opens with "The Soviet Union is a land at war" and then proceeds to define the areas of conflict. He places special emphasis on the part that American know-how played in the first Plan.

936.   Lipphard, William Benjamin. *Communing with Communism: a narrative of impressions of Soviet Russia*. Philadelphia, Judson Press. 1931. 153 pp. illus.

Professional lecturer leads a special party of Americans to Leningrad and Moscow on a one-month tour in 1930. In his account he comments on the position of Christianity in the Soviet Union.

937. Mackiewicz, Stanislaw. *Russian minds in fetters.* London, Allen & Unwin, 1932. pp. 1–182. index.

Polish journalist, with a smattering of Russian, is in Moscow in 1930. He presents a very impressionistic account with comments on sex (which he characterizes as puritanical), religion, education, and daily life (". . . in Russia, if you are hungry, you can die.").

938. Rowan-Hamilton, Norah. *Under the red star.* London, Jenkins, 1930. 316 pp. illus. port. index.

British professional writer approaches objectivity in her presentation of both sides of the situation in the Soviet Union after her journey to Moscow, Novgorod, and Kiev in 1930. She deals with religion, law, marriage, housing, the rural situation, etc.; and the reader should especially notice the section on "Dope—white and red."

939. Sibley, Robert. *America's answer to the Russian challenge. In which electric power, as a common denominator, is requisitioned to throw light on the Russian enigma and the challenge it presents to western civilization.* San Francisco, Farollon Press, 1931. pp. 33–72. illus.

American delegate to a worldwide power conference in Berlin in 1930 journeys into Russia, traveling from Leningrad to the Black Sea. He sets out to appraise Lenin's dictum that Sovietism plus Electrification equals Communism and arrives at the conclusion that titanic forces are in motion in the Soviet Union and the free world should be warned and aware.

940. Taylor, Sidney. *Soviet and soul; Russia through the eyes of youth.* London, Houghton, 1931. 164 pp. illus.

A journey of 1,200 miles to Leningrad and Moscow is made by a British student in 1930. He is deeply impressed by the idealism of the people and the fact that no one appears to want war.

941. Tweedy, Owen. *Russia at random.* London, Jarrolds, 1931. 192 pp. illus.

In 1930 a British traveler and writer spends three days in Leningrad and Moscow with a group of 500 people from a tour ship. He uses a metaphor and compares the Russians to seals who have good living conditions, are always half-afraid of their keeper, but are perhaps happy.

942.   Van Paassen, Pierre. *Visions rise and change.* New York, Dial, 1955. 400 pp.

Looking back twenty-five years, Dutch writer recalls his journey to the Soviet Union in 1930, primarily to examine the state of religion in an atheistic state. He is impressionistic in his descriptions of police persecution, a visit to an old folk's home, the life of the people in the cities, and other similar experiences.

943.   Johnson, John. *Russia in the grip of Bolshevism; a vivid story of a trip to the land of the Soviets.* New York, Revell, 1931. 160 pp.

An American's account of his travels in Russia (Leningrad and Moscow) in March–April, 1930. He is very critical of the Soviet Union's persecution of Christians and emphasizes the impact of godlessness and atheism on the church as an organization and on the faith of the people.

944.   O'Flaherty, Liam. *I went to Russia.* London, Jonathan Cape, 1931. 299 pp. port.

Irish film director writes a satiric account of his visit to Leningrad and Moscow in April–May, 1930, in which he observes that the evangelistic communists are on top, the greedy, ambitious careerists beneath. See especially the dialogue between Walter Duranty (see no. 790 and 791) and O'Flaherty.

945.   Bourke-White, Margaret. *Eyes on Russia.* New York, Simon & Shuster, 1931. 135 pp. illus.

Associate editor of *Fortune* spends five weeks in European Russia during the summer of 1930 photographing a sympathetic portrait of industrial development under the first Five Year Plan.

946. Friedman, Elisha M. *Russia in transition: A business man's appraisal.* New York, Viking, 1933. 582 pp. app. index.

After a journey to Moscow and European Russia in July–August, 1930, American businessman advocates recognition of the Soviet Union if she pays her debts to the United States.

947. Yeghenian, Aghavnie Yeghia. *The red flag at Ararat.* New York, The Women's Press, 1932. 170 pp. illus. map.

Free-lance journalist, Armenian-American, journeys to Soviet Armenia in August, 1930, to observe the impact of communism on the way of life and, considering the circumstances, writes a fairly objective report.

948. Polunin, Nicholas. *Russian waters.* London, Edward Arnold, 1931. pp. 47–266. illus. map. port.

In September, 1930, a Russian-speaking Oxford student ships out as deck hand on a British timber boat running between England and Russia. His account is a detailed description of his experiences in the tiny town of Soroka, located at the mouth of a river flowing out of Lake Onega.

949. Tagore, Rabindranath. *Letters from Russia.* Translated by S. Sinha. Calcutta, Visva-Bharati, 1960. 222 pp. illus.

Hindu poet, musical composer, and painter, is in Moscow for five days, September 20–25, 1930. From there he writes favorable, but critical, comments in which Communist Russia is seen as a mighty future force, with equality and no human greed.

950. Harben, Henry Devenish. *Diary written during a visit to Russia in September and October, 1930.* London, privately printed, 1930. 94 pp. app.

Film writer and businessman, a guest of the Soviet Union, sees the people as being permitted to criticize the administration but not the principles of the system. He justifies the secret police as a necessary preventive to sabotage.

951.   Harrison, Juanita. *My great wide wonderful world.* Mildred
        Morris, editor. New York, Macmillan, 1936. pp. 277–82.

On a trip around the world, a Mississippi-born Negro travels from
Leningrad to the Manchurian border on the Trans-Siberian Railway, September 2–15, 1930. Special treatment by the functionaries
and the people evokes a friendly judgment.

952.   Long, Ray. *An editor looks at Russia; one unprejudiced
        view of the land of the Soviets.* New York, Long & Smith,
        1931. 114 pp.

American publisher claims to have visited Moscow and Leningrad
in October–November, 1930, with no preconceptions and with no
desire to prove anything. His account proves to be very informative on Soviet writers and writing.

953.   Burrell, George A. *An American engineer looks at Russia.*
        Boston, Stratford, 1932. 324 pp. illus.

Petroleum engineer, eighteen months in Grozny in 1930–31, comments on what he refers to as "hokum" in the West about the
Soviet Union. He has many useful things to say about the way of
life and observes that communism and capitalism will eventually
meet as each modifies in the direction of the other.

954.   Burr, Malcolm. *In Bolshevik Siberia. The land of ice and
        exile.* London, Witherby, 1931. 224 pp. illus. map. index.

British geologist looking for gold in the winter of 1930 to the
winter of 1931 describes a journey down the Lena river from
Irkutsk to Svetloie. He claims he has no axe to grind—only to
tell the story of nature and of his fellow man.

955.   Beal, Fred E. *Proletarian journey. New England, Gastonia,
        Moscow.* New York, Hillman-Curl, 1937. pp. 225–344. illus.
        port.

Disillusioning experiences of an American socialist, 1930–33, who
emerges as a "fugitive from Capitalist and Bolshevik justice." He
provides a moving description of famine in Russia in 1933.

956. Hall, P. E. "Sport." In Griffith, editor, *Playtime in Russia*, pp. 184–204. illus. (See no. 1439.)

London journalist's comments on Soviet amateur sports, 1930–34. He believes that Moscow's purpose is to organize youth around the social organism, making them efficient in industry and defense.

957. Street, Lucie, editor. *I married a Russian; letters from Kharkov*. New York, Emerson Books, 1947. 331 pp. map.

English girl accompanies Russian scientist husband to the Ukraine. In these letters she describes her adjustment to a new way of life, 1930–45. An especially valuable account because it takes the reader inside Russian homes.

958. Craig-McKerrow, (Mrs.) Margaret (Reibold). *The iron road to Samarcand*. London, De La More Press, 1932. 143 pp. illus.

Readable commentary on Transcaspia in 1931. After eighteen days on a crowded train she was convinced that many Russians still retained their prerevolutionary customs and attitudes (see no. 536); and after some time in Samarkand, she was convinced that the Soviet authorities would like to liquidate all persons over forty years of age.

959. Eastman, Max. *Great companions*. New York, Farrar, Straus & Cudahy, 1959. pp. 151–69.

American socialist (see no. 806) and writer reports on a twelve-day visit with Leon Trotsky, who was in exile on the island of Prinkipo in 1931. In this brief report he emphasizes the "bloodless" characteristic of Trotsky's personality.

960. Fischer, Louis. *Men and machines in Russia*. New York, Harrison Smith, 1932. 283 pp. illus.

Russian-born American correspondent stationed in Moscow, 1921–39, to represent the *Nation*. At first sympathetic, he is later disillusioned by the purges, and urges rejection of both communism and fascism. Beautifully and strikingly illustrated by the photogra-

phy of Margaret Bourke-White (see no. 945), the book describes
the progress of the first Five Year Plan by 1931.

961.   Forman, Archibald Thomas. *From Baltic to Black Sea.*
        Impressions of Soviet Russia today. London, Low, Marston,
        1932. 333 pp. illus. map. index.

British lawyer journeys from Leningrad to the Caucasus on a
4,000-mile tour in 1931 and writes an observant account of the
people and their way of life. In the last sentence of his story he
asks: "Where will it lead? Will it be a success? The future can
alone discuss the answer."

962.   Frank, Waldo. *Dawn in Russia. The record of a journey.*
        New York, Scribner's, 1932. 272 pp.

American journalist attempts to reveal the soul of the Russian
people in this account of his travels to Leningrad, Moscow, and
the Volga River area in 1931.

963.   Freeman, Joseph. *The Soviet worker. An account of the*
        economic, social and cultural status of labor in the U.S.S.R.
        New York, Liveright, 1932. 344 pp. app. index.

American, sympathetic to the aims and ideals of the Soviet Union,
journeys through European Russia in 1931 gathering data on the
Russian working man. His account uses Soviet statistics for many
of his conclusions but is comprehensive in its scope if this is taken
into consideration. There is a model of a collective agreement in
the appendix.

964.   Griffith, Hubert Freeling. *Seeing Soviet Russia, an informa-*
        tive record of the cheapest trip in Europe. London, John
        Lane, 1932. 199 pp. map. index.

London theater critic travels to Leningrad, Moscow, and Nizhni-
Novgorod in 1931 to discover the truth behind the Soviet Union's
revolutionary changes and, favorably impressed, contrasts the sur-
plus and waste of the West with the communist production for
use.

965. Hindus, Maurice Gerschon. *Humanity uprooted*. Garden City, New York, Blue Ribbon Books, 1932. 369 pp. illus.

His 1931 journey through European Russia and Transcaspia leads Hindus (see nos. 711, 839, and 917) to the conclusion that "hardly an institution—property, religion, morality, family, love—has escaped the blasts of the Revolution."

966. Huxley, Julian. *A scientist among the Soviets*. New York, Harper, 1932. 142 pp.

British biologist and author, grandson of Thomas Henry Huxley, who was Charles Darwin's foremost supporter and a lecturer in King's College, London, visits Leningrad and Moscow in 1931 as the guest of the Soviet Union. In his account he likens the first Five Year Plan to the human embryo.

967. Jones, Gareth V. *Experiences in Russia—1931: a diary*. Pittsburgh, The Alton Press, 1932. pp. 43–235. illus. app.

The account of a thirty-nine day journey to Leningrad, Moscow, and rural areas around them in which the high tide of collectivization under the first Five Year Plan is described.

968. * Nurenberg, Thelma. *This new red freedom*. New York, Wadsworth, 1932. 327 pp. illus.

969. Raiguel, George Earle, and William Kistler Huff. *This is Russia*. Philadelphia, Penn Publishing Co., 1932. 423 pp. illus. map. index.

A very useful guide to the cities of Leningrad and Moscow in 1931 prepared by two travelers who illustrate their comments with dozens of excellent photographs.

970. Robinson, William Josephus. *Soviet Russia as I saw it; its accomplishments, its crime and stupidities*. New York, International, 1932. 224 pp. index.

Member of an American medical tour in 1931 favors recognition of Russia even though he recognizes that Stalin and the first Five Year Plan are hurting the peasants.

971.   Strong, Anna Louise. *From Stalingrad to Kuzbas; sketches of the Socialist construction of the U.S.S.R.* New York, International Publishers, 1932. 72 pp. illus.

American sympathizer of Soviet aims (see nos. 782, 792, 896, 915, and 926) travels through southern Russia and east into Siberia in 1931, placing an emphasis in her account on Americans employed in factories in the first Five Year Plan.

972.   Walter, Ellery. *Russia's decisive year.* New York, Putnam, 1932. 269 pp. illus. app.

New York *Herald Tribune* correspondent, Russian-speaking, sets out on a journey in 1931 to study the first Five Year Plan and discovers that one must be very careful how he uses Soviet statistics. He provides a delightful account of the treatment accorded Bernard Shaw (see no. 980) and Lady Astor on their journeys through Russia.

973.   Cravath, Paul Drennan. *Letters home from the Far East and Russia, 1931.* Garden City, New York, Country Life Press, 1931. pp. 78–97.

On a trip across Siberia on the Trans-Siberian Railway to Moscow in April–May, 1931, an American offers little criticism of the Soviet system but much on its operation.

974.   Crichton, Charles Frederick Andrew Maitland-Magkill. *Russian close-up.* London, Chatto & Windus, 1932. 167 pp.

Russian-speaking British traveler makes a short visit (twelve and one-half days) to Leningrad, Moscow, and Kiev in May, 1931, and seeks to discover motivations behind Russian actions.

975.   Cummings, E[dward] E[stlen]. *Eimi (The journal of a trip to Russia).* New York, Grove Press, 1933. pp. 12–379.

American poet visits Moscow, Kiev, and Odessa, May 10–June 14, 1931. After summing up his impressions, he refers to the Soviet Union as "Hell."

976. Matters, Leonard. *Through the Kara Sea. The narrative of a voyage in a tramp steamer through Arctic waters to the Yenisei River.* London, Skeffington, 1932. 283 pp. illus. map. port.

English Member of Parliament travels to Igarka the long way in the summer of 1931 and supplies a very informative commentary on the sources of livelihood in Arctic waters.

977. Wright, Russell. *One-sixth of the world's surface.* Hammond, Indiana, privately printed, 1932. 145 pp. illus.

American tourist journeys from Leningrad to Stalingrad in the summer of 1931 and returns to describe his impressions of Soviet life in a collection of stories.

978. Lohman, Clarence. *The U.S.S.R. in 1931.* Houston, privately printed, 1945. pp. 15–40.

Texas tourist on typical tour (Leningrad, Moscow, Kiev) in June, 1931, returns home extremely critical of the entire system.

979. Shaw, Bernard. *A little talk on America. What Bernard Shaw told the Americans about Russia!* London, Friends of the Soviet Union, 1932. pp. 3–14. illus.

The famous British satirist, dramatist, and writer honored the Soviet Union by his presence, July 20–30, 1931. This pamphlet contains the diatribe Shaw launched at the United States over American radio on October 11, 1931, in which the Union of Soviet Socialist Republics is viewed as the wave of the future.

980. Shaw, Bernard. *The rationalization of Russia by Bernard Shaw.* Harry M. Geduld, editor. Bloomington, Indiana, Indiana University Press, 1964. pp. 58–117. illus. port. app.

Shaw set out here to record his impressions of his 1931 journey, but did not complete the report. The editor provides an excellent account of the Shaw journey, pp. 9–32.

981.   Koerber, Lili. *Life in a Soviet factory.* Translated from the German by Claud W. Sykes. London, John Lane, 1933. 280 pp.

For one month in August, 1931, Russian-speaking German writer works in the Leningrad Putilov factory. She describes the home life of the workers and their activities on the assembly line with sympathy and understanding.

982.   Darling, Jay N. *Ding goes to Russia.* New York, McGraw-Hill, 1932. 195 pp. illus.

American political cartoonist travels from Moscow to Sebastopol in the autumn of 1931 noting the foibles of a planned economy and sketching them in a series of delightful and enlightening cartoons. Observes: "Either you end by wanting to murder them or you are fast friends for life. With me in Russia it was the latter."

983.   Smith, Marjorie E. *From Broadway to Moscow.* New York, Macauley, 1934. 317 pp.

New York correspondent goes to Russia in 1931–32 with her communist husband to explore the Soviet way of life. She describes her experiences during a ten-month stay by placing special emphasis upon the lives of workers and expressing sympathy for their aims and ideals.

984.   Seymour, (Mrs.) June. *In the Moscow manner.* London, Archer, 1935. 286 pp.

Wife of Canadian engineer in Moscow, 1931–34, sings neither a hymn of unqualified praise nor a song of hate as she recalls her experiences. Instead, she tries to objectively comment on the way of life and its influence on her and her husband.

985. Weissberg, Alexander Cybulski. *Conspiracy of silence.* Translated from the German by Edward Fitzgerald. London. Hamish Hamilton, 1952. 509 pp.

Jewish scientist, member of the Austrian Communist party, moves with his family to Kharkov in 1931. Arrested in 1937, he confesses to plotting the deaths of Stalin and Voroshilov and is sent to a labor camp, from which he is released to the Nazis in 1940. He survives to write one of the best and most revealing of the personal accounts by victims of the 1937 trials.

986. Wood, William. *Our ally. The people of Russia as told to Myriam Sieve.* New York, Scribner's, 1950. 287 pp.

American engineer and his wife live in the Soviet Union, 1931–34, in 1937, and in 1941, while he is under contract to the government. He carefully describes his relations with the bureaucracy and also with the United States government in arranging to go to Russia. His chapters dealing with everyday life are excellent, as are his comparisons of the way he was treated with the way Russian engineers were exploited by the state.

987. Smith, Homer. *Black man in red Russia: a memoir.* Chicago, Johnson Publishing Co., 1964. 214 pp. illus. port. index.

Journey of disillusionment by Minnesota Negro who flees the depression and segregation to become a newspaper correspondent in Moscow. There he marries and life is smooth until the novelty of the Negro in Russia declines with increasing numbers. Finally, in 1946, he and his wife leave the promised land where race hatred appears to him to be increasing at frightening speed. Excellent photographs illuminate this unusual account.

988. Abbe, James E. *I photograph Russia.* New York, McBride, 1934. 324 pp. illus.

American reporter-photographer is commissioned by German newspaper owners, Ullsteinhaus, to photograph Stalin and Russia. In

1932 Abbe proceeds to Moscow, where he secures permission, interviews and photographs a smiling Stalin. After this, he describes the Soviet way of life in word and picture, then joins the Soviet Photo Trust to secure permission to photograph in restricted areas. Arrest and eviction from the Soviet Union follows several daring exploits. His account includes eighty excellent photographs.

989.   Brown, Edwin Tyler. *This Russian business.* London, Allen & Unwin, 1933. 255 pp. index.

In 1932 British writer makes the usual tour (Leningrad, Moscow, and Kiev) to study "The Red Room." He sees the Bolsheviki as winning but inevitably changing.

990.   Durant, Will. *The tragedy of Russia. Impressions from a brief visit.* New York, Simon & Schuster, 1933. 164 pp.

American historical writer, reacting to the American depression in 1932, finally concludes that communism is the world's only hope for peace and plenty. After a journey to Moscow, he is led to "look in horror and pity upon the land of our dreams." He sees the enthroning of the weak to control the strong as a heroic but futile experiment.

991.   Fischer, Louis. *Soviet journey.* New York, Harrison Smith and Robert Haas, 1935. 308 pp. illus. map.

Fischer (see no. 960) records sympathetic impressions of 1932 journey in which the attempt is made to enable the reader to see, hear, feel, and smell Russia by crowding the pages with human beings.

992.   Grierson, John. *Through Russia by air.* London, Foulis, 1934. 174 pp. illus. port.

British student and amateur pilot makes a solo flight to Tashkent in 1932 and comes away with the observation that the "U.S.S.R. is the new world, the Aeroplane the key."

993.   Hoyland, John S. *The new Russia. A Quaker visitor's impressions.* London, Allenson, 1933. 89 pp.

British observer looks at the positive aspects in Leningrad and Moscow in 1932. He expresses admiration for the average man, the equality of sexes, the rehabilitation of criminals, the emphasis on children, and finds the people to be "remarkably gentle, courteous, and lovable. . . ."

994. Lecler, Paula (Vaughn Henry, pseudonym). "The dead hour (Russia 1932)." In Overseas Press Club of America, compiler, *As we see Russia,* pp. 93–115. (See no. 1458.)

A critical analysis by an American reporter in 1932 of the overweening ambition and dishonesty in a Soviet man, based on her association with Max, an Intourist guide. Her account appears to demonstrate how the need for the basic necessities of life breeds a new exploiter class.

995. Low, David. *Low's Russian sketchbook.* London, Gollancz, 1932. 141 pp. illus.

British cartoonist visits Leningrad, Moscow, and the Volga River area in 1932 to sketch the Soviet scene. Text is by Kingsley Martin.

996. Dominique, Pierre (pseudonym of Pierre Lucchini). *Secrets of Siberia.* Translated from the French by Warre B. Wells. London, Hutchinson, 1934. 288 pp. illus.

French Russian-speaking journalist visits Magnitogorsk in 1932 and describes the crude way of life lived by the people in a growing steel-producing city—a city that did not exist in 1929.

997. Lyall, Archibald Laurence. *Russian roundabout. A nonpolitical pilgrimage.* London, Desmond Harmsworth, 1933. 207 pp.

Professional British traveler and writer, journeying with a Russian-speaking companion, visits most of European Russia in 1932. Part of his purpose was to observe English admirers of the Soviet Union as they see the existing conditions firsthand, in much the same way that Stephen Graham did earlier in *With the Russian pilgrims to Jerusalem* (see no. 576).

998.   Oberndorf, Clarence Paul. *A history of psychoanalysis in America*. New York, Grune & Stratton, 1953. pp. 192–93.

Medical doctor, psychoanalyst, journeys to Leningrad in 1932, where he is assured that there is no need in Soviet Russia for mental treatment.

999.   Patrick, Mark. *Hammer and sickle*. London, Mathews & Marrot, 1933. 243 pp.

Member of Parliament in Moscow, 1932, concludes that big business has recovered leadership, although the Soviet leaders still profess socialist ideals.

1000.   Wells, Carveth. *Kapoot. The narrative of a journey from Leningrad to Mount Ararat in search of Noah's Ark*. New York, McBride, 1934. 251 pp. illus. app.

Professional traveler and lecturer from the United States concludes that the Soviet system has broken down, although it still provides benefits for those who are managing it. His account of a 1932 visit finds little to admire in Russia.

1001.   Williams, Frankwood Earl. *Russia, youth, and the present day world. Further studies in mental hygiene*. New York, Farrar & Rinehart, 1934. pp. 3–74, 88–263. illus. index.

American psychiatrist journeys 10,000 miles through European Russia in 1932 to study Russia's mental hygiene program and her use of psychiatry. Detailed and well-written, his account also is concerned with the program for children and the treatment of alcoholics. Excellent cartoons are included.

1002.   Winter, Ella (Mrs. Joseph Lincoln Steffens). *Red virtue; Human relationships in the new Russia*. New York, Harcourt, Brace, 1933. 313 pp. illus. app. biblio. index.

In 1932 New York *Post* correspondent journeys to Moscow, where she records her first impressions on women's rights, sex education, the rehabilitation of prostitutes and criminals, and the general way of life.

1003. Byron, Robert. *First Russia, then Tibet*. London, Macmillan, 1933. 151 pp. illus.

British artist, critical of the machine cult emerging from the first Five Year Plan, visits Leningrad, Moscow, and Kiev in January–February, 1932. He provides excellent descriptions of churches, icons, painting, and architecture.

1004. Murchie, Guy, Jr. *Men on the horizon*. Boston, Houghton Mifflin, 1932. pp. 229–309. illus. map.

An American seaman, at the end of a world tour, journeys from Vladivostok to Moscow by railroad, January 25–April 5, 1932, and comments on sights he observes from his car window and the treatment he receives. His comments are not profound but have some use because of his unusual opportunity.

1005. Griffin, Frederick. *Soviet scene; a newspaperman's closeups of new Russia*. Toronto, Macmillan, 1932. 279 pp.

Toronto Star reporter journeys from Moscow south to Stalingrad in the summer of 1932 and makes a study of Russia's institutional structure from education through art, etc. He is definitely in favor of the Soviet system and does not appear to concern himself about the means used, as long as the ends are achieved.

1006. Koerber, Lenka von. *Soviet Russia fights crime*. Translated from the German by Mary Fowler. New York, Dutton, 1935. 240 pp. illus.

German prison official, with a smattering of "1000 words for daily living," journeys through European Russia and western Siberia during the summer of 1932. Her comments on Soviet attitudes toward crime and punishment are informative and useful, as is her visit to rehabilitated Tjumen, the former exile prison visited by Kennan (see no. 359).

1007. Jarman, T. L. *Through Soviet Russia. The diary of an English tourist*. London, Houghton, 1933. 119 pp. illus.

Economics student from Britain travels through European Russia, June–July, 1932, and finds conditions to be crude and rough. He comments critically on the shoddy workmanship that he observes.

1008.   Lamont, Corliss and Margaret L. *Russia day by day; a travel diary.* New York, Covici-Friede, 1933. pp. 24–244. map.

American writer and his wife journey to the land that they consider to be the promise of a bright future, visiting from Leningrad to Moscow and down the Volga River and returning north through Kiev, July–September, 1932. Their comments indicate that their prior judgment was correct: the Soviet Union is pregnant with a bright future for the common man.

1009.   Newsholme, (Sir) Arthur, M.D., and John Adams Kingsbury. *Red medicine: Socialized health in Soviet Russia.* Garden City, New York, Doubleday, Doran, 1933. 312 pp. index.

British physician and American companion travel through European Russia, August–September, 1932. Their report is a full account of Soviet medical practices as well as the way of life.

1010.   Purves-Stewart, (Sir) James. *A physician's tour in Soviet Russia.* New York, Frederick A. Stokes, 1933. 176 pp. illus. index.

As a guest of the Soviet Union, British medical doctor tours from Leningrad through Moscow down the Volga River and west into the Ukraine, August 14–September 7, 1932. He comments on medical matters but includes observations on the people, characterizing the Soviet Union as a "curious sort of purgatory" where the population is joyless and cowed. Four cartoons are included.

1011.   Elmhirst, Leonard Knight. *Trip to Russia.* New York, New Republic, 1934. 213 pp. illus.

On a journey from Moscow through Central Asia, observer comments on the impact of collectivization and wonders if secrecy and force will backfire in the next generation. His trip during September–October, 1932, leaves Elmhirst very pessimistic about Russia's agricultural future.

1012. Dennen, Leon. *Where the ghetto ends; Jews in Soviet Russia.* New York, King, 1934. pp. 1–187. illus.

Born in the United States, taken to Russia by his father, and then returned to America at the age of nineteen, Dennen is a reporter on the *Moscow Daily News* staff who sees the end of the ghetto and the beginning of hope for all Jews during a 1932–33 journey. One of his best descriptions is of a Crimean collective of 29,000 Jews.

1013. Koestler, Arthur. *The invisible writing. An autobiography.* Boston, Beacon Press, 1954. pp. 49–160. map. port.

A Hungarian by birth and a member of the German Communist party, Koestler travels to Russia in 1932–33 to write a book for the Communist party of the Soviet Union in which emphasis is to be placed on the development of the Arctic, the success of the first Five Year Plan in the Ukraine, and the development of Central Asia under socialism. In his comments Koestler compares the Soviet Union as he found it and how it pictured itself to those living in foreign countries. His is an account of beginning disillusionment.

1014. Mehnert, Klaus. *Youth in Soviet Russia.* Translated from the German by Michael Davidson. New York, Harcourt, Brace, 1933. 270 pp.

In 1932–33, Mehnert (see no. 905) immerses himself in Russian life by changing his clothes, ways, and speech, and the result is an invaluable document on Soviet youth and literature.

1015. Strøm, Arne. *Uncle, give us bread.* London, Allen & Unwin, 1936. 357 pp.

Danish-American farm expert takes his wife and child with him to advise poultry farm managers at Povorino, 1932–33. He reports a disillusioning experience as he writes of seeing beggars in Moscow and finding relentless poverty in the countryside. He concludes that there appears to be no working relationship between Soviet theory and practice, between fact and fiction (Russian propaganda).

1016. Muggeridge, Malcolm. *Winter in Moscow.* London, Eyre & Spottiswoode, 1934. 252 pp.

British satirical writer expresses a strong dislike for the dictatorship of the proletariat and its "imbecilic" foreign admirers after a winter spent in Moscow, 1932–33. He considers all news from Russia to be a joke and makes no serious attempt to factually describe his adventures; instead, he develops a series of impressions.

1017. Hirsch, Alcan. *Industrialized Russia.* New York, Chemical Catalog Co., 1934. 273 pp. illus. port. biblio. index.

American consulting engineer to the Ministry of the Chemical Industry of the Soviet Union, 1932–34, presents a reasonably objective account of his activities in setting up factories around Moscow. In addition to information for businessmen, he provides data on religion, the press, the theater, education, and so on.

1018. Wells, Linton. *Blood on the moon. The autobiography of Linton Wells.* Boston, Houghton Mifflin, 1937. pp. 55–60, 113–43, 246–48, 333–56. illus. port.

International News Service roving correspondent from the United States is stationed in Moscow, 1932–34. His account is a comparison of the capital city with earlier experiences in 1914, 1919–20, and 1926, when it was dirty and overcrowded, whereas now it is still overcrowded but clean and orderly. His several journeys on the Trans-Siberian Railway illustrate the changing situation in Siberia over the years.

1019. Allan, (Mrs.) Seema Rynin. *Comrades and citizens.* London, Gollancz, 1938. 383 pp. index.

British roving *Moscow Daily News* reporter sings one long song of praise for the Soviet Union and its way of life during her three year sojourn, 1932–35. Russian-speaking, she provides information secured from conversations with people in all walks of life.

1020. Smith, Andrew. *I was a Soviet worker.* New York, Dutton, 1936. 298 pp. illus. app.

Member of the Communist party of the United States works in a Soviet electrical equipment factory, 1932–35, then returns home bitterly disillusioned. His comments on factory life are extremely informative and valuable, even though biassed.

1021. Edelman, Maurice. *How Russia prepared: U.S.S.R. beyond the Urals.* New York, Penguin, 1942. 127 pp. map.

Russian-speaking businessman in British firm trading with the Soviet Union, 1932–39, observes and comments on the industrial development that enables the Russians (in 1941–42) to resist the German invasion.

1022. Scott, John. *Behind the Urals. An American worker in Russia's city of steel.* Boston, Houghton Mifflin, 1942. 266 pp. illus. map. app.

Scott, son of Scott Nearing (see no. 842), took a job in the Soviet Union and remained there until 1941. During that time he worked as a welder in the building of the great steel works in Magnitogorsk. He concludes that Westerners can really have no part in Russia's revolution—it is her own. He provides valuable information in his comments on life among his fellow workers.

1023. Forbes, (Mrs.) Rosita (Torr). *These men I knew.* London, Hutchinson, 1940. pp. 61–94.

Subtle criticism of everything socialist in Russia by a British journalist who travels to Moscow in 1933 to interview Stalin and his wife.

1024. Goldman, Bosworth. *Red road through Asia. A journey by the Arctic Ocean to Siberia, Central Asia and Armenia; with an account of the peoples now living in those countries under the hammer and sickle.* London, Methuen, 1934. 270 pp. illus. biblio. index.

Excellent photographs and detailed description of Siberia by a British correspondent in 1933.

1025. Herriot, Edouard. *Eastward from Paris*. Translated from the French by Phyllis Megroz. London, Gollancz, 1934. pp. 125–311.

French statesman and man of letters as well as leader of the Radical Socialist party journeys to the Ukraine and Moscow in 1933. He favors what he sees and provides historical backgrounds for his comments on current problems in the Soviet Union.

1026. Maillart, Ella K. *Turkestan solo; one woman's expedition from the Tien Shan to the Kizil Kum*. Translated from the French by John Rodker. New York, Putnam, 1935. 301 pp. illus. biblio. index.

Danish-Swiss, Russian-speaking traveler journeys to the land of the Kirghiz in 1933, where she visits the people, observes their customs and manners, and records the impact of communism on their institutions.

1027. Mannin, Ethel. "Playtime of the child in modern Russia." In Griffith, editor, *Playtime in Russia,* pp. 136–83, illus. (See no. 1439.)

Labour party socialist writer, interested in children and their care, journeys to Leningrad and Moscow in 1933 with Russian-speaking friends. She describes the theater and the teaching of history along with the care of children and is highly complimentary in her analysis of Soviet propaganda techniques.

1028. Rowley, Claude Arthur. *Russia, a country up-side-down.* Painesville, Ohio, Painesville Telegraph, 1933. 196 pp. illus. map.

Painesville Telegraph reporter journeys from Leningrad to the Black Sea by way of the Volga River in 1933. He recommends some Russian practices, especially the Soviet court system, which appears to him to be more efficient than that of the United States of America.

1029. Tobenkin, Elias. *Stalin's ladder. War and peace in the Soviet Union*. New York, Minton, Balch, 1933, 294 pp. biblio. index.

Russian-speaking American social worker comments on war, peace, and prisons after a ten-month journey in 1933, with observations on the way of life, the intelligentsia, the Jews, and the courts.

1030. Travers, P. L. *Moscow excursion*. New York, Reynal & Hitchcock, 1937. 121 pp.

Viewing the Soviet Union in 1933, British tourist observes: "In a world rocking madly between Fascism and Communism the writer prefers the latter form of tyranny if the choice must be made."

1031. Buchwald, N. *From peasant to collective farmer*. New York, International Publishers, 1933. 102 pp. illus.

Left-wing British correspondent attends the Congress of Collective Farmers in Moscow, February, 1933. He finds no evidence of force or suffering as Soviet farmers get rid of "old junk" and adopt modern ideas, methods, and machinery.

1032. Cummings, Arthur John. *The Moscow trial*. London, Gollancz, 1933. 287 pp.

In March, 1933, London *News Chronicle* correspondent travels to Moscow to report on the trial of six British engineers (on contract to Soviet industry) arrested and accused of espionage and sabotage. In spite of the state of terror dominating the city, the engineers received light sentences and, after the British government imposed a trade embargo, they were soon released.

1033. Hamilton, Cicely Mary. *Modern Russia as seen by an English-woman*. New York, Dutton, 1934. 235 pp. illus. app.

Correspondent journeys through European Russia in the summer of 1933. An excellent writer, she holds the reader's attention on a variety of subjects: children, art and propaganda, birth control, the theater, marriage customs, religious practices, travel hints, the Soviet attitude toward foreigners, etc.

1034. Hindus, Maurice Gerschon. *The great offensive*. New York, Harrison Smith and Robert Haas, 1933. 368 pp. map.

Journey in the summer of 1933 by American observer (see nos. 711, 839, 917, and 965) emphasizes the impact of "the efforts of the Communist Party and of the Soviets to recast human society and to reconstruct human personality. . . ." Special comments are made on prostitution and the treatment of crime and criminals.

1035. Durstine, Roy Sarles. *Red thunder*. New York, Scribner's, 1934. pp. 1–124.

American advertising man journeys to Moscow in November, 1933, and returns with an enthusiastic description of music and the theater with little evidence of prejudice or special pleading on his part.

1036. Hughes, James Langston. *I wonder as I wander. An autobiographical journey*. New York, Rinehart, 1956. pp. 69–235.

Friendly report on his visit to Moscow and journey east to Vladivostok in 1933–34, by Negro American poet, with a humorous and perceptive description of a Russian film group's uninformed efforts to make a movie on Negro-white labor relations in which the plot is supposed to mirror life in the United States' Deep South.

1037. Silver, Boris. *The Russian workers' own story*. London, Allen & Unwin, 1938. 251 pp.

Journey from Moscow to Odessa in the winter of 1933–34 by a left-wing Russian-speaking Belgian worker with Socialist Revolutionary connections, who saw Russians as "all inmates of a great prison." He travels without the services of Intourist guides and is treated contemptibly. His description of the Little Berditchev (Jewish) kolkhoz is excellent. To him, the letters U.S.S.R. equal "United Soviets, Stalin's realm."

1038. Kleist, Peter. *G.P.U. justice.* Maurice Edelman, editor. London, Allen & Unwin, 1938. 207 pp.

German engineer describes his arrest and acquittal in the years 1933–37, and also comments on the foreign engineers' view of Russian casualness in building construction.

1039. Thayer, Charles Wheeler. *Bears in the caviar.* Philadelphia, Lippincott, 1950. 303 pp.

Russian-speaking American embassy secretary, 1933–41, delineates diplomatic life and is especially informative, in a very casual manner, about the establishment of the United States embassy in Moscow after recognition of the Soviet Union in 1933.

1040. Amba, Achmed. *I was Stalin's bodyguard.* Translated from the Turkish by Richard and Clara Winston. London, Frederick Muller, 1952. 256 pp.

Russian-speaking Turkish scientist acts as guard and describes life in Stalin's "court," 1933–42.

1041. Baughan, E. A. "Politics in the theatre." In Griffith, editor, *Playtime in Russia,* pp. 19–44. illus. (See no. 1439.)

British theater critic attends the Moscow Theater Festival in 1934 and finds the theater too much involved in politics. In the streets Baughan observes much poverty but no apparent hopelessness.

1042. Blanch, (Mrs.) Lesley. "The ballet in Russia, 1934." In Griffith, editor, *Playtime in Russia,* pp. 83–94. (See no. 1439.)

Ballet designer from Covent Garden visits Moscow in 1934 and provides a complimentary description of modern techniques being used with ancient ballet forms.

1043. Brown, John. *I saw for myself.* London, Selwyn & Blount, 1935. pp. 171–277. port.

British socialist accepts the challenge of Lord Nuffield (Morris Motor Works) and travels to Russia in 1934 to see Russian socialism in action. He finds the Soviet system to be a shamble of deserted ideals where four times as many men are used to do a piece of work that turns out to be shoddy and unattractive.

1044. Callcott, Mary Stevenson. *Russian justice*. New York, Macmillan, 1935. 265 pp.

American labor and prison specialist does research on Russian law and court system during the summer of 1934, aided by special permissions from Andreyev Vishinsky. She provides excellent descriptions of Sokolniki (the men's prison), the Moscow Women's Prison, and the relationship between children and the law. The Russian theory that crime arises from class distinctions and will disappear in a classless society is also explored.

1045. Chesterton, (Mrs.) Ada Elizabeth (Jones). *Sickle or swastika?* London, Paul, 1938. 268 pp. illus.

Attending a Writers' Congress in Moscow, 1934, Mrs. Chesterton (see no. 932) compares conditions in Russia and Germany and answers the question implied in the title of her account in favor of the Soviet Union.

1046. Eddy, Sherwood. *Russia today. What we can learn from it.* New York, Farrar & Rinehart, 1934. 276 pp. app. index.

In 1934 Eddy (see nos. 547 and 559) made his tenth journey to the Soviet Union. He suggests that we should fear and respect the Soviet Union as we do sulphuric acid. In his Appendix he includes what he considers to be the cause of the Jewish problem in Russia.

1047. Franck, Harry A. *A vagabond in Sovietland. America's perennial rambler goes tourist.* New York, Frederick A. Stokes, 1935. 267 pp. illus. map.

Professional traveler and lecturer spends thirty days in the Soviet Union in 1934 and decides that his stay more than equals the thrills of many years' journeys in other parts of the world. Includes forty-five excellent photographs of people, places, and things.

1048. Gauvreau, Emile Henry. *What so proudly we hailed.* New York, Macauley, 1935. pp. 19–182. illus.

The editor of the New York *Daily Mirror* and a severe critic of life in America discusses the best features of the Soviet Union and the worst aspects of the United States after 1934 journey to Leningrad and Moscow. He underscores his caustic comment with anti-American cartoons.

1049. Griffith, Hubert Freeling. "Moscow Theater Festival." In Griffith, editor, *Playtime in Russia,* pp. 205–49. illus. (See no. 1439.)

British critic attends the Moscow Theater Festival in 1934 and takes a vacation train journey to the Crimea. He comments on the ten plays he saw and describes the favored position of the intellectuals, referring to Gorky as "a petted Pope."

1050. Mattern, James. *Cloud country.* Chicago, Pure Oil Co., 1936. 58 pp.

Friendly impressions result from an airplane journey made by an American aviator who flew through Siberian country in 1934.

1051. * Maybury, H. *The land of 'Nichevo.'* Liverpool, Daily Post Printers, 1935. 161 pp.

1052. Phillips, G. D. R. *Dawn in Siberia. The Mongols of Lake Baikal.* London, Frederick Muller, 1943. 192 pp. illus. map. index.

British socialist journeys to the land of the Buryiats in 1934 and 1936, where he observes how communism has helped them to realize their potentials and aspirations.

1053. Plievier, Hildegard Piscator. *With my dogs in Russia.* Translated from the German by Vivian Melroy and Eric Mosbacker. London, Hammond, Hammond, 1961. 190 pp.

The wife of the German novelist, Theodore Plievier, attending the Soviet Writers' Congress in 1934 with her husband, leaves him for a short journey down the Volga River.

1054. Waters, (Brigadier General) Wallscourt Hely-Hutchinson. *Russia then and now.* London, John Murray, 1935. 296 pp. index.

Making a return visit in 1934 (see no. 639), Waters observes the paradox of lazy Russians versus Soviet idealism. He concludes that the system that has finally emerged is really more state capitalism than socialism.

1055. Wells, Herbert George. *Experiment in autobiography. Discoveries and conclusions of a very ordinary brain (since 1866).* London, Cresset Press, 1934. II, 799–809. port.

British novelist (see no. 754) returns to the Soviet Union in 1934 to interview Stalin. He compares the Russian leader with Franklin D. Roosevelt and concludes that Stalin is "candid, fair and honest." See no. 1056.

1056. *Wells, Herbert George. *Stalin-Wells talk. The verbatim record and a discussion by G. B. Shaw, H. G. Wells, J. M. Keynes, E. Toller, and others, with three caricatures and cover design by Low.* London, New Statesman and Nation, 1934. 47 pp. illus. (See no. 1055.)

1057. Holmes, Burton. *The traveler's Russia.* New York, Putnam, 1934. 246 pp. illus.

Holmes returns to Russia in 1934 (see no. 474) to journey from Moscow south to the Crimea and then north to Leningrad. His comments and photographs are excellent, especially the descriptions of a walk in Moscow's Red Square, celebrations on May Day, and "traveling with a girl guide." He is critical of the dirt and drabness.

1058. Munday, Madeleine Constance. *Far East.* London, Stanley Paul, 1935. pp. 156–75. port.

British traveler and writer crosses Siberia by railroad on her way from Shanghai to London, May 3–May 18, 1934. Train life en route and in the stations is detailed; she states that travelers were forced to spend a certain amount of money each day or have the difference confiscated during customs inspection.

1059. Bellman, (Sir) Harold. *Baltic backgrounds. Pages from a diary kept on a visit to the Baltic, with excursions within Russia, and calls at the northern capitals.* London, privately printed, 1934. pp. 38–89. illus.

After a four-day visit to Leningrad and Moscow in August, 1934, British businessman sees Russia on the way to respectable republicanism.

1060. Halliburton, Richard. *Seven league boots.* Indianapolis, Bobbs-Merrill, 1935. pp. 100–228. illus.

American globetrotter (see nos. 803 and 804) describes his journey to Leningrad, Moscow, Sverdlovsk, and the Caucasus in October–November, 1934. He locates and interviews the commander of the squad that executed Nicholas II and his family in 1918 and later visits the descendants of Crusaders living in the Caucasus Mountains.

1061. Crowther, James Gerald. *Soviet science.* New York, Dutton, 1936. 336 pp. illus. biblio. index.

American historian of science, friendly to Soviet aims, is a guest of the Soviet Union in 1934–35. He examines the organization and aims of the Russian science institutes and provides valuable information about the way scientists live and how they are treated by their government.

1062. Houghton, Norris. *Moscow rehearsals. An account of methods of production in the Soviet Theater.* New York, Harcourt, Brace, 1936. 265 pp. illus. app. index.

Financially aided by a Guggenheim grant, Russian-speaking American theater expert spends September, 1934–February, 1935, 1 Moscow. He concludes that all roads lead to the capital city of tl Soviet Union for the artist of the theater.

1063. Tendulkar, Dinanath Gopal. *30 months in Russia.* Bombay, Karnatak, 1943. 96 pp. illus.

East Indian student, twenty-six years of age, earns a living with a Leica camera and his pen and ink during 1934–36. He admits to observing some ugly elements, but has high praise for the people.

1064. Wiley, Irena. *Around the globe in twenty years.* New York, David McKay, 1962. pp. 3–61, 97–109. illus.

Sculptress wife of United States foreign service officer stationed in Moscow embassy, 1934–36. Of Polish ancestry and Russian-speaking, she provides a description of food, servants, protocol, and parties, mixed with love for the common people and a deep hatred for the Soviet system and the Communist party.

1065. Miller, Wright W. *Russians as people.* London, Phoenix House, 1960. 202 pp. illus. index.

Russian-speaking British correspondent journeys many times to European Russia between 1934 and 1960 and here provides a genuine account of the people through the seasons, the Russian scene, on being a Russian, the common people, the lot of the minority, etc.

1066. Clark, Frederick LeGros, and L. Noel Brinton. *Men, medicine and food in the U.S.S.R.* London, Lawrence & Wishart, 1936. 167 pp. biblio. index.

Invited by the Soviet Union to study the problem of social feeding, Clark, Russian-speaking British nutritionist, visits Moscow and its rural surrounding. He forecasts prosperity for Russia in the near future, but admits belts will have to be tightened in 1935.

1067. Harris, Audrey. *Eastern visas.* London, Collins, 1939. pp. 11–20, 380–92. map. port.

In 1935 British tourist crosses Siberia by rail and describes her treatment on the train and the sights she sees in the stations and along the road. In 1936 she travels from the Afghanistan border to Moscow and comments on experiences in Russian Central Asia.

1068. London, Kurt. *The seven Soviet arts.* Translated from the German by Eric S. Bensinger. New Haven, Yale University Press, 1938. 365 pp. illus. index.

Art expert is highly critical of artists in the Soviet Union for not realizing their potentials, and his comments reflect the tense atmosphere of the purges of the thirties. He includes magnificent illustrations of all the arts in this account of a journey in 1935.

1069. Mannin, Ethel. *South to Samarkand.* New York, Dutton, 1937. 348 pp. illus. map. index.

British socialist (see no. 1027) travels to Tamerlane's tomb with a Russian companion in 1935 on what she claims was an unconducted tour. She observes things that do not relate to ideal socialism, and, disillusioned by the end of her tour, her final word is "Nevermore."

1070. Wilson, Edmund. *Red, black, blond and olive. Studies in four civilizations: Zuni, Haiti, Soviet Russia, Israel.* New York, Oxford University Press, 1956. pp. 153–384. Also in *Travels in two democracies.* New York, Harcourt, Brace, 1936. pp. 147–322.

Edmund Wilson is an American writer who has done considerable research into Russian history, especially the background and events of 1917. Between May and October, 1935, he travels from Leningrad to Odessa by way of the Volga River, and has a number of unusual adventures that he describes in a moody and impressionistic manner. Even though extremely critical at times, he is inclined to favor the Soviet Union's way of life.

1071. Smith, Vern Ralph. *In a collective farm village.* Moscow, Co-operative Publishing Society of Foreign Workers in the U.S.S.R., 1936. 229 pp. app.

American, friendly to the Soviet Union, visits various collective farms during the summer of 1935 and writes an account that provides most of what needs to be known about their origin and operation, the people and their manner of life, the relation of the kolkhoz to the state, etc. He includes the "Model Rules of the Agricultural Artel" in the appendix.

1072. Carr, Brownell (pseudonym of Lionel Tompkins). *Black bread and cabbage soup.* Cincinnati, Powell & White, 1936. pp. 29–320. illus.

American writer tours European Russia from Leningrad to the Black Sea in July, 1935, making the journey to discover whether all Russian life is one gray mass without smiling and happy people. His account is critical of what he sees, but he tempers his judgment with a sense of humor.

1073. Christopher, Mari. *No soap and the Soviet.* Plainfield, New Jersey, Red Ram Press, 1936. 101 pp. illus.

This account by a woman member of an American tour group in Leningrad and Moscow, July, 1935, is written with a fully developed sense of humor and is dedicated to the land where there is no privacy, where all seem to live in a huge public fishbowl. The author covers a wide variety of subjects not usually dealt with in tourist accounts, such as bathing (infrequent), "roosting" (housing), and love life (no prostitution).

1074. Citrine, (Sir) Walter McLennan. *I search for the truth in Russia.* New York, Dutton, 1937. 362 pp. illus. port. index. For a shorter account see *A Trade Unionist looks at Russia.* London, Trade Union Congress General Council, 1936. 108 pp.

The general secretary of the Trade Union Congress, Labour party official, and president of the International Federation of Trade Unions summarizes his September, 1935, journey to Leningrad and Moscow. In the shorter account he places emphasis on housing, wages, costs, etc. In the longer account he adds more detail on the Soviet way of life and attempts to understand the Russian point of view. This account contains excellent photographs.

1075. Pares, Bernard. *Moscow admits a critic.* London, Nelson, 1936. 94 pp.

After prying a visa from the reluctant Soviet officials, Pares (see nos. 450, 451, 503, 515, and 600) journeys through European Russia in 1935–36 comparing and analyzing the positive and negative features of life under socialism. His account contains a good deal that is appreciative of the Soviet experiment, but he also observes that there is little respect for personality in almost every area of human activity.

1076. Sigerist, Henry Ernest. *Socialized medicine in the Soviet Union*. New York, Norton, 1937. 310 pp. illus. app. index.

Johns Hopkins professor presents a detailed and appreciative description of Soviet medical organization and practices after two summers spent in Moscow (1935) and in the Caucasus (1936). He includes fourteen comprehensive appendixes on all aspects of Soviet medicine.

1077. Hampel, (Mrs.) Elizabeth (Coffey). *Yankee bride in Moscow*. New York, Liveright, 1941. 319 pp.

Wife of embassy electrician, responsible for Spaso House (the embassy) while Ambassador Bullitt is absent, comments on her experiences, 1935–37. She provides an excellent insight into the problems of running a foreign diplomatic post.

1078. Leonhard, Wolfgang. *Child of the Revolution*. Translated from the German by C. M. Woodhouse. Chicago, Henry Regnery, 1958. pp. 17–286.

Taken to the Soviet Union by his mother in 1935, Leonhard describes the decade of training he received in Moscow and Karaganda before he returned to Eastern Germany with Walter Ulbricht to participate in the founding of the German Democratic Republic. This account is extremely valuable because very few high-placed communists have left the Soviet Union and told their experiences to the West.

1079. Magidoff, Robert. *In anger and in pity, a report on Russia*. Garden City, New York, Doubleday, 1949. 269 pp. app.

National Broadcasting Company–Associated Press correspondent
of Russian descent is stationed in Moscow, 1935–47. He demon-
strates a deep love for the people but is very critical of the Soviet
system and analyzes the positive and negative features of every
aspect of life. When he is accused of being a spy, he fights back,
and the appendix contains letters on this subject.

1080. Bigland, Eileen. *Laughing Odyssey*. New York, Macmillan,
       1938. 307 pp.

Long-time British friend of Russian civilization and culture travels
to Leningrad, Moscow, and the Ukraine in 1936. She comments
on her experiences by comparing them favorably with what she
considers to be a desertion of civilization in Nazi Germany.

1081. Brown, John. *The road to power*. London, Selwyn & Blount,
       1937. pp. 67–75. port.

Brown (see no. 1043) makes a return visit (incognito) in 1936
to the Ukraine to check on his earlier judgment, and concludes
that Britain must somehow find a third way between communism
and fascism.

1082. *Bullitt, (Mrs.) Nora (Iasigi). *Three weeks in Russia*.
       Louisville, privately printed, 1936. 105 pp.

1083. Cohen, Lester. *Two worlds*. New York, Covici-Friede, 1936.
       pp. 71–198. illus. map.

A critical look at Leningrad, Moscow, Kiev, and Minsk in 1936
by a Hollywood film writer who visits Russia on his way around
the world seeking answers to the differences between various ways
of life.

1084. Conolly, Violet. *Soviet tempo: a journal of travel in Russia*.
       New York, Sheed & Ward, 1937. 189 pp.

American writer makes a trip from Leningrad to the Caspian Sea
in 1936 and returns to describe the tired, pasty faces of over-
worked Russian women whom she saw everywhere. She comments

on her impressions of a land where the creative spirit is in chains and the whole system is an organized tissue of lies.

1085. Forbes, (Mrs.) Rosita (Torr). *Forbidden road—Kabul to Samarkand*. London, Cassell, 1937. pp. 48–281. illus. map. index.

Mrs. Forbes (see no. 1023) comments on the Europe-Asia confrontation as the Communist party sets out to change the Asiatic. Her detailed report on the way of life and its changing patterns includes her adventures with officialdom on this 1936 journey.

1086. Gide, André P. G. *Return from the U.S.S.R.* Translated from the French by Dorothy Bussy. New York, Knopf, 1937. pp. 3–62. app.

French philosopher and novelist travels to European Russia in 1936. Sympathetic to the Russian experiment, he observes that the basic theories have been warped by Stalin, but the Soviet Union is still a land "where Utopia was in the process of becoming reality." He comments that it is unfortunate that the people's faith in religion has suffered by the punishment leveled upon the hierarchy of the church.

1087. Gide, André P. G. *Afterthoughts on the U.S.S.R.* Translated from the French by Dorothy Bussy. New York, Dial Press, 1938. 142 pp. app.

Gide modifies his earlier adulation by certain retractions after his critics attacked him personally in review of *Return from the U.S.S.R.* and exposed his contradictions.

1088. Lee, Hubert. *Twenty years after. Life in the U.S.S.R. today*. London, Lawrence & Wishart, 1937. 172 pp.

American communist, contributor to periodicals, lives in the Soviet Union, 1929–36. His report is sympathetic to Soviet aims, and he provides no evidence on the purge atmosphere that prevails at this time.

1089. Lehmann, John. *Prometheus and the Bolsheviks.* New York, Knopf, 1938. 256 pp. illus. map.

British writer journeys from Moscow to the Caucasus in 1936 and returns to report that the Bolsheviki are successfully remolding the Georgians into the image of the new Soviet man.

1090. Lubinski, Kurt. *This is our world.* London, Hodder & Stoughton, 1938. pp. 99–154. illus. port.

Austrian actor tours the land of the Kazakhs in 1936. His account is beautifully written, with excellent photographs, and it concludes: ". . . taking with us the protean picture of a land of the future."

1091. Marchant, Herbert Stanley. *Scratch a Russian.* London, Drummond, 1937. 210 pp. illus. map. index.

British journalist travels from Leningrad to the Rumanian border through Moscow and Kiev in 1936. After he views the efforts of the Communist party to transform the people, he concludes that communism will not come to Russia because the ideal is unattainable.

1092. Miles, Frederic James. *Changing Russia.* London, Marshall, Morgan & Scott, 1936. 144 pp.

Former British tour director and international secretary of the Russian Missionary Society journeys through European Russia in 1936 to study the Communist party attack on religion. Knowledge of the language enables him to comment intelligently on many aspects of life, and he concludes that the socialists cannot succeed in eliminating religion and religious practices but can only make it difficult for the communicants to worship.

1093. Sloan, Pat. *Soviet democracy.* London, Gollancz, 1937. 288 pp.

British communist, teacher in a technical school in the Soviet Union, 1931–36, defends Soviet democracy by analyzing the 1936

Constitution. Pages 224–40 are especially useful, providing a list of communist reasons why no opposition is permitted against the Soviet system.

1094. Smolka, Harry Peter. *40,000 against the Arctic. Russia's polar empire.* London, Hutchinson, 1937. 275 pp. illus. map. app. index.

Russian-speaking London *Times* correspondent journeys along the Arctic coast and up the Yenisei River in 1936, visiting the colonies that have been established as prison labor camps. His comments are very informative on the emerging way of life, and he illuminates his account with fifty-three excellent photographs. By way of a summary judgment he observes that the formerly keen desire of the communists to conquer the world appears to be subsiding.

1095. Stucley, Peter. *Russian spring.* London, Selwyn & Blount, 1937. 286 pp. illus.

British journalist, using tourist Russian, sets out to get the truth about the Soviet Union in 1936 and returns to write a gay but perceptive account of his experiences. He concludes that in his opinion no elixir of success has yet been compounded by the Kremlin alchemists.

1096. Gould, Margaret. *I visit the Soviets.* Toronto, Francis White Publications, 1937. 166 pp.

Russian-speaking executive secretary of the Toronto Child Welfare League spends April, 1936, touring Leningrad, Moscow, and the Black Sea area. She sees the Soviet Union "getting ahead" as she journeys unrestricted through the country visiting her relatives.

1097. King, Beatrice. *Changing man: the education system of the U.S.S.R.* London, Gollancz, 1936. 265 pp. app. index.

English schoolteacher writes a sympathetic account of her tour to Leningrad, Moscow, and Kiev in April–June, 1936. She expresses her confidence that "I never was a tourist" as she studies the education of Soviet youth with the generous help of the officials. Useful material on courses and class time-schedules is included in an appendix.

1098. Luck, Sidney I. *Observations in Russia*. London, Macmillan, 1938. 339 pp. illus.

Volunteer technical helper of British solar eclipse expedition to Omsk, Siberia, April 22–July 22, 1936, comments on all aspects of Russian life. Having lived in Russia the first eighteen years of his life, Luck is able to report definite improvement under the communists.

1099. Delafield, Edmée (pseudonym of Edmée Elizabeth Monica de La Pasture). *I visit the Soviets*. New York, Harper, 1937. 344 pp. illus.

During the summer of 1936 British writer visits Leningrad, Moscow, and the Seattle Commune, located near Rostov-on-Don, a community settled by dissatisfied Americans (see no. 792 for Anna Louise Strong's account of the founding of the Seattle Commune). Her report is sympathetic to the efforts of the people to build a new way of life.

1100. Willett, George. *A few days in Russia*. New York, George F. O'Connell, 1936. 46 pp.

American tourist visits Leningrad in July, 1936, and combines his personal observations with those of other travelers' accounts.

1101. *Collard, Dudley. *Soviet justice, and the trial of Radek and others*. London, Gollancz, 1937. 208 pp.

English lawyer, present at Radek's trial, January 23–30, 1937, explains why he believes in the innocence of the accused. See Grierson, *Books on Soviet Russia* (no. 1438).

1102. Timbres, Harry and Rebecca. *We didn't ask Utopia. A Quaker family in Russia*. New York, Prentice-Hall, 1939. 290 pp. map.

American medical doctor, his wife, and their two children live and work in a small village near Kazan, Marbumstroy, June, 1936–July, 1937. The Timbres family involves itself in the life of the village and thus is provided an unusual and very informative account of how ordinary people live away from the great urban centers. The Timbres were in the village as participants in a malaria control project.

1103. Davies, Joseph E. *Mission to Moscow.* New York, Simon & Schuster, 1941. 513 pp. illus. app. index.

Ambassador to the Soviet Union from the United States, 1936–38, presents a sympathetic but uncritical report of his mission from official reports, private letters, and his personal diary. His account is a mine of information about Russia during the purge trials.

1104. Ciliberti, Charles. *Backstairs mission in Moscow.* New York, Booktab Press, 1946. 128 pp. illus. map. port.

Ambassador Davies' chauffeur learned Russian and used his position to establish relations with the common people. His account is almost the exact opposite of his employer's, for whereas the ambassador was intrigued and fascinated, the chauffeur was repelled and disgusted—not by the ordinary people but by the Communist party members and the secret police.

1105. * Dawson, Percy Millard. *Soviet samples: diary of an American physiologist.* Ann Arbor, Michigan, Edward Brothers, 1938. 538 pp.

1106. Francis, Peter Geoffrey. *I worked in a Soviet factory.* London, Jarrolds, 1939. 228 pp. illus. port.

Detailed account of factory life in Orekhovo-Zuyevo (near Moscow) in 1937 by a British student who lived with the people and spoke their language. Not a communist, he provides an objective report on life at work and in the home.

1107. Harris, Thomas Lake. *Unholy pilgrimage.* New York, Round Table Press, 1937. 185 pp.

In 1937 British Episcopal rector of Philadelphia journeys to Moscow and the Volga region to examine the damage done to religion after twenty years of atheism. Speaking Russian, he travels alone to remote areas, observing that (1) Soviet man excels in "goodness" (truthful, courageous, neighborliness), but is not religious, and (2) the Orthodox church received the kind of treatment it deserved.

1108.   * Mauer, James H. *It can be done*. New York, Rand School, 1938.

1109.   Newman, Bernard. *Ride to Russia*. London, Herbert Jenkins, 1938. pp. 251–332. Illus. map. port. index.

British professional traveler and writer rides a bicycle through Europe to Odessa and Kiev in 1937 and presents a report in which he compares living conditions in the two Russian cities with those in European cities. His account is rich in information on rural conditions, and he believes peace will continue.

1110.   Feuchtwanger, Lion. *Moscow 1937. My visit described for my friends*. Translated from the German by Irene Josephy. New York, Viking, 1937. 151 pp.

German musician reports on the "invigorating atmosphere of the Soviet Union" in the spring of 1937 and makes friendly comments on work and leisure, conformism and individualism, war and peace, Stalin and Trotsky, etc.

1111.   Bowen, Catherine Drinker. *Adventures of a biographer*. Boston, Little, Brown, 1959. pp. 3–42.

American biographer of Anton and Nicholas Rubinstein journeys to Moscow, Leningrad, and Klin in April–May, 1937, to see firsthand the things she had described from sources. She comments on the dirt and poverty that are very evident at this time and speaks about the tenseness of the people.

1112. Hooper, (Major) A. S. *Through Soviet Russia and Soviet Finnish campaign 1940.* London, privately printed, 1944. pp. 7–139.

Soldier and journalist, Major Hooper writes a report whose character is indicated by his dedication: "Dedicated to those who buy a copy." Bernard Shaw and Hewlett Johnson (see nos. 979, 980, and 1134) praised Hooper's account as truthful and the first to give accurate information about daily life in the Soviet Union at a popular price. The 1937 journey was made during April–June.

1113. Pope-Hennessy, (Dame) Una Birch. *The closed city. Impressions of a visit to Leningrad.* London, Hutchinson, 1938. 254 pp. illus.

In August–September, 1937, British writer makes a journey to Leningrad to get material for a biography of Lady Muriel Paget, founder of a relief center for distressed British subjects in the Soviet Union. She comments on the obvious preparations being made to defend the city in the event of war and describes her difficulties in moving about among the suspicious population and bureaucracy.

1114. Maclean, Fitzroy. *Escape to adventure.* Boston, Little, Brown, 1950. pp. 3–136. map.

British foreign office clerk, Russian-speaking, attempts to travel in the Soviet Middle East, 1937–39. In addition to his travels he describes the purge of the Old Bolsheviks in a graphic way that illustrates Andreyev Vishinsky's trial techniques.

1115. Buber-Neumann, Margarete (pseudonym of Margarete Buber). *Under two dictators.* Translated from the German by Edward Fitzgerald. London, Gollancz, 1949. pp. 1–166. index.

In 1931 German communist goes to Moscow, sees the poverty, but retains her faith in socialism. Between 1937 and 1940, she and her husband were under protective custody, prisoners in every sense of the word but allowed to work as translators. In her account she carefully distinguishes between the harsh treatment accorded her by Communist party members and the kindnesses shown by Russians. For another side of her story see Karl Kindermann, no. 832, falsely accused by Margarete Buber-Neumann.

1116.   Lipper, Elinor. *Eleven years in Soviet prison camps.* London, Hollis & Carter, 1951. 310 pp. map.

German, sympathetic to communism, works in Moscow as a translator before she is arrested, tried, and imprisoned in labor camps from Kolyma to Vladivostok, 1937–48. She believes that most of the people in the camps were innocent and that they were set up to provide slave labor.

1117.   Coblentz, L. A. *Russia up to date. As seen by a Minnesota farmer, together with an account of the world's most horrible atrocities.* Red Lake, Minnesota, privately printed, 1938. pp. 1–57.

Report of a tour to Moscow and south to the Crimea in 1938. The title is satirical.

1118.   Gruber, Ruth. *I went to the Soviet Arctic.* New York, Simon & Schuster, 1939. 333 pp. map.

American sociologist receives assignment from Leningrad Arctic Institute to study lives of white women living in the Arctic and presents a report that is very readable but somewhat uncritical. Speaking from firsthand experience after being taken into the women's confidence, Dr. Gruber observes: "Women in the Arctic were not leading the lives of the wealthy woman in the West; they had no silk clothes and limousines and villas. Yet most of them seemed hopeful, and the idealistic ones were completely happy."

1119.   Utting, Mattie Johns. *Arctic fringe. A day by day cruise.* Boston, Christopher Publishing House, 1939. pp. 133–61. illus.

American member of a cruise ship visits Leningrad and Moscow in 1938 and comes away from a tour to Peterhof (Peter's version of Versailles to the southwest of Leningrad) with the observation that it was a "charming rendezvous for the workman."

1120. Mora, Constantcia de la. *In place of splendor. The autobiography of a Spanish woman.* London, Michael Joseph, 1940. pp. 345–51.

Mother of daughter sent to the Soviet Union and enrolled in a Moscow school for Spanish refugees visits her daughter in January–February, 1938, and comes away with a favorable report of a world happy and successful.

1121. Levin, Deana. *Children in Soviet Russia.* London, Faber & Faber, 1942. 151 pp. app.

Excellent summary of Russian pedagogical methods by a Russian-speaking, British, English-language teacher in Moscow, 1938–42. Comments are made on the organization of the school system, the pupils, teachers, summer camps, extracurricular activities, trade unions, and holidays. Useful appendixes include examination questions and extracts from textbooks.

1122. Chesterton, (Mrs.) Ada Elizabeth (Jones). *Salute the Soviet.* London, Chapman & Hall, 1942. 215 pp. illus. app.

British journalist (see nos. 932 and 1045) writes a sympathetic account of her journey through European Russia in 1939. She comments on the improvement in living standards and the opportunities that are available to the young.

1123. Forman, Harrison. *Horizon hunter. The adventures of a modern Marco Polo.* New York, McBride, 1940. pp. 259–82.

American plane salesman and movie-maker visits Moscow in 1939 and witnesses an air show of Soviet military strength just before the signing of the Nazi-Soviet pact in August. He sees Russia as a gigantic failure maintaining a façade of success.

1124. Cowles, Virginia Spencer. *Looking for trouble.* London, Hamish Hamilton, 1941. pp. 201–42. index.

American correspondent is assigned to cover the Russian situation in February–March, 1939. She reports on her findings in Moscow and Kiev, emphasizing the shortages and the pale faces of weary people.

1125. Barber, Noel. *Trans-Siberian.* London, Harrap, 1942. 180 pp. illus. map.

Escaping from threatening events in the Far East, British writer and his wife cross Siberia by train in the spring of 1939 to report on the great promise of a vast land.

1126. Gliksman, Jerzy. *Tell the West. An account of his experiences as a slave laborer in the Union of Soviet Socialist Republics.* New York, Gresham, 1948. pp. 23–353.

Polish socialist, arrested in 1939, spends two years in a Soviet prison camp being "remolded" through "productive work and suitable educational approach." He describes his remolding as systematic starvation, ill treatment, and hopelessly high daily work quotas—endured until he was released in 1941 to fight the Germans.

1127. Wittlin, Tadeusz. *A reluctant traveller in Russia.* Translated from the Polish by Noel E. P. Clark. London, William Hodge, 1952. 237 pp.

Fleeing from German-occupied Warsaw, Russian-speaking Polish writer escapes across Siberia, 1939–42. His account is very impressionistic and ranges from objective to friendly.

1128. *Halpern, (Dr.) Ada. *Conducted tour.* New York, Sheed & Ward, 1945. 145 pp. map.

Daughter of Polish bank manager, a doctor of mathematical science, is deported to Kazakhstan, 1939–43, to work as a librarian. Her report emphasizes the poor treatment accorded political deportees

—her phrase is "liberation—Russian style." For this data see *Book Review Digest,* 1945.

1129. * Kreusler, Abraham A. *A teacher's experiences in the Soviet Union.* 1965. 194 pp.

1130. Maks, Leon. *Russia by the back door.* Translated from the Polish by Rosamond Batchelor. New York, Sheed & Ward, 1954. 264 pp. map.

Russian-speaking Polish soldier serves in Russian armies and lives in Russia as a native, 1939–44. Comments on the friendliness of the people but considers the Soviet system to be destructive to personality.

1131. Noble, John H., and Glenn D. Everett. *I found God in Soviet Russia.* New York, St. Martin's Press, 1959. pp. 98-192.

German-American photographic supplies manufacturer describes his imprisonment in a Russian labor camp, 1939–45, and tells of finding a deep spiritual hunger among his fellow-prisoners.

1132. González, Valentín (El Campesino). *El Campesino. Life and death in Soviet Russia.* New York, Putnam, 1952. 218 pp. port.

Unique point of view of Soviet oppression by a Spanish Republican who went to Russia in 1939 to train for underground activity, was accused of being a Trotskyite, and imprisoned until 1949.

1133. Armonas, Barbara, and A. L. Nasvytis. *Leave your tears in Moscow.* Philadelphia, Lippincott, 1961. 222 pp. map.

In 1935 Barbara Armonas, her husband, and children returned to Lithuania from the United States to visit and to take care of some business matters. Four years later they were caught when the Soviet Union overran Lithuania; she was imprisoned and the others permitted to leave (she had been born in Lithuania, her husband was born of Lithuanian parents who had migrated to Cleveland, Ohio). Twenty years later, in 1960, she was released and returned to write this account of her stay in Irkutsk as a prisoner.

1134. Johnson, Hewlett. *The Soviet power. The socialist sixth of the world.* New York, International Publishers, 1940. 346 pp. illus. map. port. biblio. app.

The Dean of Canterbury Cathedral, who is often referred to as the "Red Dean" because of his sympathies for communism and its methods in the Soviet Union, journeys through European Russia in 1940 and returns to report favorably about conditions. He comments widely and strongly on practically every aspect of life there and often appears to justify Soviet actions by saying that others are doing certain things, and therefore, why not the Russians.

1135. Trivanovitch, Vaso. *Crankshafts or bread.* Ridgefield, Connecticut, Acorn Publishing Co., 1940. 236 pp.

Russian-speaking Yugoslavian sets out to expose the evils of the Soviet Union in this account published soon after the Nazi-Soviet pact of August, 1939. The title of this account is intended to symbolize the failure of industry and agriculture to meet the needs of the people.

1136. Herling, Gustav. *A world apart.* Translated from the Polish by Joseph Marek. New York, New American Library (Mentor), 1952. 243 pp. app.

Accumulated horror of daily prison life near Archangel, 1940–42, by a Polish intellectual caught trying to join the Polish army of resistance after Nazi-Soviet pact, 1939–41.

1137. Feld, Mischa Jac, and Ivan H. Peterman. *The hug of the bear.* New York, Holt, Rinehart & Winston, 1961. 305 pp.

Latvian Jew, with a knowledge of the Russian language, is arrested in 1940 when the Russians overrun Latvia, is sent to Siberian labor camp, and escapes in the guise of a Polish communist. He serves as a *Komissar* for a time, joins the Soviet army, travels throughout the Soviet Middle East, and finally escapes in 1946.

1138. Ciszek, Walter J. (S.J.), and Daniel L. Flaherty (S.J.). *With God in Russia*. New York, McGraw-Hill, The American Press, 1964. 302 pp. map.

American priest serving his church in Poland travels incognito with workers to the Ural Mountains in the spring of 1940. After the Germans invade Russia in 1941, he is identified as a priest and sent to Lubianka prison for five years and then to the labor camps for another ten, being released in 1962. Leaving Moscow by plane, he indicates his continuing concern for the Russian people and his own spirit of forgiveness by his blessing: "Slowly, carefully I made the sign of the cross over the land I was leaving."

1139. Elvin, Harold. *A cockney in Moscow*. London, Cressett, 1958. 222 pp.

British embassy employee comments on the impact of the German invasion during April–October, 1941. It would appear from the nature of his report that life went on in very much the usual fashion at the embassy in spite of the increasing restrictions imposed by a nation fighting a mortal enemy.

1140. Bourke-White, Margaret. *Shooting the Russian war*. New York, Simon & Schuster, 1942. 287 pp. illus. app.

American photographer (see nos. 945 and 960) prepares a sympathetic, well-written, and superbly photographed account of Moscow and its people just after the German invasion in 1941 (account covers May–October), with an interesting and informative chapter entitled "I photograph Stalin." See no. 1141.

1141. Caldwell, Erskine. *All out on the road to Smolensk*. New York, Duell, Sloan & Pearce, 1942. 230 pp.

Famous American novelist and his wife, Margaret Bourke-White (see no. 1140), arrive in Moscow in May, just before the German invasion, and leave in October. A sympathetic and very moving description of Russia's first resistance to Hitler's armies.

1142. Moats, Alice-Leone. *Blind date with Mars.* Garden City, New York, Doubleday, Doran, 1943. pp. 165–454.

Collier's war correspondent is in the Soviet Union, May 7–November 12, 1941, and witnesses the impact of the German invasion on Moscow, Leningrad, and Baku. A good deal of her account is a commentary on the life of foreign correspondents in the capital city, and she feels she would "die of melancholia" if she had to live in Russia for any length of time.

1143. Haldane, Charlotte Franken. *Russian newsreel. An eyewitness account of the Soviet Union at war.* London, Secker & Warburg, 1942. 207 pp. illus.

British correspondent (see no. 890) dedicates her account to the "Red Army and the heroic defenders of Moscow" and follows with a detailed and well-written report on the Russian resistance to the German invasion. Her comments are illuminated by well-chosen posters and photographs of the summer-autumn, 1941, journey.

1144. Werth, Alexander. *Moscow war diary.* New York, Knopf, 1942. 297 pp.

Russian-speaking London theater critic and Reuter's special correspondent reports on the changing Soviet scene after periodic journeys beginning in 1941. A British subject, Werth lived in St. Petersburg until he was sixteen. He describes the capital city during Hitler's initial onslaught, July–October, 1941. His comments indicate that in the midst of war the cultural life of the Soviet Union continued to flourish, especially the theater, which was used by the state as an effective device to maintain a high morale among the people.

1145. Ingersoll, Ralph McAllister. *Action on all fronts. A personal record of this war.* New York, Harper, 1941. pp. 67–198. illus. map.

American correspondent of New York newspaper, *PM,* journeys from Alma Ata to Moscow and returns to exit through Baku, August–September, 1941. His comments are especially informative on "Foreigner in Moscow" and "Soviet Society."

1146. Carroll, Wallace. *We're in this with Russia.* Boston, Houghton Mifflin, 1942. 264 pp.

United Press correspondent from the United States reports on the conditions at the Russian-German front, August–November, 1941. His descriptions of the early stages of resistance by the Russians are useful, and he includes an interesting section on "Exiles in Utopia"—the Americans who went to the Soviet Union in the 1930's.

1147. Reynolds, Quentin James. *Only the stars are neutral.* New York, Random House, 1942. pp. 63–298.

Collier's war correspondent reports on the Stalin-Beaverbrook-Harriman conference in Moscow, September–December, 1941. See especially the section on "Dinner with Stalin," a record of feasting in the midst of austerity.

1148. Citrine, (Sir) Walter McLennan. *In Russia now.* London, Hale, 1942. 154 pp. illus.

British laborite (see no. 1074) journeys to Moscow through Archangel in October, 1941, to arrange for co-operation between British and Russian trade unions. Observes the "miracle" of resistance to Hitler and urges "all aid to Russia."

1149. Eden, Anthony (Earl of Avon). *The reckoning; the memoirs of Anthony Eden, Earl of Avon.* Boston, Houghton Mifflin, 1965. pp. 332–52, 476–85, 556–65, 593–601. index.

Sir Anthony describes his first journey to Moscow by way of Murmansk, December 12–22, 1941, and his meeting with Stalin on December 16 as the German guns pound outside the capital city; his second trip, October 18–November 3, 1943, to the Foreign Ministers' Conference in Moscow; his third journey and second meeting with Stalin, October 9–19, 1944, when the futures of Poland, Germany, and Yugoslavia were discussed; and his fourth visit, February 3–14, 1945, at Yalta, with perceptive comments on Franklin D. Roosevelt's health and on Stalin as a negotiator— "toughest proposition."

1150. Czapski, Joseph. *The inhuman land.* Translated from the French by Gerard Hopkins. London, Chatto & Windus, 1951. 301 pp. illus.

Polish artist, prisoner of the Russians from 1939 to 1941, joins them against the Germans, 1941–42, and assists in leading a large contingent of Polish refugees to freedom in Iran.

1151. Lesueur, Laurence. "The Soviet army." In Overseas Press Club of America, compiler, *As we see Russia.* pp. 234–44. (See no. 1458.)

Columbia Broadcasting System correspondent describes the iron discipline imposed on the Russian army, 1941–42.

1152. Jordan, Philip. *Russian glory.* London, Cresset Press, 1942. 181 pp.

London *News Chronicle* special correspondent claims to be the first British reporter on Russian invasion scene until November, 1941. He claims that Lenin's body was moved to Sverdlovsk during the peak of danger to Moscow, a report confirmed by the Soviet Union in 1966.

1153. Lesueur, Laurence. *Twelve months that changed the world.* New York, Knopf, 1943. 345 pp.

Correspondent (see no. 1151) describes wartime Moscow, October 31, 1941–October 22, 1942. One of his many interesting observations is that Russians are very easy to like in a non-political situation.

1154. Cassidy, Henry C. *Moscow dateline, 1941–1943.* Boston, Houghton Mifflin, 1943. 367 pp. map. app. index.

Sympathetic description of Russia at war by Associated Press and National Broadcasting Company correspondent, 1941–43. There is much about Stalin of an uncritical nature, especially the famous "by mail" interview. His early comments are on Moscow just before the German invasion, and he includes an appendix of Soviet leadership as of February, 1943.

1155. Malaparte, Curzio (pseudonym of Curt Erich Suckert). *The Volga rises in Europe.* Translated from the Italian by David Moore. London, Alvin Redman, 1957. pp. 19–281.

Italian, friendly to the Soviet Union and the only front-line war correspondent in the summer of 1941 (according to him), states that communism is European and not Asiatic (the Volga rises in Europe!). He observes that World War II is "one of those social wars which always precede, and clear the ground for, a new political and social world-order." He describes the siege of Leningrad, 1941–43, from within the city.

1156. Wettlin, Margaret. *Russian road. Three years of war in Russia as lived through by an American woman.* London, Hutchinson, 1945. 126 pp. illus. port.

Tourist, sympathetic to communist aims, marries a Russian stage director in 1932 and between then and 1941 travels to Siberia and Mongolia and later to the United States with her son to lecture on the Soviet Union. In this account she provides details about war-time Russia not available to even the most capable foreign correspondents, June, 1941–June, 1944.

1157. Hughes, William R., compiler. *Those human Russians. A collection of incidents related by Germans.* London, Gollancz, 1950. 128 pp.

Accounts of anonymous aid and succor given to German soldiers and civilians in areas overrun by the Soviet armies, 1941–46. The purpose of this publication was to slow down the growth of anti-Russian attitudes in the West.

1158. Gilmore, Eddy. *Me and my Russian wife.* New York, Doubleday, 1954. 313 pp.

Russian-speaking Associated Press correspondent in European Russia, 1941–53, observes that communism "was state capitalism to me, rigidly and brutally enforced by the secret police." An especially useful part of his account describes how he finally got his wife out of the country, and he is informative on Stalin's death and funeral.

1159. Einsiedel, (Count) Heinrich von. *I joined the Russians. A captured German flier's diary of the Communist temptation.* New Haven, Yale University Press, 1953. 295 pp. illus. map. index.

In 1942 Einsiedel was given the opportunity to attend an antifascist school where he tried his best to become a communist. This is a useful and informative account that helps the reader to understand the backgrounds in the creation of East Germany (the German Democratic Republic).

1160. Hindus, Maurice Gerschon. *Mother Russia.* New York, Garden City Publishing Co., 1943. 395 pp. illus.

The purpose of this 1942 journey (see nos. 711, 839, 917, 965, and 1034) was to examine the impact of war on "the dark masses." Hindus comes away with a deep respect for the people and their heroism in the face of invasion.

1161. Segal, Louis. *The real Russia.* London, Evans, 1943. 160 pp. illus. map.

Segal (see no. 918) journeys through European Russia in 1942 and returns to extol the Soviet Union to the West. He comments on the right of the ordinary man to criticize the administration so long as he did not question the principles of communism.

1162. Snow, Edgar. *Journey to the beginning.* New York, Random House, 1958. pp. 276–341, 356–70. index.

Saturday Evening Post roving correspondent in the Soviet Union and longtime friend of communism's aspirations comments here on the life of war correspondents in Moscow in 1942 and the costs of the war as shown in the lives of the people by 1945. He remarks that the earlier fervor of the Communist party members has somewhat diminished by the end of the war as communism tends to become "good form" and party ranks are swelled by opportunists.

1163. Stowe, Leland. "Soviet unpreparedness for world leadership." In Overseas Press Club of America, compiler, *As we see Russia,* pp. 21–30. (See no. 1458.)

Chicago *Daily News* correspondent examines the characteristics of Soviet leadership after his experience in Moscow in 1942.

1164. Williams, Albert Rhys. *The Russians, the land, the people, and why they fight.* New York, Harcourt, Brace, 1943. 239 pp. index.

This is essentially a tract, written in 1942 by a friend of the Soviet Union (see no. 703), to explain the Russians to the West. It is especially effective in explaining the relationship between the Communist party and the governmental structure; that is, the image the Communists wish to project.

1165. Willkie, Wendell L. *One world.* New York, Simon & Schuster, 1943. pp. 50–102.

In 1940 Willkie, who had been a Democrat, was defeated as the Republican candidate for the presidency of the United States. Appointed by President Roosevelt as his personal representative, the former utilities executive journeyed around the world, traveling through Russia, September–October, 1942. He observes that Russia is an effective society and that the United States and the Soviet Union must work together in the postwar world when Russia will need products from America and the United States will require Soviet resources.

1166. Curie, Eve. *Journey among warriors.* New York, Doubleday, Doran, 1943. pp. 115–276. map. index.

French war correspondent journeys from Teheran to Moscow, January 6–29, 1942. Casts light on the life of women, from the ballet dancer to the welder; describes the liberation of Tolstoi's home.

1167. Churchill, Winston Leonard Spencer. *The hinge of fate.* Boston, Houghton Mifflin, 1950. pp. 472–500.

Between August 12–15, 1942, the Prime Minister of Great Britain is in Moscow conferring with Joseph Stalin. Here he describes his task of informing the Russian leader that an invasion of the Continent to take the pressure off western Russia is impossible at this time, a piece of information that leads Stalin to express some doubts about Allied promises.

1168. Chaplin, William Watts. *Seventy thousand miles of war: being one man's odyssey on many fronts.* New York, Appleton-Century, 1943. pp. 159–283.

International News Service war correspondent emphasizes the trivia that he believes reveals the character of a nation and its people in wartime. He also comments on how a foreigner is made to feel like an alien at all times in his tour in Moscow, September–November, 1942.

1169. Brown, James E. *Russia fights.* New York, Scribner's, 1943. 276 pp.

United Press correspondent comments on the visits of Churchill and Willkie (see nos. 1165 and 1167) in 1942 and on the morale and activities of the Russian men and women as Russia begins her counterattack against the Nazi armies.

1170. Emmens, (Lieutenant Colonel) Robert G. *Guests of the Kremlin.* New York, Macmillan, 1949. 291 pp.

Five American aviators, forced to land in the Soviet Union after the Doolittle raid on Tokyo, are interned as guests "without choice" for one year and one month, 1942–43. Emmens observes: ". . . a population, controlled by terror and violence, nurtured on fear and suspicion."

1171. Jacob, Alaric. *A traveller's war. A journey to the wars in Africa, India and Russia.* New York, Dodd, Mead, 1944. pp. 148–59, 326–90.

London *Daily Express* war correspondent's impressions of the Caucasus and Moscow, April, 1942, and June 13–September 20, 1943. Jacob praises the Russian army in Azerbaijan in these words: "We have never had allies quite like these before—tough guys with souls of artists, who sing as well as they fight."

1172. Reynolds, Quentin James. *The curtain rises.* London, Cassell, 1944. pp. 28–155.

American journalist (see no. 1147) comments on the impact of war on Soviet institutions and the people's way of life, April, 1942–June, 1943.

1173. Standley, (Admiral) William H., and A. A. Ageton. *Admiral ambassador to Russia.* Chicago, Regnery, 1955. 524 pp. index.

This is the account of an unhappy man in Moscow, April, 1942–October, 1943. Imagining himself slighted during Wendell Willkie's visit and completely alienated from the system around him, the ambassador refers to communism as "a religion of the devil; it is a distillation of evil; it is the very anti-Christ."

1174. Graebner, Walter. *Round trip to Russia.* Philadelphia, Lippincott, 1943. 216 pp. illus.

A friendly report by *Time-Life* correspondent on a journey through European Russia, July, 1942–January, 1943, in which he shares impressions of Winston Churchill and Wendell Willkie in Moscow, with added comments on how Americans are acting in wartime Russia.

1175. Kerr, Walter B. *The Russian army. Its men, its leaders and its battles.* New York, Knopf, 1944. 250 pp. map. index.

New York *Herald Tribune* correspondent studies the organization, training, personnel, and general character of the Soviet army, 1942–44.

1176. Snow, Edgar. *People on our side.* New York, Random House, 1944. pp. 67–255. illus. map. index.

Correspondent (see no. 1162) describes life in beleaguered Moscow, 1942–44, with sympathy and understanding.

1177. Lawrence, John. *Life in Russia.* London, Allen & Unwin, 1947. 239 pp. illus. map. app. index.

Well-written and perceptive comments by British correspondent stationed in Moscow, Sverdlovsk, and Archangel, 1942–45. He is especially informative on "The Russian character" and on the use of influence in business dealings, which the Russians call "Blat."

1178. Winterton, Paul. *Report on Russia.* London, Cresset Press, 1945. pp. 1–137.

After many visits since 1928 (see no. 899), London correspondent reveals what he could not say between 1942 and 1945. Commenting on wartime conditions, he sees the Russian people as friendly to the West but views the government as suspicious and falsely cordial, especially during wartime conferences.

1179. Bauer, Joseph Martin. *As far as my feet will carry me.* Translated from the German by Lawrence Wilson. London, Andre Deutsch, 1957. 254 pp.

Captured by the Russians in 1942, Clemens Forell (pseudonym), German soldier, is taken to East Cape camp, near the Bering Strait, from which he escapes, strikes south to Chita and west to the Caucasus. He escapes from the Soviet Union into Iran after a three-year journey, 1949–52.

1180. Wigmans, Johan H. *Ten years in Russia and Siberia.* Translated from the Dutch by Arnout de Waal. London, Darton, Longman & Todd, 1964. 234 pp. map.

Forced to fight in the German army, Wigmans deserts to the Russians in 1942. Three years in Russia as a prisoner of war, five years in a Siberian labor camp, and two years returning to the West after release leads Wigmans to promise never to forget Russia: ". . . Your millions of prisoners drawn from your own blood and country, who would sometimes share with me, a foreigner, their meagre ration of bread, your beguiled workers and girls who thirst after a different life."

1181. Lauterbach, Richard E. *These are the Russians.* New York, Harper, 1945. 359 pp. index.

Time-Life war correspondent, assigned to Moscow for Kharkov atrocity trials and Katyn investigation, sets out to provide Americans with "a picture of how the Russians tick" in wartime, 1943. He comments in some detail on the high life lived by the rulers and describes the peoples' image of Stalin as godlike.

1182. Stevens, Edmund. *Russia is no riddle.* Cleveland, World Publishing Co., 1945. 300 pp.

Stevens represented the *Christian Science Monitor* in Moscow, 1940–49. Russian-speaking and married to a Russian, he was very friendly at first, but gradual disenchantment set in as he became better acquainted with conditions as they really were. This is an account of Moscow in 1943, and Stevens is sympathetic to the suffering about him. He comments on the constant diplomatic activity; and the food, drink, and talk are described in detail. Especially interesting and informative are his sections on "Christmas in Moscow" and the "Katyn massacre."

1183. Downs, William Randall, Jr. "A cake of soap." In Overseas Press Club of America, compiler, *As we see Russia,* pp. 125–28. (See no. 1458.)

Downs provides a tender reminiscence of an encounter with a Russian girl in February, 1943, when he was in Moscow representing the Columbia Broadcasting System.

1184. Werth, Alexander. *Leningrad.* New York, Knopf, 1944. 189 pp.

In this account Werth (see no. 1144) describes the siege of Leningrad and the heroic resistance of the people, September, 1943.

1185.   Salisbury, Harrison Evans. *Russia on the way*. New York
        Macmillan, 1946. 414 pp. index.

Chief of the United Press Bureau, 1944–46, and *New York Times* correspondent in Moscow, 1949–54, Salisbury made his most recent visits in 1959 and 1961. Accused of being overly optimistic in his continued assessment of the Soviet regime, he has been described as wishing to be thought more of a political prophet than a reporter (see Abraham Brumberg, "The same old Salisbury," *Reporter,* September 27, 1962, pp. 48–51). *Russia on the way* is Salisbury's account of the Soviet Union as the Nazi armies are brought to a halt in 1943–44 and the counteroffensive begins. He refers to Stalin as "fatherly and benevolent."

1186.   Winter, Ella (Mrs. Joseph Lincoln Steffens). *I saw the
        Russian people*. Boston, Little, Brown, 1945. 299 pp. illus.

New York Post correspondent (see no. 1002) details wartime conditions in Moscow, 1943–44, not sparing in her praise and criticism of schools, free markets, beauty parlors, etc.

1187.   Deane, John R. *The strange alliance. The story of our
        efforts at war-time cooperation with Russia*. New York,
        Viking, 1947. 333 pp. index.

American major general assigned to Ambassador W. Averell Harriman, whose purpose was to expedite relations with the Soviet Union, 1943–45, sees the leaders as sincere but severely handicapped by their constant jockeying for Stalin's favor. He comments in some detail on the lives of the common people and expresses admiration and respect for them and their efforts.

1188.   Maloney, James Joseph. *Inside red Russia*. Sidney, Angus
        & Robertson, 1948. 198 pp. index.

Australian minister to Moscow, 1943–45, presents a "frank record of an appalling system." As a "Labour man officially visiting a supposed socialist state," he comments on the Soviet way of life from birth to death.

1189. * Lundberg, Yngve and Soren Hellstrom. *So this is Russia.*
London, Falcon, 1949. 95 pp.

1190. Djilas, Milovan. *Conversations with Stalin.* Translated from
the Serbo-Croatian by Michael B. Petrovich. New York,
Harcourt, Brace & World, 1962. pp. 39–186. app. index.

Djilas, close friend of Yugoslavia's President Tito and instru-
mental with him in bringing Yugoslavia into the communist camp,
describes the three journeys he made to confer with Stalin in
1944, 1945, and 1948. Using the words "rapture," "doubts," and
"disappointments," he comments on his progressive disillusionment
with the Soviet system and the "new class" appearing in his own
country. He also provides some detail on the way Stalin lived.

1191. * Falkson, Emmanuel Leon. *A Cockney among the reds.*
London, Stockwell, 1945. 237 pp. illus.

1192. White, William L. *Report on the Russians.* New York,
Harcourt, Brace, 1945. 309 pp.

Reader's Digest roving correspondent with Eric Johnston, president of the Chamber of Commerce of the United States, during
a six-week tour in western Russia and Siberia, 1944. He attempts
to balance the disregard for individual life and liberty in the Soviet
Union with the great accomplishments achieved in wartime.

1193. Wallace, Henry A., and Andrew J. Steiger. *Soviet Asia
mission.* New York, Reynal & Hitchcock, 1946. 248 pp.
illus. map. app. index.

The Vice-President of the United States, sent by President Roosevelt to estimate the war potential of the Soviet Union, reports on
his visit to Soviet Asia, May–July, 1944. Sympathetic to Soviet
aims, Wallace describes the great efforts of the people and provides useful information on the agricultural situation.

1194. Snow, Edgar. *The pattern of Soviet power.* New York,
Random House, 1945. 212 pp. illus. map. index.

By the summer of 1944 Snow (see nos. 1162 and 1176) sees a
victorious Russia and speculates on a future when the Soviet army

returns from Europe, having seen so much and having paid so high a price. He wonders if wartime compromises with Marxist doctrine will continue into the postwar period and is especially informative on the cultural and psychological effects of war on Soviet society.

1195. Jacob, Alaric. *A window in Moscow, 1944–1945.* London, Collins, 1946. 320 pp.

British correspondent (see no. 1171) describes Moscow life and observes that wartime sympathy with the Soviet Union will produce non-interventionists in the West who will work to avoid World War III.

1196. Churchill, Winston Leonard Spencer. *Triumph and tragedy.* Boston, Houghton Mifflin, 1953. pp. 226–43, 346–94.

Visiting Moscow in October, 1944 (see no. 1167), British Prime Minister encounters "an extraordinary atmosphere of goodwill"— Stalin dines with him at the British Embassy! He also comments on Stalin and Roosevelt at Yalta in February, 1945.

1197. Moorad, George. *Behind the curtain.* Philadelph, Fireside Press, 1946. 309 pp.

Columbia Broadcasting System correspondent comments on the life of the foreign reporter and his battles with the censor during his stay in Moscow, October, 1944–April, 1945, and carefully outlines the impact of Roosevelt's death on the Soviet people and government.

1198. Alexander, Joseph Aloysius. *In the shadow. Three years in Moscow.* Melbourne, Herald and Weekly Times, 1949. 356 pp.

First secretary of the Australian legation eagerly observes "wonderful Russia," 1944–47. He comments on the people and government in war and in the postwar period and provides considerable detail on the transition era.

1199. Whitney, Thomas P. *Russia in my life.* New York, Reynal, 1962. 307 pp. illus.

Washington *Post* reporter assigned to Moscow, 1944–53, learns the language, marries a Russian girl, and here presents an intimate picture of Russian home life. In one of his most informative sections he describes Stalin's death and the events following it.

1200. Ashby, Eric. *Scientist in Russia.* Baltimore, Penquin, 1947. 252 pp. app.

Russian-speaking Australian scientist stationed in Moscow discusses the organization of scientific research and the lives of the scientists, whose activities appear to be only slightly influenced by the yoke of communism. He provides an excellent appendix with rules for scholars, syllabuses of the universities, and lesson plans for the middle schools.

1201. Fittkau, Gerhard A. *My thirty-third year. A priest's experiences in a Russian work camp.* New York, Farrar, Straus, 1958. pp. 30–248.

German priest spends nine months in a Petchora labor camp in 1945. His description of conditions there and of his journey home is full of pathos and of pity for the Russians he sees enslaved. At one point, observing some prisoners working, he remarks: "The picture was right out of the story of ancient slaves . . . every mark of the individual personality had been suppressed."

1202. George, Father (pseudonym), and Gretta Palmer. *God's underground.* New York, Appleton-Century-Crofts, 1949. pp. 152–262.

Croatian priest, incognito in the Russian army and acting in the medical corps, describes the Christian and Moslem resistance to Moscow's control in 1945. He considers the Russian Orthodox church to be a puppet of the Communist party.

1203. Lucas, William O. (William van Narvig, pseudonym). *East of the Iron Curtain.* Chicago, Ziff-Davis, 1946. 361 pp. map.

Friendly comments by one who was born in Russia, although not Russian, and lived there for twenty-five years. He claims the Soviet attitude toward the West in 1945 had been influenced by a long history of foreign interference in Russia's activities.

1204. Phillips, Tracey. "The Russians have no word for her." In Overseas Press Club of America, compiler, *As we see Russia,* pp. 139–49. (See no. 1458.)

United States correspondent's wife in Moscow, 1945, points out that there is no word in the Russian language for "housewife."

1205. Stypulkowski, Zbigniew. *Invitation to Moscow.* London, Thames & Hudson, 1951. pp. 192–360. port.

Member of the Polish resistance is captured and taken to Moscow in 1945, where he is interrogated 141 times in Lubianka prison, pleads not guilty, and survives. In addition to his comments on life in Lubianka he describes how the Soviet government sets out to discredit the Polish government in exile.

1206. Parker, John. *Forty-two days in the Soviet Union.* London, Gardner, Darton, 1946. 75 pp.

British Member of Parliament journeys south from Leningrad into the Ukraine during the final stages of World War II, January– February, 1945. He comments especially on the changes wrought by six years of war on the Black Sea areas.

1207. Leahy, (Fleet Admiral) William D. *I was there. The personal story of the Chief of Staff to Presidents Roosevelt and Truman based on his notes and diaries made at the time.* New York, McGraw-Hill, 1950. pp. 291–323.

Admiral Leahy comments on Stalin's day-to-day changes in attitude at Yalta, January 23–February 11, 1945.

1208. Stettinius, Edward R., Jr., and Walter Johnson. *Roosevelt and the Russians.* Garden City, New York, Doubleday, 1949. pp. 79–292. illus. map. app. index.

The United States secretary of state accompanies President Roosevelt to Yalta and here presents his account of events, February 4–11, 1945.

1209. McGill, Ralph. "The man in the iron lung." In Overseas Press Club of America, compiler, *As we see Russia,* pp. 184–97 (See no. 1458.)

American correspondent in Moscow in March, 1945, discusses the flow of news between the Soviet Union and the free world, pointing out that the Soviet government fears the new Soviet man it has created and is therefore reluctant to keep him fully informed.

1210. Johnson, Hewlett. *Soviet Russia since the war.* New York, Boni & Gaer, 1947. 270 pp.

In this account the "Red Dean" (see no. 1134) outlines his journey east to Transcaspia in the summer of 1945, where he sees the process of postwar reconstruction at full tide. Of the Soviet Union, he says that it is the "ally of all that is best in the religions in the world."

1211. Hiett, Helen. "Return to the Soviet." In *Deadline delayed.* Overseas Press Club of America, compiler. New York, Dutton, 1947. pp. 54–65.

National Broadcasting Company correspondent accompanies repatriated Russian prisoners of war from Italy on their return to Odessa, July, 1945. She comments on the cold and stony welcome of the ship by soldiers standing with fixed bayonets before a crowd of sullen people, one of whom informs her that they (the returnees) should not have been captured!

1212. Eisenhower, Dwight David. *Crusade in Europe.* Garden City, New York, Doubleday, 1948. pp. 457–78. illus. index.

Commander-in-chief of the Allied forces in western Europe accepts Stalin's invitation to visit Leningrad and Moscow, August, 1945. He describes how he stood for five hours beside Stalin on top of Lenin's tomb reviewing a vast parade—one of the first two foreigners (with Major General Deane, see no. 1187) to be accorded such an honor in Soviet history. He equates the ordinary Russian with what he calls an average American.

1213. Byrnes, James Francis. *All in one lifetime.* New York, Harper, 1958. pp. 326–45. index.

United States secretary of state describes his attendance at the Moscow Conference, December 12–28, 1945, commenting on the Russian officials' hours of work (afternoon to past midnight) and expressing sharp criticism of the class distinctions he encounters.

1214. Atkinson, Oriana. *Over at Uncle Joe's. Moscow and me.* Indianapolis, Bobbs-Merrill, 1947. 325 pp. illus.

Wife of *New York Times* correspondent outlines the life of a foreign housewife in Moscow in 1945–46 by describing her buying habits and problems, by reacting against the smugness of the Russians toward what they consider their rightness and democracy, and by listing some of the characteristics of the Russian, such as friendliness and an insistence on getting foreigners drunk. This account is definitely not objective in its approach to "Uncle Joe's."

1215. Smith, Jessica. *People come first.* New York, International Publishers, 1948. 254 pp.

The editor of *Soviet Russia Today* (a pro-Soviet publication) describes a journey from Moscow to Baku, autumn, 1945–winter, 1946, during which she sees a will to peace that can only be changed by foreign aggression against the Soviet Union.

1216. Price, Morgan Philips. *Russia, red or white; a record of a visit to Russia after twenty-seven years.* London, Low, Marston, 1948. 120 pp. index.

Impressions from a journey (see nos. 609 and 699) to European and Asiatic Russia, October, 1945–January, 1946. Price has become convinced that Marxism is not the only answer, so is friendly in his comments on the people but extremely critical of the Soviet system, which he believes is the old imperial economy with new names.

1217. Thompson, Craig. *The police state. What you want to know about the Soviet Union.* New York, Dutton, 1950. 248 pp. index.

Time-Life correspondent in Moscow describes how the Soviet Union oppresses its people and how they manage to survive by illegal acts, 1945–47. See no. 1218.

1218. Thompson, Edith W. (Mrs. Craig). "Mama, what shall I say?" In Overseas Press Club of America, compiler, *As we see Russia,* pp. 199–205. (See no. 1458.)

Comments on the Soviet educational system, 1945–47, which emphasizes how the post–1917 system repeats many of the pre–1917 features.

1219. Parker, Ralph. *Moscow correspondent.* London, Muller, 1949. 302 pp. app.

New York Times correspondent in Moscow, 1945–48, "attempts to do little more than describe the Soviet scene as it appeared in its changing shape and varying colors to a foreign observer." One of the most informative sections in this account is "The red army comes home."

1220. Gollwitzer, Helmut. *Unwilling journey. A diary from Russia.* Translated from the German by E. M. Delacour. Philadelphia, Muhlenberg Press, 1954. 316 pp.

Religiously-oriented German soldier, captured in Czechoslovakia, spends four years, from May, 1945, to December, 1949, in Soviet labor camps. Using the diary form to dramatize his encounter with the triumphant communists, he characterizes his prison treatment as mentally arduous but not too strenuous physically.

1221. Biemel, Rainer (Jean Rounault, pseudonym). *Nightmare.* Translated from the French by Vera Traill. New York, Crowell, 1952. 267 pp.

French journalist characterizes his eight years (1945–53) in the Soviet labor camps as nightmarish under the ever-changing rules and ordinances. He says he could never respect the Russians because of their inefficiency, but he did like them and, because of this, was able to penetrate a little distance into their lives.

1222. Noble, John H. *I was a slave in Russia. An American tells his story.* New York, Devon-Adair, 1958. pp. 70–174. illus.

Noble (see no. 1131) describes the horrors of the Stalin labor camps, especially Vorkuta, 1945–55.

1223. Parvilahti, Unto. *Beria's gardens. A slave laborer's experiences in the Soviet Utopia.* New York, Dutton, 1960. 286 pp.

Finnish businessman and liaison officer in Berlin during World War II describes his experiences, 1945–55. He is especially interesting in his comments on *tuhtaa* or "fiddling," the low cunning of prisoners in avoiding work.

1224. Fischer, John. *Why they behave like Russians.* New York, Harper, 1947. 262 pp.

Wartime official on the American Board of Economic Warfare, on a mission in 1946 to Kiev and the Ukraine, makes a dispassionate effort to explain the motives and future course of the Soviet Union.

1225. Hottelet, Richard C. "Turning Point," In Overseas Press Club of America, compiler, *As we see Russia,* pp. 274–92. (See no. 1458.)

Columbia Broadcasting System reporter, in Moscow in 1946, comments on the expansion of the membership and scope of the Communist party to take advantage of the impending "decline of the West."

1226. King, Fay [pseudonym?]. *Footloose in the Soviet Union.* London, Valiant, 1947. 144 pp. port.

British student, touring from Leningrad to the Crimea, 1946, presents "The Truth" about the Soviet Union by emphasizing all the positive features and comparing life in Russia before the 1917 Revolution with conditions after World War II.

1227. Priestly, John Boynton. *Russian journey.* London, Writers Group for Cultural Relations of the U.S.S.R., 1946. 40 pp. illus.

British novelist, guest of the Soviet Union during a journey in 1946, offers a strong plea to build bridges of understanding between Russia and the West.

1228. Strohm, John. *Just tell the truth. The uncensored story of how the common people live behind the Russian Iron Curtain.* New York, Scribner's, 1947. 243 pp. illus. port. index.

The editor of *Prairie Farmer,* an American rural periodical, challenges Stalin to permit an uncensored and unrestricted journey into the Soviet Union in 1946. His account reflects the amicable Russian-American feeling just before the cold war began. Excellent illustrations.

1229. Lauterbach, Richard E. *Through Russia's back door.* New York, Harper, 1946. 219 pp. illus. map. app.

American journalist (see no. 1181) journeys west from Vladivostok to Moscow in June, 1946, on the Trans-Siberian Railway. The theme of his account is "the dwindling peace," and he is shocked to hear American newspapermen talking about "war with the Soviet Union as though it were as inevitable as next June." He illuminates his account with excellent photographs, especially of Siberia.

1230. Grimm, Peter. *Russia seen from within: an account of a relief mission visit.* New York, Carnegie Endowment for International Peace, 1947. pp. 119–42.

New York state chamber of commerce president describes devastation after a journey from Leningrad to the south, summer, 1946, and predicts an era of exploding competition between the Soviet Union and the United States.

1231. Smith, Walter Bedell. *My three years in Moscow*. Philadelphia, Lippincott, 1950. 335 pp. illus. port. index.

American ambassador to the Soviet Union, 1946–48, describes life
in the embassy and the restrictions when outside. Critical of the
Communist party, he is very sympathetic to the Russian people
but sees a rising tide of suspicion and distrust as Russian-American
relations worsen and the cold war begins.

1232. Peterson, Maurice. *Both sides of the curtain: an autobiography*. London, Constable, 1950. pp. 254–99. illus. port. index.

British ambassador in Moscow, 1946-49, outlines the cold war
harrassment accorded his office after 1947 and observes that
"Stalin's post-box" (a hole in the Kremlin war for supplicants in
czarist times) is not the best substitute for Western-type justice.

1233. Peltier, (Rear Admiral) Marius. *Soviet encounter*. Translated from the French by T. C. Butler. London, Geoffrey
Bles, 1955. 244 pp. illus. port.

After four years in Moscow, 1946–50, the French *Attaché naval
à Moscou* concludes that Russians, like all men, are full of hopes
and fears. He comments on the strategy of non-involvement used
by ordinary men who might otherwise tend to become robots under
the system.

1234. Clifford, Alexander, and Jenny Nicholson. *The sickle and
the stars*. London, Peter Davies, 1948. pp. 9–252.

This account is made up of letters to a fellow correspondent in
the United States by a British delegate to the Foreign Ministers
Conference in Moscow, who also visits Stalingrad in 1947. He is
critical of the Soviet way of life, especially the failure to align
practice with theory.

1235. Dallas, Don. *Dateline Moscow*. London, Heinemann, 1952.
260 pp. app. index.

British writer travels to Moscow and through European Russia
in 1947 and records impressions ranging from funerals to Stalin to

tea-drinking, and all between. He includes in the Appendix such things as the state-secrets law, the church in Russia, divorce law, and restrictions on foreign travel.

1236. Steinbeck, John. *A Russian journal.* New York, Viking, 1948. 220 pp. illus.

American novelist and his photographer companion, Robert Capa, journey to Moscow, Kiev, Stalingrad, and the Georgian Republic in 1947, and return to record one of the best and earliest postwar accounts from the standpoint of both writing and photography.

1237. * Ward, Paul W. *Life in the Soviet Union.* Baltimore, *Baltimore Sun,* 1947. 75 pp.

1238. Welles, Sam. *Profile of Europe.* New York, Harper, 1948. pp. 17–190. map.

Time-Life correspondent with a knowledge of Russian characterizes the Soviet Union in 1947 as the "most wasteful form of society in human history." He devotes a number of his comments to the absurdities of Russian science in the early stages of the cold war.

1239. Nyárády, Miklós. *My ringside seat in Moscow.* New York, Crowell, 1952. 297 pp. index.

Hungarian diplomat recounts the difficulties he experiences on a mission to negotiate a Soviet demand for $200,000,000 in "German assets," May–December, 1947. In addition he supplies interesting information on courtship and marriage, the place of woman, religion, the new classes, and other details about the way of life.

1240. Hilton, Donald. *Military attaché in Moscow.* London, Hollis & Carter, 1949. 225 pp. port. app. index.

Russian-speaking major general offers details on the gray life of sad and sour adults, 1947–48. He critically comments on the Soviet mentality, the light side of Russian life, communism in theory and practice, and the difficulty of discovering the truth about anything in the Soviet Union.

1241. Werth, Alexander. *Musical uproar in Moscow.* London, Turnstile Press, 1949. 103 pp.

In 1948 Werth (see nos. 1144 and 1184) describes and indicts Zhdanov's reach for control of Russian music at the Conference of Musicians, Central Committee of the All-Union Communist Party, in January.

1242. Stevens, Leslie Clark. *Russian assignment.* Boston, Little, Brown, 1953. 552 pp. illus. index.

United States embassy naval attaché who speaks Russian is stationed in Moscow, 1947–49, during the first two years of the cold war. He writes a full account of his life in and out of the embassy and comes to the conclusion that the Russian people are fundamentally decent and will eventually eliminate the "darkness of communism."

1243. Johnstone, Archie. *Ivan the not-so-terrible.* London, British Soviet Friendship Society, 1956. 164 pp. illus.

British (Scotch) journalist, editor of the *British Ally,* a foreign office newspaper published by the British in the Soviet Union, resigns and goes over to the communists, remaining in Moscow with his Russian wife. His account from 1947 to 1954, is especially valuable because it is an intimate pro-Soviet account by a foreigner.

1244. Rupert, Raphael. *A hidden world.* Anthony Rhodes, editor. London, Collins, 1963. pp. 1–220. map. app.

Son of a liberal Hungarian politician, Rupert was arrested as an alleged British spy in 1947, and here describes the living conditions, the work, the attempts to save human dignity, the activities of camp bandits, and other details experienced during eight years in various Soviet labor camps.

1245. Roberts, Leslie. *Home from the cold wars.* Boston, Beacon Press, 1948. pp. 36–124.

Canadian journalist sees what he refers to as the "real Russia" during his journey in 1948. Anti-American and pro-Russian, he discovers that the people of the world fear both the United States and the Soviet Union.

1246. Lindsay, Jack. *A world ahead; journal of a Soviet journey.* London, Fore publications, 1950. 164 pp. illus.

British writer and his wife attend Pushkin celebration in Leningrad and Moscow in June, 1949, and comment in this account on Soviet arts and artists, writing, and writers.

1247. Kelly, Marie Noële. *Mirror to Russia.* London, Country Life Ltd., 1952. 242 pp. illus. map. port. index.

British correspondent of *Country Life Magazine* journeys with her son from Leningrad to the Black Sea, 1949–51. She writes a full account and illuminates it with excellent photographs, mentioning but not overemphasizing the sordid aspects of life they encounter.

1248. Sassoon, Penelope. *Penelope in Moscow.* London, Weidenfeld & Nicolson, 1953. 157 pp. illus.

Wife of French correspondent stationed in Moscow informs the West about life in Russia after a journey from Leningrad to Moscow and on to the Georgian Republic, April, 1949–January, 1951. There is a breathless quality about this account, as if the author had just discovered the Soviet Union.

1249. Kirk, Lydia. *Postmarked Moscow.* New York, Scribner's, 1952. 278 pp.

The wife of the United States ambassador to Moscow, June, 1949–October, 1951, might have justifiably entitled her account "How to run an embassy," for this is a delightfully written description of embassy housekeeping, with a fine attention to detail.

1250. Salisbury, Harrison Evans. *American in Russia.* New York, Harper, 1955. 321 pp. ilus. map. index.

Here Salisbury (see no. 1185) describes the transition period from Stalin's last years through his death to the leadership of Georgi

M. Malenkov, 1949–54. He describes his journeys away from Moscow and provides an interesting commentary on a voyage down the Volga River, during which he observed the Russian passengers enjoying themselves in much the same way as their contemporaries would on a Rhine River boat. He also comments on the similarities between the Russo-British relations in the nineteenth century and the Russian-American relations in the twentieth century.

1251. Salisbury, Harrison Evans. *Moscow journal. The end of Stalin.* Chicago, University of Chicago Press, 1961. 441 pp. index.

In 1962 Salisbury published another account of his years in the Soviet Union between 1949 and 1954, in which he places in brackets all the censored materials not seen in *American in Russia* (see no. 1250).

1252. * British Workers' Delegation. *Russia with our own eyes. The full report of the British Workers' Delegation to the Soviet Union, 1950.* London, British Workers' Delegation, 1950. 128 pp.

1253. Laycock, Harold. *Moscow close-up.* London, Dennis Yates, 1951. 224 pp.

One of the reporters on the *British Ally* (see no. 1243) describes how the Soviet Union succeeded in destroying it in 1950.

1254. Stevens, Edmund. *This is Russia uncensored!* New York, Eton Books, 1951. 214 pp.

Upon returning to the United States after his assignment in Moscow, 1940–49 (see no. 1182), Stevens published this account in which he exposed what he termed the real Russia. Going down the list of Soviet institutions—economics, family, education, religion, etc.—he comments on the Communist party's methods of restricting and destroying liberty. The account is one of bitter disillusionment.

1255. Gordey, Michel. *Visa to Moscow*. Translated from the French by Katherine Woods. New York, Knopf, 1952. 419 pp.

Russian-speaking *France Soir* correspondent is admitted to Russia for sixty-three days in the spring of 1950 and returns to present an informative account on almost every aspect of Soviet life, based chiefly on conversations with the common people and with members of the Communist party. He has an especially interesting section on "America: Soviet version."

1256. Marion, George. *All quiet in the Kremlin*. New York, Fairplay Publishers, 1951. 183 pp.

American author of a book published in Moscow that appears to prove that the United States is really responsible for the cold war is invited to the Soviet Union by Andreyev Vishinsky during the summer of 1950 to spend the accumulated royalties. Upon his return to America he states somewhat categorically that there are "no iron curtains, secret police, labor camps and heavens knows what other hellish inventions" in Russia.

1257. Scholmer, Joseph. *Vorkuta*. Translated from the German by Robert Kee. London, Weidenfeld & Nicholson, 1954. pp. 32–304.

German political prisoner in Vorkuta forced labor camp, 1950–54, comments on life there, especially the strike in 1953 that occurred immediately after Stalin's death.

1258. *Canadian workers look at the Soviet Union; statements made by two Canadian trade union delegations which visited the Soviet Union in 1951 and 1952*. Moscow, Foreign Language Publishing House, 1953. 95 pp.

Journeys made from Leningrad to Odessa with resulting statements by members, who describe the people as well dressed and report that housing is being built.

1259. * Delegation of Trade Unionists. *Russia—the truth. Official report of the elected delegation of trade unionists to the U.S.S.R., 1951*. London, 1951. 71 pp.

1260. Harding, Sidnie Milana (Mrs. J. P.). *The Soviet Union today; a scientist's impressions.* London, Lawrence & Wishart, 1952. 132 pp. illus. map. index.

Woman Reader in the University of London is one of a thousand admitted as guests of the Soviet Union, 1951. She advocates a cultural exchange program as a means of bridging the misunderstanding between Soviet Russia and the West.

1261. Carter, Charlotte and Dyson. *We saw socialism.* Toronto, Canadian-Soviet Friendship Society, 1951–52. 396 pp. illus. port.

Canadian research scientist and his wife (a nurse) travel through European Russia in May, 1951, as guests of the state. Their account is detailed on Soviet medicine and science, and they claim to present the truth about a nation that has no forced labor camps and where anyone who can read a foreign language may read newspapers from abroad without restriction.

1262. *We have learned the truth about the Soviet Union, say British, Americans, French, Italians, Canadians, Danes, Dutch, Swedes, Icelanders, Finns, and Austrians, who visited the U.S.S.R. in May 1951.* London, Soviet News, 1951. 64 pp. illus.

A series of highly complimentary statements by members of various tour groups.

1263. National Union of Students of the Universities and Colleges of England, Wales, and North Ireland. *British students visit the Soviet Union; a report of a delegation of the National Union of Students.* London, K-H Services, 1951. 96 pp.

An interesting reaction to a journey into the Soviet Union as guests of the state by British students, who complain that there is too much wining and dining and too few statistics.

1264. American Trade Union Delegation. *American workers look at the Soviet Union; impressions of the American Trade Union Delegation.* Moscow, Foreign Language Publishing House, 1951. 96 pp. illus.

A visit to Leningrad and Moscow, June–July, 1951, brings friendly reports from members of the delegation.

1265. Lonsdale, Kathleen, editor. *Quakers visit Russia*. London, Friends House, 1952. 145 pp.

A Quaker team journeys to Leningrad, Moscow, and Kiev, July 14–27, 1951, to test the sincerity of the Russian peace testimony. Speaking for the team, Lonsdale discovers life to be more normal than she expected, and finds that the people express immense pride in their system, although it appears obvious that begging and drunkenness are still present. See no. 1266.

1266. Cadbury, Paul S. *A personal diary of the Quaker mission to Russia*. Birmingham, England, privately printed, 1951. 24 pp.

Managing director of British chocolate firm responds in friendly fashion to Soviet Peace Committee reception, July 14-27, 1951. See no. 1265.

1267. Hardy, Frank J. *Journey into the future*. Melbourne, Australian Book Society, 1952. 336 pp. illus.

Pro-communist Australian writer and his wife tour Leningrad and Moscow in September, 1951, and write a commentary dealing with education, sports, religion, and the way of life, with a strong plea for world disarmament.

1268. Rounds, Frank, Jr. *A window on Red Square*. Boston, Houghton Mifflin 1952. 304 pp. map. index.

Russian-speaking American embassy employee comments on life in, and out of, the embassy grounds, January 10, 1951–June 5, 1952. His comments are interesting and useful because of their emphasis upon the ordinary man.

1269. Donnelly, Desmond. *The March wind. Exploration behind the Iron Curtain*. New York, Putnam, 1960. pp. 26–35, 120–34, 190–216. illus. index.

Member of Parliament and editor of *Town and Country Planning* makes three journeys to European Russia and Siberia in 1952, 1954, and 1957. He says anger against communism is not enough, that we must try to understand the challenge that it offers to capitalism and seek effective counter-challenges. He feels it is not possible to make peace with communism, for peace means surrender.

1270. Kyaw Min, U. *Through the Iron Curtain via the back door.* London, Ernest Benn, 1953. pp. 1–187.

Burmese lawyer, member of a delegation to the International Economic Conference in Moscow, March, 1952, comments like a typical tourist on his journey, although his remarks on Soviet amusements are informative.

1271. * Watkins, Harold Mostyn. *The dove and the sickle.* London, Fore Publications, 1953. 118 pp. biblio.

1272. Vassilieff, Elizabeth Sutton. *Peking-Moscow letters; about a four month's journey, to and from Vienna, by way of Peoples' China and the Soviet Union.* Melbourne, Australian Book Society, 1953. pp. 155–237.

Australian writer, guest of the Soviet Peace Committee, December, 1952–January, 1953, journeys west across Siberia to Moscow and Leningrad. She records her experiences with Soviet writers and peace workers and concludes that the differences between communism and capitalism can be resolved; in fact, they will have to be resolved because socialism is here to stay.

1273. Menon, Kumara Padmanabha Siva-Sankara. *The flying troika: extracts from a diary by K. P. S. Menon, India's Ambassador to Russia, 1952–1961.* London, Oxford University Press, 1963. 318 pp. index.

This account is chiefly a narrative of diplomatic relationships and an attempt to interpret the Russians to India. For Menon's account of life outside the Indian embassy in Moscow, see no. 1274.

1274. Menon, Kumara Padmanabha Siva-Sankara. *Russian panorama: Moscow, Georgia, the Crimea, Azerbaijan, Nizhni-Novgorod, Leningrad, Stalingrad, the Ukraine, the Volga, Siberia, Soviet and Chinese Central Asia, the Arctic and Baltic, Poland, Hungary.* Bombay, Oxford University Press, 1962. 273 pp. illus. map. index.

Menon (see no. 1273) describes the beauty of places and people and illuminates his narrative with excellent photographs. He depicts the periods immediately before and after Stalin's death, with friendly comments on a variety of topics related to the life of the common people.

1275. MacDuffie, Marshall. *The Red Carpet. 10,000 miles through Russia on a visa from Khrushchev.* New York, Norton, 1955. 319 pp. illus. index.

In 1953 *Collier's* writer is granted a visa and proceeds to visit eight of the Soviet republics with 90 per cent of the Russian population. Having been in the Soviet Union in 1946, he is able to make intelligent comparisons; and he manages to visit enough places and interview enough people (through his interpreter) to provide a useful and informative survey of the country just after Stalin's death. Especially interesting are his sections on the "Minsk auto plant," "Oil city," and his "Interview with 'Mr. Communist'" (Khrushchev).

1276. Vaikunthavasan, K. *Three months in New China and Soviet Union.* Colombo, Ceylon, Peoples' Press, 1953. pp. 57–147. illus. map.

East Indian member of Congress of Peoples for Peace describes his sojourn in Moscow in 1953 and comments in a highly complimentary way about the way of life he observes.

1277. Mahmuduzzafar, S. *Quest for life, a record of five months in the Soviet Union.* Bombay, Peoples' Publishing House, 1954. 155 pp. illus.

During July–December, 1953, East Indian writer and his wife were in Moscow—he had brought her there for cancer treatment (she died in Moscow). After living in Moscow and later in the

Crimea, he describes Moscow and the Soviet system as an answer to his dreams for peace and the good way of life.

1278.   Stockwood, (Canon) Mervyn. *I went to Moscow*. London, Epworth Press, 1955. 198 pp. illus. port.

With the London *Daily Herald* paying his way, Canon Stockwood went to the Soviet Union primarily to interview Alexis, patriarch of the Russian Orthodox church. He tries to communicate with the people in order to understand their relationship to the Soviet system and observes that although the difficulties are great, the West must make an effort to understand the communist way of life.

1279.   Bissonnette, Georges. *Moscow was my parish*. New York, McGraw-Hill, 1956. 272 pp.

Assigned to Moscow to care for the needs of Roman Catholics in the foreign colony, Chaplain Bissonnette describes the obstacles he encountered in dealing with the Soviet bureaucracy in an attempt to carry out his duties. During the two years (1953–55) in European Russia he travelled by automobile from Moscow to the Black Sea and the Caspian, and his comments provide the reader with useful data about Russia just after Stalin's death.

1280.   Boffa, Giuseppe. *Inside the Khrushchev era*. New York, Marzani & Munsell, 1959. 226 pp.

Italian correspondent, in complete sympathy with communism, is in European Russia, 1953–58, and concludes that it is only a question of time before the Russian standard of living rises. He sees economic security as the greatest benefit derived from socialism for the new Soviet man.

1281.   Cartier-Bresson, Henri. *The people of Moscow*. New York, Simon & Schuster, 1955. 163 pp. illus.

In 1954 French photographer and his wife receive permission from the Soviet Union to photograph as they wish, without restrictions of any kind. The result is a magnificent book of pictures in which the text is a friendly commentary on their visit.

1282. Chappelow, Allan. *Russian holiday.* London, Harrap, 1955. 190 pp. illus.

National Union of Students of Great Britain organizes a non-delegation, non-political tour "at £95 per head" in 1954, and the group journeys to Moscow, Stalingrad, the Volga area, Sochi, and Leningrad. This account, by the tour director, is a friendly, but occasionally critical, description of things and people.

1283. Egginton, Joyce. *Excursion to Russia.* London, Hutchinson, 1955. 164 pp. illus. map. index.

British writer travels from Leningrad to the Caucasus in 1954 and returns to record some typical, if critical, observations of the tourist. There are some excellent photographs included with the text.

1284. Lazareff, Helene and Pierre. *The Soviet Union after Stalin.* London, Oldhams Press, 1955. 247 pp. illus. port. index.

Paris Soir correspondent and his Russian-speaking wife, accompanying the Comédie Française to Moscow, extend their journey to Leningrad and the Black Sea in 1954. Their account, which deals with the life of the common people, is reasonably fair and objective.

1285. MacColl, René. *Just back from Russia. 77 days inside the Soviet Union.* London, Beaverbrook Newspaper, Ltd., 1954. 224 pp. illus.

Daily Express correspondent describes conditions away from the tourist sites as "the iceberg you don't see." He sees Moscow just after Stalin's death on his way to Stalingrad and Transcaspia, 1954.

1286. Whyte, Christopher. *A conservative looks at Russia.* London, British Soviet Friendship Society, 1954. 47 pp. illus.

Aircraft electrician for British Overseas Airways Corporation is elected a delegate to the meeting of Soviet trade unions in 1954 and reports on the existence of a class system in the land of a classless society.

1287. Hecht, Rudolph S. *Dancing with the bear. A capitalist's impressions of Soviet Russia.* New Orleans, Publications Press, 1954. 105 pp. illus.

American businessman travels from Leningrad to Transcaspia in May, 1954, spending a great deal of time in shops because he assumes that what is sold in them indicates the standard of living.

1288. Phillips, Morgan. *East meets west, a pictorial story of the Labour Party Delegation to the Soviet Union and China.* London, Lincolns-Prager, 1954. pp. 10–26. illus. port.

August, 1954, journey through the Soviet Union in a party that includes Clement Atlee and Aneurin Bevan. Meetings with Georgi Malenkov and Nikita Khrushchev are described.

1289. Sharma, Satya Dev. *In the shadow of the Kremlin.* Delhi, Siddhartha, 1957. 91 pp. port.

East Indian student teacher with twenty-six delegates to the Soviet Union's World Federation of Democratic Youth travels to Leningrad, Moscow, Kiev, Stalingrad, Armenia, and Georgia, September–October, 1954. Special attention is given to Soviet educational procedures in his account, which also describes experiences in Moscow in detail.

1290. Sergeant, Patrick. *Another road to Samarkand. Leningrad-Moscow-Kharkhov-Kiev-Yalta-Tiflis-Barnaul-Siberia-Tashkent-Samarkand.* London, Hodder & Stoughton, 1955. 157 pp. illus.

Correspondent of the London *Daily Mail,* who does not speak Russian, journeys through European Russia to Transcaspia, September–November, 1954, talking to the people (through an interpreter) and noting their way of life.

1291. Higgins, Marguerite. *Red plush and black bread.* Garden City, New York, Doubleday, 1955. 256 pp. illus. map.

New York *Herald Tribune* correspondent journeys 14,000 miles by air, train, and automobile from Leningrad to Kiev, Yalta, Novosibirsk, and Alma Ata in 1955. Russian-speaking, she talks to everyone and concludes that "George Orwell was wrong," that in refusing to recognize that men work best for their own private interests, the Communist party has failed to alter human nature in any significant way.

1292. Levine, Irving R. *Main street, U.S.S.R.* New York, Doubleday, 1959. 408 pp. illus. port. index.

Russian-speaking American correspondent in Moscow, 1948–59, makes a 10,000–mile journey in 1955 with the American Agricultural Delegation and comments on every aspect of Russian life—chiefly, however, from the Moscow point of view. Some of the more interesting and informative sections of the book are: "Agitator's Notebook"; "Boy loves girl loves tractor"; "Ne Kulturny"; and "Why was the anti-religious museum liquidated?"

1293. MacGregor-Hastie, Roy. *Don't send me to Omsk! A sort of travel book.* London, MacDonald, 1961. 240 pp. illus.

British correspondent in Moscow in 1955 uses his knowledge of the language to record some very flippant criticisms of Soviet pretensions, excellently illuminated by photographs.

1294. Miller, Maurice Solomon. *Window on Russia. A doctor in the U.S.S.R.* London, Lawrence & Wishart, 1956. 102 pp. illus.

Journey from Leningrad to Tashkent by British medical doctor in company with a tour group, 1955. Special treatment by the Soviet Union does not prevent Miller from making a number of critical observations about medical practices.

1295. Sinha, Satyanarayan. *Flight to Soviets.* Bombay, Bharatiya Vidya Bhavan, 1956. pp. 33–118. illus.

Member of the Indian Parliament visits Moscow, European Russia, and Transcaspia, and comments on the friendly treatment he receives "living as Russian."

1296. Zelliott, Eleanor, editor. *Meeting the Russians. American Quakers visit the Soviet Union.* Philadelphia, American Friends Service Committee, 1956. 94 pp. illus. map. port.

Edited comments of six Quakers on a thirty-day journey in 1955 to many cities of European Russia and to Tashkent, Alma Ata, and Akmolinsk. Friendly but critical impressions are expressed by each member of the group, whose primary purpose was to report on the state of religion in the Soviet Union where antireligious practices were employed. Included is the account of an additional thirty-day stay in the Soviet Union by William Edgerton to do research on Nikolai Leskov. Russian-speaking, he has a very busy month attending receptions and dinners given for him by Soviet writers and their friends (pp. 80–88).

1297. Hearst, William Randolph, Jr. *Report on Russia . . . uncensored.* New York, Hearst Corporation, 1955. 48 pp. illus. port.

In February, 1955, Hearst, American editor and owner of a large newspaper chain, arrived in Moscow as Georgi Malenkov was being demoted and proceeded to interview many prominent figures, including Nikita Khrushchev and the daughter of Joseph Stalin. He comments on the Soviet system and its relationship to the people and the Communist party, pointing out that the people support the principles behind the system but feel free to criticize its administration. See no. 1298.

1298. Hearst, William Randolph, Jr., Frank Conniff, and Bob Considine. *Ask me anything. Our adventures with Khrushchev.* New York, McGraw-Hill, 1960. pp. 19–59, 106–56, 187–231.

Hearst (see no. 1297) and two of his fellow reporters visit Moscow in 1955, 1957, and 1959, in time to witness the downfall of Malenkov (1955), to interview Khrushchev upon the occasion of the fortieth anniversary of the 1917 Revolution, and to witness and report the confrontation of United States Vice-President Richard Nixon and Prime Minister Khrushchev. Hearst comments here on whatever interests him, and the whole spectrum of Soviet life appears to be in that category. For the Nixon version, see no. 1369.

1299. Douglas, William O. *Russian journey*. New York, Doubleday, 1956. 244 pp. illus. map. port. index.

United States Supreme Court justice comments as objectively as an American liberal can in reporting on his journey from Leningrad to Novosibirsk and Sverdlovsk during the summer of 1955. He places special emphasis on liberty in the Soviet Union, the administration of the law, and the system of Soviet courts, all well illustrated by excellent photographs.

1300. Crankshaw, Edward. *Russia without Stalin: the emerging pattern*. New York, Viking, 1956. 219 pp. illus. app. index.

Russian-speaking British journalist whose specialty is Soviet affairs and who is considered to be an authority on the Kremlin reports on his September, 1955, journey. He comments on many topics, including the use of influence to achieve purposes within a restrictive state, the presence of freedom within limits set by the Communist party, the literary "Thaw," the new generation of young people—all excellently described and illustrated with cartoons and moral lessons from the press included in the appendix.

1301. Benton, William. *This is the challenge. The Benton reports of 1956–1958 on the nature of the Soviet threat*. New York, Associated College Presses, 1958. 254 pp. port. app.

Former United States senator from Connecticut and publisher of *Encyclopedia Brittanica,* accompanied by his wife, thirteen-year-old son, and by Robert Tucker, specialist on the Soviet Union, journeys to Moscow in November, 1955, to explore the communist challenge to American education. He observes that the Communist party views education as a training ground for state service and that religion, art, the press, and culture in general, along with education, are all parts of communist-directed propaganda.

1302.   Capote, Truman. *The muses are heard*. New York, Random
         House, 1956. 182 pp.

In December, 1955, American novelist accompanies a Negro musical comedy troupe to Leningrad. He reports on the Russian reactions to the Negro players and their response, as well as his own experiences in the northern city.

1303.   Davidson-Houston, James Vivian. *Armed diplomat. A mili-
         tary attaché in Russia*. London, Hale, 1959. 186 pp. illus.
         map. port. index.

The author describes a two-year tour of duty (1955-57) with his wife during which they journey from Leningrad eastward through Siberia. He is inclined to be critical of conditions he observes, especially in the area of sports where he has much to say.

1304.   Cohen, David. *A socialist summer*. New Delhi, Peoples'
         Publishing House, 1956. pp. 39–49.

Correspondent for the *New Age* spends six days in Moscow and Tashkent attending meetings of the International Union of Journalists, 1956. He is definitely pro-communist in his sympathies, although critical of some aspects.

1305.   Evans, Joseph E. *Through Soviet windows*. New York,
         Dow Jones, 1957. 125 pp. map.

Associate editor of the *Wall Street Journal* visits Moscow and its surroundings in 1956 and returns with penetrating comments on farming, factories, shops, businesses, and what he terms "the perils of planning." He includes a chapter of humorously critical remarks on Intourist under the title "The compleat tourist."

1306.   Gunther, John. *Inside Russia today*. New York, Harper,
         1957. 550 pp. map. app. biblio. index.

Foreign correspondent with an international reputation for examining and then reporting on the institutional life of entire nations and continents spends two months in Russia in 1956 on a journey to Leningrad, Moscow, Kiev, and other cities, as well as to western Siberia. His account is a judicious combination of data gleaned from histories and encyclopedias along with his own experiences in interviewing significant figures and in observing the people.

1307. Metaxas, Alexander. *Russia against the Kremlin*. Cleveland, World Publishing Co., 1957. 181 pp. index.

French Russian-speaking free-lance journalist in Leningrad and Moscow in 1956 probes beneath the surface dressed for the part in an old raincoat, unshaven, and without a tie. He observes that the term "Russian" can now be applied to all people in the Soviet Union and that these same people are now anxious to shed the threadbare "soviet communism."

1308. Minney, Rubeigh James. *Next stop—Peking. Record of a 16,000 mile journey through Russia, Siberia and China.* London, George Newnes, 1957. pp. 1–27, 175–92. illus. map.

British writer attends the Bernard Shaw Centenary celebration in China, 1956, and writes a series of comments on Soviet experiences resulting from stops in stations while traveling on the Trans-Siberian Railway.

1309. Ward, Yvette. *American women behind the Iron Curtain.* Hudson, Wisconsin, Star-Observer, 1959. pp. 5–36. illus. port.

Publisher of the *Star-Observer,* on tour with newspaperwomen in 1956, contrasts the lot of Soviet and American women by observing that the latter are treated like "queens of the earth."

1310. Fischer, Louis. *Russia revisited. A new look at Russia and her satellites.* New York, Doubleday, 1957. pp. 9–122. index.

Return journey (see nos. 960 and 991) is made in the summer of 1956 to see old friends and how they have fared and to visit places and people. His account is rich in comment based on "frank, revealing conversations" with all levels of Soviet citizens.

1311. Allyn, S. C. *U.S.S.R.—1956. Behind that curtain. A report on Russia today.* Dayton, Ohio, National Cash Register Co., 1956. 62 pp. illus. map. port.

President of the National Cash Register Company is guest of the Soviet Ministry of Foreign Trade during June–July, 1956, as he and his three companions journey from Leningrad to the Black Sea and from Odessa to Tashkent and Samarkand. His report, with excellent photographs, emphasizes business practices and other areas of life such as religion and culture.

1312. Field, Mark G. *Doctor and patient in Soviet Russia.* Cambridge, Massachusetts, Harvard University Press, 1957. pp. 45–224. app. index.

American medical doctor, member of a medical tour for nine days and subsequently on his own for three weeks in Moscow, September, 1956, deplores the low status of doctors and the poor services available to their patients.

1313. Staf, Karl. *Yakutia as I saw it.* Moscow, Foreign Languages Publishing House, 1958. 114 pp. illus.

German correspondent on Moscow *Ny Day* gives unqualified endorsement to communist activity in Siberia, September, 1956, observing that "Siberia today is the promised land . . . A new America in the East? No, the comparison is ridiculous. No capitalist country can tackle the problems which today face Siberia."

1314. Kalb, Marvin L. *Eastern exposure.* New York, Farrar, Straus & Cudahy, 1958. 332 pp.

Russian-speaking press attaché in the American embassy in Moscow from January, 1956, to February, 1957, arrives at certain conclusions: (1) the Russian people really desire peace; (2) the Soviet system has grave faults but it works; (3) communist ideology is increasingly viewed with skepticism by the Russian youth; and (4) the entire country and its institutions are in transition from the old manners and customs and ways of doing things to the new.

1315. Norton, Howard. *Only in Russia*. Princeton, Van Nostrand, 1961. 236 pp. index.

Baltimore Sun correspondent stationed in Moscow with his wife and four children, January, 1956–June, 1959, makes a number of journeys throughout European Russia and into Soviet Asia. In this account he comments on every aspect of life from birth to death, furs to funerals, working conditions and wage scales, plus an account of sports, science, toys, and even "the maid problem."

1316. Cusack, Ellen Dymphna. *Holidays among the Russians*. London, Heinemann, 1964. 281 pp.

British writer with a working knowledge of Russian visits the Soviet Union five times 1956–61. Here she describes in detail her latest journey from Leningrad through Moscow to the Caspian Sea, with beautifully written comments on artists and the cultural life.

1317. Bach, Marcus. *God and the Soviets*. New York, Crowell, 1961. 214 pp.

American sociologist and anthropologist, a specialist in researching religious groups, visits Leningrad and Moscow in 1957. After various observations and interviews, he concludes that (1) religion has not been destroyed by the Soviet Union, and a new generation is rebuilding religious faith, and (2) communism as a way of life is here to stay and must be understood and lived with.

1318. Bell, Robert. *By road to Moscow and Yalta*. London, Alvin Redman, 1959. 292 pp. illus. map. index.

Professional British traveler reports on his journey in 1957 by automobile and provides useful and informative advice for the future sojourner.

1319. Godley, John (Lord Kilbracken). *Moscow gatecrash. A peer behind the curtain*. Boston, Houghton Mifflin, 1959. 240 pp.

Irish country squire and part-time reporter for the London *Daily Express* is assigned to cover the fortieth anniversary of the 1917 Revolution in 1957 and manages to interview Khrushchev and Boris Pasternak. His report is casual, entertaining, and urbane— so much so that the reader wonders where the line between fact and fiction is located.

1320.   Schakovskoy, Zinaida. *The privilege was mine. A Russian princess returns to the Soviet Union.* Translated from the French by Peter Wiles. New York, Putnam, 1959. 318 pp.

Born in 1907 to an ancient noble family descending from Rurik, the writer was taken out of Russia in 1917. She returns as the wife of a Western European diplomat in 1957 and discovers the Soviet Union to be a dictatorship over the proletariat, and a very cruel one. She reports an especially dramatic meeting with Ivan A. Serov, chairman of the Committee of State Security (the secret police).

1321.   Taylor, Kathleen. *Going to Russia? A popular guide for tourists.* London, Lawrence & Wishart, 1958. 186 pp. illus. map.

British tourist in Leningrad, Moscow, and the Black Sea area in 1957 prepares a useful and informative guide for future travelers to the Soviet Union.

1322.   * United States Public Health Mission. *Report of the U.S. Public Health Mission to the U.S.S.R.* Washington, Department of Health, Education, and Welfare, 1959.

1323.   Dunsheath, Joyce. *Guest of the Soviets. Moscow and the Caucasus, 1957.* London, Constable, 1959. 180 pp. illus. map. port.

British sportswoman and mountain climber is guest of the All-Union Sports Committee of the Soviet Union in the summer of 1957. She is invited to climb Mt. Elbrus in the Caucasus and is the first British woman to do so. Her account is polite and friendly, but she expresses the usual criticisms about there being no telephone directories and no plugs in the wash sinks.

1324. Jupp, G. Alex. *A Canadian looks at the U.S.S.R. A firsthand view of Russian life during the World Youth Festival.* New York, Exposition Press, 1958. 58 pp.

Interesting report of events in Moscow during the summer of 1957 with some observations on the way of life as he sees it during long walks about the city.

1325. Alt, Herschel and Edith. *Russia's children.* New York, Bookman Associates, 1959. 237 pp. index.

American social workers, specialists in the study of the care of children, journey to Leningrad, Moscow, and Kiev in July–August, 1957. With some knowledge of the language, they are able to get beyond the barrier of the Intourist guides, and they come away disappointed with child-rearing values and methods.

1326. Roosevelt, Eleanor. *On my own. The years since the White House.* New York, Harper, 1958. pp. 229–77. index.

Widow of the President of the United States, Franklin D. Roosevelt, describes her journey to Leningrad, Moscow, Tashkent, Yalta, etc., in September, 1957. Accompanied by her secretary and a Russian-born medical doctor, she visits a state farm, a nursery, the Moscow Baptist Church, a Russian home, and the usual tourist sites. She observes that those who believe in her brand of human freedom could not live in Soviet Russia.

1327. Ellender, (Senator) Allen J. *A review of United States foreign policy and operations.* Washington, Government Printing Office, 1958. pp. 6–84, 228–31, 236–97. app.

United States senator from Louisiana travels to eleven cities in Soviet Russia, September 7–October 9, 1957, on an inspection tour of American aid. He is reasonably objective in his report, which is greatly detailed on the Soviet way of life and which recommends much less emphasis in the United States on the inevitability of war with the communists. Included is the report of Thomas Venables, a member of the United States embassy staff in Moscow who accompanied Senator Ellender on his travels.

1328. Nearing, Scott and Helen. *The brave new world*. Harborside, Maine, Social Science Institute, 1958. pp. 15–89.

Long-time friends of the Soviet Union (see nos. 842 and 848) return to Russia, traveling through Leningrad and Moscow and on to Tashkent, 1957–58. The title of their report is not intended to be cynical, for they appear to have accepted what they saw at face value and without much criticism.

1329. Belfrage, Sally. *A room in Moscow*. New York, Reynal, 1958. 186 pp.

Twenty-one-year-old American attends the Moscow Youth Festival in 1957, gets a job in the Foreign Languages Publishing House and—incredible feat—finds a single room. Her report is a record of life among Russian youth her own age, as well as the frustrations of American correspondents.

1330. Bowers, Faubion. *Broadway, U.S.S.R. Ballet, theater, and entertainment in Russia today*. New York, Thomas Nelson, 1959. 215 pp. illus. index.

Bowers, his wife Santha Rama Rau (see no. 1331), their son, and his Negro nursemaid travel from Moscow through European Russia to the Transcaspia in 1957–58. His account is a beautifully written report on Soviet entertainment, especially the puppet theater and the circus.

1331. Rama Rau, Santha. *My Russian journey*. New York, Harpers, 1959. 300 pp.

East Indian writer and her American theater critic husband (see no. 1330) make a pleasant journey, and she records here a woman's point of view of the Russian way of life.

1332. Novak, Joseph (pseudonym). *The future is ours, Comrade. Conversations with Russians*. Garden City, New York, Doubleday, 1960. 286 pp.

A minor bureaucrat from a satellite country stationed in Leningrad and Moscow, 1957–59, describes the defects of the Soviet system, an account very impressionistic and suggestive rather than factual.

1333. Bigland, Eileen. *Russia has two faces*. London, Oldhams Press, 1960. 240 pp. illus. map. port.

Return visit (see no. 1080) made "with love" in 1958. Her report catalogues material improvement, and she sees happier faces on bodies that are better clothed and better housed.

1334. Clark, Charles Manning Hope. *Meeting Soviet man*. Sidney, Angus & Robertson, 1960. 117 pp.

Member of the Commonwealth Council of Fellowship of Australian Writers journeys to Moscow in 1958 to a meeting of the Union of Soviet Writers, where he sees the system putting the emphasis on the present, and man for the first time the master of his fate. In the Appendix various items of Soviet writing are included.

1335. * Groettrup, Irmgard. *Rocket wife*. London, Deutsch, 1959. 188 pp. illus.

1336. Hindus, Maurice Gerschon. *House without a roof. Russia after forty-three years of revolution*. Garden City, New York, Doubleday, 1961. 550 pp. map. index.

Long-time friend and frequent traveler to the Soviet Union (see nos. 711, 839, 917, 965, 1034, and 1160) returns in 1958 and 1960. In this report he concludes that the revolution is still unfinished and emphasizes peasant life and the general condition of the Christian church.

1337. Kent, Rockwell. *Of men and mountains; being an account of the European travels of the author and his wife, Sally, following their release from continental imprisonment*. Ausable Forks, New York, Asgaard Press, 1959. pp. 21–46.

American commercial artist registers the need for more cultural interchange between the United States and the Soviet Union after journeying from Leningrad through Moscow and Kiev to the Black Sea as a guest of the government in 1958. His report combines personal observations with historical backgrounds.

1338. Lathe, Heinz, and Günter Meierling. *Return to Russia.* Translated from the German by Charlotte Dixon. London, The Galley Press, 1961. 123 pp. illus. map. index.

Two former German soldiers (one Russian-speaking), prisoners of war in Russia until 1949, journey by automobile in 1958 to Moscow and south to the Crimea. They note considerable progress in remedying those conditions that prevailed in 1949.

1339. Maclean, Fitzroy. *Back to Bokhara.* London, Jonathan Cape, 1959. 156 pp. illus. map.

Russian-speaking reporter makes a return visit to Soviet Central Asia (see no. 1114) in 1958. He compares conditions with those in 1937–39, noting the change in the atmosphere with the death of Stalin and the successful orbiting of the first Sputnik. He is especially informative where he deals with the influence of the West on Russian life through the Soviet youth's adoption and adaptation of Western music, clothing, manners, etc.

1340. Mair, George Brown. *Destination Moscow.* London, Herbert Jenkins, 1960. 183 pp. illus. port. index.

British university professor and wife travel to Moscow by way of Smolensk and Minsk in 1958, later recording an account of perseverance in penetrating the Iron Curtain to observe change and progress.

1341. Stevenson, Adlai Ewing. *Friends and enemies. What I learned in Russia.* New York, Harper, 1959. 102 pp. illus.

Governor of Illinois, Democratic nominee for President of the United States in 1952, and formerly foreign correspondent in Russia for the International News Service travels with his son (who knows some Russian) to Leningrad and then east to Central Asia and Siberia in 1958. He comments on the "hasty pudding" character of Moscow and the "midwest" atmosphere of farming in Siberia. He observes that the West must gird itself to meet the remorseless challenge of the Soviet Union.

1342. * Tucker, Robert L. *Impressions of Russia in 1958, a trip report.* Santa Monica, California, Rand Corp., 1958. 195 pp.

1343. Wallace, John A. *Getting to know the U.S.S.R.* New York, Coward-McCann, 1959. 62 pp. illus. index.

A book for children by the American chairman of the Council on Student Travel, who traveled to the Soviet Union in 1958 to arrange for a student exchange program. He provides basic details accompanied by excellent photographs.

1344. American Steel and Iron Ore Delegation. *Steel in the Soviet Union. The report of the American Steel and Iron Ore Delegation's visit to the Soviet Union. May and June 1958.* Edward L. Ryerson, compiler. New York, American Iron and Steel Institute, 1959. 376 pp. map. index.

In the first section of this report Ryerson, chief of the American Steel and Iron Ore delegation, describes the friendly treatment accorded the nineteen American steel executives on their visits to steel and iron centers as far east as Sverdlovsk and Stalinsk. The remainder of the report is an extremely detailed account of every aspect of the iron and steel industries in the Soviet Union, complete with numerous graphs, tables, etc.

1345. Edmonds, Richard. *Russian vistas; the record of a springtime journey to Moscow, Leningrad, Kiev, Stalingrad, the Black Sea and the Caucasus.* London, Phene Press, 1958. 133 pp. illus.

Member of British Town Planning Delegation reports on the cordial treatment he and the delegation received on their journey during May–June, 1958. He is not too enthusiastic about contemporary housing from an architectural standpoint, but most of his comments are complimentary, especially on the apparent improvement in living conditions.

1346. Derthick, Lawrence G. *Soviet commitment to education. Report of first official United States Mission to the U.S.S.R.* Washington, Government Printing Office, 1959. 116 pp. illus. map. port. app.

Commissioner Derthick, in the United States Department of Health, Education, and Welfare, describes a journey of 7,000 miles, May 8–June 6, 1958. He comments on the team's findings in the areas of general, teacher, and technical education in eight Soviet cities: Leningrad, Moscow, Minsk, Kazan, Sverdlovsk, Tashkent, Alma Ata, and Sochi. Russian-speaking members of the group helped to overcome the usual obstacles to accurate communication, and the result is a report of valuable information about current conditions and impending changes.

1347. Ball, William H. *Talmanac goes to Russia.* Chicago, Talman Federal Savings and Loan Association, 1958. 33 pp. illus.

Employee of Talman Federal Savings and Loan Association, Chicago, and editor of *Talmanac News* comments on extensive conversations he had with the Russian people on a journey to Moscow, Kharkov, and Leningrad with a tour group of industrial editors, summer, 1958. After only three months training in the Russian language, he deals with such subjects as: "Who buys communism?", "How to make them intelligent and keep them dumb," and other topics, including some remarks about "bad" Americans on tour.

1348. Daiches, Lionel. *Russians at law.* London, Michael Joseph, 1960. 208 pp. illus. index.

As a guest of the Soviet Union, Daiches journeys from Britain in the summer of 1958 to study Russian law, justice, and administration. He observes that the entire system of dealing with crime and criminals appears to be preventive rather than punitive.

1349. Hunt, (Sir) John and Christopher Brasher. *The red snows. An account of the British Caucasus Expedition 1958.* London, Hutchinson, 1960. pp. 15–154. illus. port. app. index.

Sir John's diary provides the bulk of content from which Brasher writes the account of the expedition, its contacts with the Russian bureaucracy, people, and other climbers before and during climbing in June, July, and August, 1958.

1350. Harnwell, Gaylord P. *Russian diary*. Philadelphia, University of Pennsylvania Press, 1961. 125 pp. illus. map. port.

University of Pennsylvania president tape-records his diary of American college presidents' tour financed by the United States State Department, June 27–July 11, 1958. He comments on the friendly treatment accorded the group as it visits eight cities from Moscow to Samarkand, by air, to study the processes of higher education.

1351. Warp, Harold. *Russia as I saw it*. Chicago, Warp Bros., 1958. 70 pp. map. port.

American businessmen Harold and John Warp journey from Leningrad to Kharkov in July, 1958. Harold Warp's comments show his sympathy for the people but his criticism of the system, which he believes to be extremely backward but capable of power in the immediate future.

1352. Ethridge, Willie Snow. *Russian duet, the story of a journey*. New York, Simon & Schuster, 1959. 313 pp.

Wife of the publisher of the *Louisville Courier Journal and Times* visits the Soviet Union with her Russian-speaking friend Nila Magidoff, July 17–September 6, 1958. Her comments cover all aspects of Russian life in a friendly and humorous fashion and are especially interesting and informative because her companion came into intimate contact with the people, who quickly learned of her Russian birth and American home.

1353. Lippmann, Walter. *The Communist world and ours*. Boston, Little, Brown, 1959. pp. 3–56.

Lippmann, political analyst from the United States, interviews Nikita Khrushchev in October, 1958, and observes: "Theirs is a grim and purposeful society in which one who is used to the American air finds it hard to breathe." He also registers the power that he believes is potential in Russia's future.

1354. Mosby, Aline. *The view from No. 13 People's Street.* New York, Random House, 1962. 308 pp.

An interesting and informative account of correspondent's tour of duty at United Press International Moscow office, 13 Narodnaya Ulista, 1958–61. Very breezy but balanced, her attitude is that Russians are people, and her comments are chiefly about how they live, work, and play.

1355. Brown, John. *Russia explored.* London, Hodder & Stoughton, 1959. 222 pp.

Another visit (see nos. 1043 and 1081) by British socialist who thoroughly dislikes Russian communism. Here he describes his journey from Leningrad to Samarkand, financed by his dealing in the black market in 1959. He observes: "In planning, error equals mass multiplied by the speed of the slowest."

1356. Harriman, William Averell. *Peace with Russia?* New York, Simon & Schuster, 1959. 174 pp.

American statesman who first visited Siberia in 1899 with his father, arranged a manganese contract with the Soviet Union in 1926, negotiated for war aid to Stalin's Russia in 1941, and was ambassador in Moscow, 1943–46, revisits European Russia and Siberia in 1959. He suggests that a ruined world awaits the failure of the United States and the Soviet Union to live in peace.

1357. Hodges, Luther H. *A Governor sees the Soviet.* Raleigh, North Carolina, privately printed, 1959. 100 pp. illus.

Governor of North Carolina admits to being impressed by Soviet power on a governors' tour to Moscow in 1959 and concludes that Russians and Americans must get along together.

1358. Levine, Irving R. *Travel guide to Russia.* Garden City, New York, Doubleday, 1960. 400 pp. index.

Russian-speaking Moscow correspondent (see no. 1292) provides advice for travelers to Russia, implying that it is now perfectly safe although not the ideal place for having fun. He suggests that the Intourist route from Leningrad to Samarkand will enable the sojourner to taste, literally and figuratively, a variety of experiences with people and things.

1359. Newman, Bernard. *Visa to Russia.* London, Herbert Jenkins, 1959. pp 42–231. illus. map.

Travel writer journeys alone to the Soviet Union in 1959, where he compares improved conditions over an earlier experience (see no. 1109). He illuminates his observations on Leningrad, Moscow, and Minsk with excellent photographs.

1360. Rickover, (Vice Admiral) Hyman George. *Report on Russia.* Washington, Government Printing Office, 1959. 82 pp. index.

After a journey to Leningrad and Moscow in 1959, Admiral Rickover, outspoken critic of United States college and university education, describes education in the Soviet Union as superior because it meets the needs of a science-oriented world by producing great numbers of engineers.

1361. Salisbury, Harrison Evans. *To Moscow—and beyond. A reporter's narrative.* New York, Harper, 1959. 291 pp. illus. map. port. index.

New York Times correspondent (see nos. 1185, 1250, and 1251) makes 30,000-mile journey from Moscow to Irkutsk in 1959 to refresh his knowledge and understanding of the Soviet Union. He returns to describe the first stirrings of the "beat generation" and the great changes in socialist realism in the arts. He views the reappearance of prostitutes as a sign of the decay of communism.

1362. Hughes, Emrys. *Pilgrims' progress in Russia.* London, Housemans', 1959. 167 pp. illus.

Socialist Member of Parliament and critic of Harold Macmillan lampoons the Prime Minister's travels to Moscow, February 21–

March 3, 1959. Having been in the Soviet Union in 1929, Russian-speaking Hughes comments on the apparent changes in Moscow, as well as in Leningrad and Kiev. He turns out what is really an anti-Tory political pamphlet, illustrated by excellent cartoons and photographs.

1363. Hope, Bob. *I owe Russia $1200*. Garden City, New York, Doubleday, 1963. pp. 215–56. illus. port.

In March, 1959, the American movie, radio, and television actor-comedian visits Moscow to prepare a television show for viewing in the United States. Hope makes the usual remarks of the tourist, but does have some interesting data about his dealings with the Soviet bureaucracy.

1364. Hallinan, Vivian and Vincent. *A clash of cultures. Some contrast in American and Soviet morals and manners*. San Francisco, American-Russian Institute, 1960. 72 pp.

American lawyer and his wife visit Moscow in April, 1959, and return to comment in friendly fashion on their experiences. Their report doesn't measure up to the promise of its title.

1365. James, Frank Cyril. *On understanding Russia*. Toronto, University of Toronto Press, 1959. 63 pp.

Principal of McGill University, on a Ford Foundation–financed tour, April 13–May 11, 1959, provides useful and informative comments on university studies, Soviet culture, and the state of religion in Leningrad and other cities as far east as Irkutsk. The group had its own interpreter.

1366. Wurmser, André. *The U.S.S.R.—with an open heart*. Translated from the French by Victor M. Schneierson. Moscow Foreign Languages Publishing House, 1960. 74 pp. illus.

Pro-communist French writer and his wife visit Leningrad, Moscow, and Kiev in May–June, 1959. His comments are all complimentary and non-critical as he describes improved conditions over an earlier time when he had been in the Soviet Union.

1367. Henderson, Larry Wills. *A journey to Samarkand.* Toronto Longmans, 1962. 153 pp. illus. index.

Canadian journalist journeys through European Russia to Georgia and Transcaspia in the summer of 1959. His comments are friendly about the people and their way of life, and he illuminates his report with excellent photographs.

1368. Kalb, Marvin L. *Dragon in the Kremlin. A report on the Russian-Chinese alliance.* New York, Dutton, 1961. pp. 89–113.

Kalb (see no. 1314) provides information about the success of the American Exhibition in Moscow in July, 1959, along with informative comments on the emerging fear in the Soviet Union of the mid-twentieth century "Yellow Peril."

1369. Nixon, Richard Milhous. *Six crises.* Garden City, New York, Doubleday, 1962. pp. 253–314, 472–80. port. app.

The Vice-President of the United States describes his journey to open the American Exhibition in Moscow in July, 1959, and his verbal interchange with Prime Minister Nikita Khrushchev over a comparison of the ways of life of the two nations.

1370. Shepard, Elaine. *Forgive us our press passes.* Englewood Cliffs, New Jersey, Prentice-Hall, 1962. pp. 39–68. illus. port.

American actress who became an international correspondent comments on her experiences in Moscow, July, 1959, during the showing of the American Exhibition. Her comments are commonplace and often appear to be made with her best profile to the camera.

1371. Baty, Eben Neal. *Citizen abroad. An American finds out about his country's decade of decline while going around the world by freighter and car.* New York, Viking, 1960. pp. 226–62.

Retired businessman-banker and his wife visit Leningrad for three days in August, 1959. His comments are chiefly concerned with

Alec, the Intourist guide, whom he tried to convert to capitalism, and with his assessment of "Russia—its debits and credits."

1372. Price, Morgan Philips. *Russia forty years on. An account of a visit to Russia and Germany in the autumn of 1959.* London, Allen & Unwin, 1961. pp. 20–88, 110–22. illus. port. app. index.

Author and his wife return (see nos. 609, 699, and 1216) to the Soviet Union on board the "Baltika," journeying from Leningrad south through the Ukraine and reminiscing on their earlier visits by combining historical background with their own past and present. Price includes an appendix of quotations by prominent westerners about Russia and by Russians about themselves and their role in Europe.

1373. Werth, Alexander. *Russia under Khrushchev.* New York, Fawcett World Library, 1962. 342 pp. index.

British journalist (see nos. 1144 and 1184) returns to the Soviet Union in the autumn of 1959. His report is a careful dissection of the way of life based on intimate conversations with citizens in all walks of life, including data on music, literature, the Jews, and the observation that Russians view all Germans as dangerous and believe them to be preparing for World War III.

1374. Bourdeaux, Michael. *Opium of the people. The Christian religion in the U.S.S.R.* London, Faber & Faber, 1965. 233 pp. illus. map. app. index.

Russian-speaking British Council exchange student attends Moscow University, 1959–60. He provides an excellent combination of personal experience and historical background in describing university life, the students, and people, whom he indicates as ranging from mocking atheists to secret converts to Christianity.

1375. Ronchey, Alberto. *Russia in the thaw.* Translated from the Italian by Raymond Rosenthal. New York, Norton, 1963. 239 pp. illus. port.

Italian Russian-speaking correspondent of *La Stampa* points up the sharp contradictions within the Soviet Union on his tour of duty in Moscow, 1959–61. His comments include observations on every aspect of activity open to public inspection; they include also some exasperated comments on the omnipresence of security police. During his stay Ronchey travels across Siberia and takes a trip down the Volga River, both of which deepen his awareness of the dichotomy of freedom and restraint that persists.

1376. Atkinson, Alex, and Ronald Searle. *By rocking chair across Russia*. New York, Grosset & Dunlap, 1961. 91 pp. illus. index.

British humorist Atkinson and cartoonist Searle take an imaginary journey across the Soviet Union and, never having been there in their lives, are free to show us the real Russia, the Russia few tourists will ever see. This lampoon of a typical tourist's journal uses contemporary sources of real journeys as did the account of John Milton (see no. 17).

1377. Byford-Jones, W. *Uncensored witness*. London, Hale, 1961. 180 pp. illus. map. port. app. index.

British correspondent in Moscow to cover Gary Powers' trial in 1960, combines the assignment with a journey down the Volga River. His commentary on the treatment of the American pilot of the shot-down U-2 reconnaissance plane is objectively done, as are his remarks on life as he saw it along the Volga.

1378. Carlisle, Olga Andreyev. *Voices in the snow: encounters with Russian writers*. New York, Random House, 1962. 224 pp.

Granddaughter of Leonid Andreyev, reared in Paris and married to an American painter, is assigned to interview Boris Pasternak in 1960 for the *Paris Review*. Her report is friendly to the Soviet Union, reflecting the high regard accorded her as a relative of Andreyev. From her comments it would appear that she accepts what she hears without asking embarassing questions.

1379. Conner, William N. *Cassandra looks at the face of Russia.*
       London, Daily Mirror, 1960. 28 pp. illus.

British columnist journeys to the Black Sea area in 1960 and returns to comment critically on his contacts and experiences, illustrating his report with useful photographs.

1380. Jacquet, Elaine. *High heels in Red Square.* New York,
       Holt, Rinehart & Winston, 1961. 209 pp.

French student studies the Russian language in Moscow in 1960.
Although vague in many areas of Russian life, her report is useful
simply because it apparently records only what she saw and
experienced. She outlines her year as she describes dormitory life,
her fellow students, art and architecture, and the difficult business
of providing herself with the daily necessities of living.

1381. Neugebauer, Katherine. *Russia as I saw it. The journal of
       a tour in 1960.* New York, Exposition Press, n.d. 82 pp.

American tourist of Russian ancestry visits European Russia
(Leningrad, Moscow, Kiev, Yalta, Simerpol) with her Russian-
speaking husband. Her remarks are commonplace about people
and places, although she does have the unusual opportunity of
visiting with Russian relatives.

1382. Sejersted, Francis. *Moscow diary.* London, Ampersand,
       1961. 129 pp. illus. port.

Twenty-five-year-old member of the Norwegian Conservative
party studies the Russian language at the University of Moscow
during January–July, 1960. Although brief, his commentary on
university life is rich in detail and anecdote, and is an outstanding
panorama of student life, Russian and foreign, sympathetically
presented.

1383. DeLong, Russell V. *What we can do about Communism.*
       New York, Avon Book Div., Hearst Corp., 1963. pp. 7–66.

Anticommunist crusader, president of Pasadena College (California), journeys through eight cities of the Soviet Union in the

summer of 1960. He approves little of what he sees and condemns much. As he crosses the border into Finland, he mentions seeing a stand where one could buy "a good old American hamburger and hotdog and a Coke and 7-up. You could feel the freedom—almost smell it."

1384. Hingley, Ronald. *Under Soviet skins. An untourist's report*. London, Hamish Hamilton, 1961. 224 pp. illus.

Oxford lecturer in Russian journeys through European Russia during the summer of 1960 recording the Soviet way of life for the London *Sunday Times*. Avoiding the tourist spots, he describes outdoor Russia, getting and spending, housing, family life, religion, education, etc. A friendly reaction to a "going concern."

1385. Fischer, Bertha Markoosha. *Reunion in Moscow. A Russian revisits her country*. New York, Harper & Row, 1962. 240 pp.

In June, 1960, Mrs. Fischer returns to the Soviet Union (see no. 796), where she visits old friends rehabilitated from Stalinist labor camps and witnesses what she describes as a decline in idealism. She observes: ". . . mostly I saw ordinary people busy with everyday living. The book is about them." Her account is beautifully written and filled with useful and informative comment.

1386. U.S. Petroleum Industry Exchange Delegation. *U.S. oil men take a look at Russia*. Los Angeles, American Petroleum Institute, 1960. 34 pp. illus. map.

Ten oil industry executives journey chiefly by air from Leningrad to Baku through Moscow and Stalingrad, August 2–31, 1960. In addition to a description of their treatment by their Russian counterparts, their account includes useful charts and tables of Soviet petroleum statistics.

1387. Houghton, Norris. *Return engagement. A postscript to Moscow rehearsals*. New York, Holt, 1962. 205 pp. illus. index.

Return to Moscow (see no. 1062) in the autumn of 1960 enables theater critic to record the emergence of the "star system" and the continuing conflict between the old guard and those who would revive the Meyerhold tradition.

1388. Belli, Melvin M., and Danny R. Jones. *Belli looks at life and law in Russia.* Indianapolis, Bobbs-Merrill, 1963. 364 pp. illus. map. port. index.

California trial lawyer describes his and his partner's experiences during their travels from Moscow to Transcaspia and Siberia with their wives in early 1961. Belli claims he had complete freedom to attend trials in Russia, and much of his book is a comparison of law practices in the United States and the Soviet Union. He adds additional comments on education, sex, the theater, the price of food in non-Intourist restaurants, etc.

1389. * Ispahani, Mirza Abol Hassan. *Leningrad to Samarkand.* Karachi, Forward Publications Trust, 1962. 151 pp. illus.

1390. * Chapman, J. Vincent. *Education in the Soviet Union: report of a College of Perceptors Delegation, May, 1961.* London, College of Perceptors, 1962.

1391. Miller, Jessie L. and James G. *Behavioral scientists visit the Soviet Union. A report of a trip.* Ann Arbor, Michigan, University of Michigan, 1962. 36 pp. illus. map.

American psychologist and his wife report on the experiences of an exchange delegation to European Russia and Transcaspia, May, 1961, in which they provide excellent notes on the Soviet attitude toward the behavioral sciences and the paramount influence of Pavlov and relative unimportance of Freud.

1392. Ruggles, Melville J., and Raynard C. Swank. *Soviet libraries and librarianship: report of the visit of the delegation of U.S. Librarians to the Soviet Union, May–June, 1961, under the U.S.–Soviet Cultural Exchange Agree-*

ment. Chicago, American Library Association, 1962. 121 pp. biblio.

The authors comment briefly on travel conditions and the treatment the delegation received, but the bulk of their report is on the organization and operation of Soviet libraries. Very useful and informative, with tables and statistics supplied.

1393. Jones, Mervyn. *The antagonists*. New York, Clarkson N. Potter, 1962. 328 pp.

British novelist, theater critic, and traveler, the son of Freud's most noted biographer, journeys with Russian-speaking Canadian companion to the United States and the Soviet Union in the summer of 1961. He sets out to compare the two countries much as the American Curtis Guild did (see no. 364) in comparing Russia with Great Britain after a journey to both in 1886. Extraordinarily well written, Jones's account examines almost every aspect of Soviet life, with special emphasis on the standard of living, which he considers to be "the central battleground of the antagonists."

1394. Westbrook, Robert. *Journey behind the Iron Curtain*. New York, Putnam, 1963. pp. 48–148. illus. index.

Fifteen-year-old American boy journeys with nine other teen-agers to Moscow, Leningrad, and Kiev in the summer of 1961, where they associate with Russian teen-agers in town and in a Soviet youth camp near Kiev. He has a basic knowledge of Russian, and his account is fresh and interesting, although somewhat flamboyant—not a disadvantage when dealing with some of the images Americans have of Russians and vice versa.

1395. Davidson-Houston, James Vivian. *Russia with your eyes open. A background book*. Chester Springs, Pennsylvania, Dufour Editions, 1962. 122 pp. app.

Traveler returns to Russia in June, 1961 (see no. 1303). He prepares this short and well-written handbook, full of details about hotels, transportation, and prices.

1396. Hartsough, David. *Discovering another Russia. The journal of a camping trip*. Philadelphia, American Friends Service Committee, 1962. pp. 3–31.

Howard University student and four friends journey to Moscow, Kharkov, Kiev, and Lvov, August 5–September 3, 1961, in a Volkswagen. He provides a good deal of interesting and useful information for future travelers by automobile who wish to camp along the way, but the promise of his title is not altogether fulfilled.

1397. Salisbury, Harrison Evans. *A new Russia?* New York, Harper & Row, 1962. 137 pp. index.

American correspondent returns to the Soviet Union in the autumn of 1961 (see nos. 1185, 1250, 1251, 1361), where he observes the decline of Chinese influence, the rise of political anti-Semitism, and the attacks on "Stalinist bullyboys."

1398. Paar, Jack. *3 on a toothbrush. Adventures and encounters around the globe*. Garden City, N.Y., Doubleday, Doran, 1965. pp. 1–25, illus. port.

American television interviewer of celebrities and commentator on the United States entertainment world is in Moscow in September, 1961, where he visits Lenin's suite in the Kremlin and engages in other tourist activities. These brief comments are not outstanding.

1399. Slesser, Malcolm. *Red peak. A personal account of the British-Soviet Pamir Expedition*. New York, Coward-McCann, 1964. pp. 40–250. illus. map. port. app. index.

British mountain climber and lecturer provides details on the joint climbing in the Pamirs, November, 1961–August, 1962. He is especially informative on mountain village life and includes an Appendix that contains a contract between the British and the Soviet Union in which respective rights and responsibilities are carefully outlined.

1400. Beauvoir, Simone de. *Force of circumstances*. Translated from the French by Richard Howard. New York, Putnam, 1965. pp. 625–639.

French novelist, sympathetic to the Soviet Union, describes the bettered conditions of artists and writers on a journey to Moscow, Rostov, Kiev, and Leningrad in 1962. She says that architects fare better under Khrushchev because he likes simplicity in buildings, and the "style of ugly ostentation so dear to Stalin is now a thing of the past. . . . She further observes that "one senses in the people, especially among the youth, a passionate desire to know and to understand. . . ."

1401. Eskelund, Karl. *Black caviar and red optimism. Travels in Russia.* London, Alvin Redman, 1962. 169 pp. illus. map. index.

British professional traveler (in seventy countries) discovers the impossibility of getting away from Intourist guides, even when accompanied by a Russian-speaking friend in 1962. He observes conditions in Leningrad and Moscow and then describes his journey southeast to Bukhara. In a section entitled "The old order changeth not" he compares the Soviet Union in the 1960's with Custine's (see no. 215) Russia of 1839.

1402. Feifer, George. *Justice in Moscow.* New York, Simon & Schuster, 1964. 346 pp. app.

Russian-speaking student of criminal law from the United States attends the University of Moscow in 1962 and returns to present an excellent and informative account of his impressions from having been present at actual trials in the peoples' courts. He also provides a considerable amount of data on living conditions and the way people entertain themselves along with his comparisons of law practice in the Soviet Union and the United States.

1403. Mace, David Robert and Vera. *The Soviet family.* Garden City, New York, Doubleday, 1963. 397 pp. biblio. index.

Two British sociologists, their family, and friends journey 3,500 miles through European Russia by Volkswagen, to Leningrad, Moscow, Kharkov, Kiev, and Lvov, to study family institutions in co-operation with the Soviet Women's Committee in 1962. The first chapter in their account describes their travel experiences in the auto camps where they met and associated with the people. The remainder is a mine of information about family relationships.

1404. McKnight, Felix R. *The Russia I saw*. Dallas, Southwest Review, 1962. 129 pp. map. port. app.

Executive editor of *Dallas Times Herald* visits Leningrad, Moscow, and the east (to Tashkent) for twenty-three days in 1962. He is extremely critical of the Soviet way of life although impressed with the presence and dynamism of Khrushchev, whom he interviewed.

1405. * Miller, Paul. *Russia: 1962*. Rochester, New York, privately printed, 1962. 63 pp. illus.

1406. Drane, (Father) James F. *Pilgrimage to Utopia*. Milwaukee, Bruce, 1965. 155 pp. illus.

During the summer of 1962 American priest studying in Europe joins an undesignated communist group and tours European Russia, practically at Communist party expense. He comments on the homes, churches, stores, schools, factories, and farms, about which he learned by speaking German. He claims to detect religious feelings in old and young, and ends his report with "Prophetic zeal of the Utopian religion," in which he sees communism as a religion.

1407. Royster, Vermont. *Journey through the Soviet Union*. New York, Dow Jones, 1962. pp. 1–89.

Editor of *Wall Street Journal* tries to be fair in relating his journey from Leningrad to Tashkent in the summer of 1962. He comments on many of the aspects related to his profession as well as making observations on the life of the people—data gathered through an American interpreter traveling with the group. He feels that his interview with Prime Minister Khrushchev is novel but does not add anything that will enable him to resolve the paradoxes he encounters on every side.

1408. Corsini, Ray Pierre. *Caviar for breakfast. An American woman's adventures in Russia*. Indianapolis, Bobbs-Merrill, 1965. 288 pp.

Free-lance writer and correspondent, whose Russian parents had fled to the United States after October, 1917, and banned all things Russian from their home including the language, describes her visit to Leningrad and Moscow in September, 1962. She emphasizes her encounters with writers and their writing, other aspects of culture, and the equality of women.

1409. Reeve, Franklin D. *Robert Frost in Russia.* Boston, Little, Brown, 1963. pp. 19–130. illus. port.

Wesleyan University professor of Russian and poet accompanies eighty-eight-year-old Robert Frost to the Soviet Union in September, 1962. Frost, sent by the President of the United States, John F. Kennedy, as a member of a cultural exchange group, visits Moscow, Leningrad, and Gagra, where Prime Minister Khrushchev sent his own personal physician to treat the ailing poet. Reeve's personal experiences are detailed in his account, but, of course, the most interesting and informative data he supplies deals with Frost's occasionally successful attempts to leap barriers of language and semantics to communicate with his Russian peers and the people.

1410. Gooding, John. *The catkin and the icicle. Aspects of Russia.* London, Constable, 1965. 213 pp.

British exchange student attends Moscow University in 1962–63 and returns to "share fragments of baggage acquired"—comments on university life and culture in Moscow, combining the personal, current, and historical. The objectivity of his account is illustrated by his observation: "A good country I have left, but very bad. A monstrously bad country, yet good. A raw and fledgling country, yet old." His account is beautifully written and a delight to read.

1411. * Brigham, Gertrude Richardson, and Victor Flambeau. *Tovarich: more red-letter days.* Boothbay Harbor, Maine, Boothbay Register, 1964. 198 pp.

1412. Gilmore, Eddy. *After the Cossacks burned down the "Y".* New York, Farrar, Straus, 1964. 245 pp.

Associated Press correspondent returns to Moscow (see no. 1158), Stalingrad, and Tiflis, where he finds conditions much improved over previous times but still far from perfect. The title refers to the lessened pressure of the Communist party on the people; the closing of Lubianka prison by the government.

1413. Levine, Isaac Don. *I rediscover Russia.* New York, Duell, Sloan & Pearce, 1964. 211 pp. index.

Russian-American correspondent and his wife revisit Moscow in 1963 (he represented the Chicago *Daily News* there in 1919–21). His account describes his attempt to solve the mystery of Gorky's death (whom he believes to have been destroyed by Stalin), and he also comments on the Soviet way of life with due recognition of the great improvements made since the early twenties. He compliments the leaders for their program of mass publishing, but criticizes them for having removed significant books from their libraries.

1414. Pollock, John Charles. *The faith of the Russian evangelicals.* New York, McGraw-Hill, 1964. 186 pp. biblio.

American writer journeys to Moscow and east to Siberia to investigate the story of the thirty-two Siberians (six men, twelve women, and fourteen children) from a small evangelical religious sect who asked aid from the American embassy in January, 1963. He describes his contacts with them and his discovery that Christianity still lives in Russia and that a smoldering religious issue may be confronting the leaders of the Soviet Union.

1415. Sillitoe, Alan. *Road to Volgograd.* New York, Knopf, 1964. 176 pp.

British novelist, critic of social conditions, journeys from Leningrad to Volgograd by way of Moscow and then east to Irkutsk and Bratsk in April, 1963. He writes beautifully, and his account is somewhat rhapsodic in its description of conditions that he feels must lead to a "dynamic and optimistic future." He reports on culture in Irkutsk and is very informative on the giant city recently developed on the Angara River, the hydroelectric city of Bratsk.

1416. Post, Laurens van der. *A view of all the Russias*. New York, William Morrow, 1964. 375 pp. map.

Novelist and world traveler journeys throughout European Russia and east to Tashkent and Samarkand viewing the people and their way of life, April–June, 1963. Post sets out to provide data on all the Soviet institutions, as well as the background history of his observations. His account is a penetrating analysis, critical but fair and reasonably objective. He especially contrasts the hideousness of Russian things with the delicacy, tenderness, and sensitivity of the people, whom he considers to be a primitive western type rather than a semi-Asiatic horde.

1417. * Folsom, Franklin. *The Soviet Union: a view from within*. New York, Nelson, 1965. 225 pp. biblio.

American traveler talks with teachers and students in cities from Leningrad to the Caucasus on a journey in 1964. His report describes the mingled horror and admiration held for Stalin by the Georgians. See *Book Review Digest*. 1965.

1418. * Refregier, Anton. *Artist's journey*. New York, International Publishers, 1965.

1419. Benton, William. *The teachers and the taught in the U.S.S.R.* New York, Atheneum, 1966. 167 pp. index.

Benton revisits the Soviet Union (see no. 1301) in May, 1964, and reports that Soviet education, teachers, and students are continuing the challenge seen in 1955, especially in the exact sciences since the first Sputnik. His account of this journey is not as full of detail about educational procedures as the previous report and often verges on the flippant, such as in his interview with "Nikita Khrushchev, 'Old Boy'."

1420. Allen, Charles R., Jr. *Journey to the Soviet trade unions. An American eyewitness report*. New York, Marzani & Munsell, 1965. 64 pp. illus. port.

Journalist associated with labor activities and trade unions spends seven summer weeks in 1964 traveling through most of European Russia and Siberia with camera and tape recorder as guest of the All-Union Central Council of Trade Unions. He writes a short report of his findings and illustrates them with generous quotations from personal interviews and excellent photographs, secured, he claims, as he went about unhindered where he wished.

1421. Grzimek, (Dr.) Bernard. *Wild animal, white man: some wildlife in Europe, Soviet Russia and North America.* Translated from the German by Michael Glenny. New York, Hill & Wang, 1966. pp. 10–173. illus.

German wildlife and land conservationist of International reputation describes people and wildlife in the Soviet Union in the summer of 1964. He reports his disappointment at finding the Soviet authorities as neglectful of wild animal life as their counterparts in capitalist countries. He illuminates his account with sixty-four photographs, eight of them in color, and provides a commentary on an aspect of Soviet life that has not appeared before in the English language.

1422. Mihajlov, Mihajlo. *Moscow summer.* New York, Farrar, Straus & Giroux, 1965. 220 pp. illus.

Thirty-year-old Yugoslavian lecturer in Slavic languages and literature at Zagreb University spends the summer of 1964 in Moscow, where he meets all the important personalities in his profession. As an exchange scholar, he becomes informed about all aspects of Soviet culture, and his commentary is a critical condemnation of "The psychology of Homo Sovieticus."

BIBLIOGRAPHY OF BIBLIOGRAPHIES

⚜

1423. Adelung, Friedrich von. *Kritisch-Literaische Übersicht der Reisenden in Russland bis 1700, deren Berichte bekannt sind.* [*Critical literary survey of travelers in Russia to 1700, whose reports are known.*] 2 vols. Amsterdam, N. Israel, 1960.

1424. *American bibliography of Slavic and East European studies, The.* Bloomington, Indiana University Press. (Becomes *The American bibliography of Russian and East European studies* after 1959.) NUMBER 10: . . . *for 1957.* Joseph T. Shaw *et al.*, editors. Published 1958. NUMBER 21: . . . *for 1959.* Joseph T. Shaw and David Djaparidze, editors. Published 1960. NUMBER 27: . . . *for 1961.* Albert C. Todd and Stephen Viederman, editors. Published 1963. NUMBER 27: . . . *for 1962.* Albert C. Todd and Stephen Viederman, editors (with Donald Rowney). Published 1964. NUMBER 32: . . . *for 1963.* Fritz T. Epstein, Albert C. Todd, and Stephen Viederman, editors (with Cynthia H. Whittaker). Published 1966. NUMBER 34: . . . *for 1964. Fritz T. Epstein, editor;* Cynthia H. Whittaker, associate editor. Published 1966.

1425. Anderson, Matthew Smith. *Britain's discovery of Russia, 1553–1815.* New York, St. Martin's Press, 1958.

1426. Astley, Thomas, compiler. *A new general collection of voyages and travels: consisting of the most esteemed relations, which have been hitherto published in any language: comprehending everything remarkable in its kind, in Europe, Asia, Africa, and America, etc.* 4 vols. London, Astley, 1745–1747.

1427. Babey, Anna M. *Americans in Russia, 1776–1917: a study of the American travelers in Russia from the American Revolution to the Russian Revolution.* New York, privately printed, 1938.

1428. Baddeley, John F. *Russia, Mongolia, China. Being some record of the relations between them from the beginning of the XVIIth century to the death of Tsar Alexei Mikhailovich, A.D. 1602–1676, rendered mainly in the form of narratives dictated or written by the envoys sent by the Russian tsars, etc.* 2 vols. London, Macmillan, 1919.

1429. Barrow, John, compiler. *Collection of authentic, useful, and entertaining voyages and discoveries, digested in a chronological series.* 3 vols. London, J. Knox, 1765.

1430. Bolles, Edwin Courtlandt. *The literature of sea travel since the introduction of steam, 1830–1930.* Philadelphia, University of Pennsylvania, 1943.

1431. Bond, (Sir) Edward Augustus, editor. *Russia at the close of the sixteenth century.* London, Hakluyt Society, 1856.

1432. Chamberlin, William Henry. "Russia under western eyes", *The Russian Review,* XVI (January, 1957), 3–12.

1433. Churchill, John, compiler. *A collection of voyages and travels, some now first printed from original manuscripts. Others translated out of foreign languages and now first publish'd in English. To which are added some few that have formerly appeared in English, but do now for their excellency and scarceness deserve to be reprinted, etc.* 4 vols. London, printed for Awnsham and John Churchill, 1704.

1434. Conover, Helen Field. *Soviet Russia: a selected list of references. Compiled by Helen F. Conover under the direction of Florence S. Hellman.* Washington, Library of Congress, Division of Bibliographies, 1943.

1435. Cox, Edward Godfrey. *A reference guide to the literature of travel.* Seattle, University of Washington, 1935.

1436. Feuer, Lewis S. "American travelers to the Soviet Union, 1917–1932: the formation of a component of New Deal ideology", *American Quarterly,* XIV (Summer, 1962), 119–49.

1437. Frewer, Louis Benson. *Bibliography of historical writings published in Great Britain and the Empire, 1940–1945.* Oxford, Blackwell, 1947.

1438. Grierson, Philip. *Books on Soviet Russia, 1917–1942: a bibliography and a guide to reading.* London, Methuen, 1943. Supplemented in *Slavonic and East European Review:* XXIV (January, 1946), 133–47; XXV (April, 1947), 508–17; XXVI (April, 1948), 512–18; XXVII (May, 1949), 556–62; XXVIII (April, 1950), 486–92; XXIX (June, 1951), 550–57.

1439. Griffith, Hubert Freeling, editor. *Playtime in Russia by various authors.* London, Methuen, 1935.

1440. Hakluyt, Richard, compiler. *The principal navigations, voyages, traffiques & discoveries of the English nation; made by sea, or overland to the remote and farthest distant quarters of the earth at anytime within the compass of these 1600 years.* 6 vols. London, Dent, 1907.

1441. Hamel, Joseph von, editor. *England and Russia.* London, Richard Bentley, 1854.

1442. Harris, John, compiler. *Navigantium atque itinerantium bibliotheca, or, a complete collection of voyages and travels.* 2 vols. London, Osborne, *et al.,* 1764.

1443. Hiebert, Peter C. and Orie O. Miller. *Feeding the hungry. Russian famine: 1919–1925.* Scottdale, Pennsylvania, Mennonite Central Committee, 1929.

1444. Horecky, Paul L., editor. *Russia and the Soviet Union: a bibliographic guide to western-language publications.* Chicago, University of Chicago Press, 1965.

1445. Howe, Sonia Elizabeth, compiler. *The false Dmitri. A Russian romance and tragedy. Described by British eye-witnesses, 1604–1612.* London, Williams & Norgate, 1916.

1446. Kerner, Robert J., editor. *Slavic Europe, a selected bibliography in the western European languages.* Harvard Bibliographies Library Series. Volume One. Cambridge, Massachusetts, Harvard University Press, 1918.

1447. Kerr, Robert. *A general history and collection of voyages and travels, arranged in systematic order: forming a complete history of the origin and progress of navigation, discovery, and commerce, by sea and land, from earliest ages to the present time.* 18 vols. Edinburgh, Blackwood, 1811–17.

1448. Kliuchevskii, V. O. *Skazaniia inostrantsev o Moskovskom gosudarstvie* [*The narratives of foreigners concerning the Moscow state*]. Moskva, Universitetskaia tipografiia, 1866.

1449. Lamb, Harold. *The City and the Tsar. Peter the Great and the move to the west, 1648–1762.* Garden City, New York, Doubleday, 1948.

1450. Lamb, Harold. *The march of Muscovy. Ivan the Terrible and the growth of the Russian Empire, 1400–1648.* Garden City, New York, Doubleday, 1948.

1451. Lensen, George Alexander, editor. *Russia's eastward expansion.* Englewood Cliffs, New Jersey, Prentice-Hall, 1964.

1452. Maggs Books, London. *Voyages and travels. A first centurie of rare adventures and painful peregrinations in divers parts of the world.*

1453. Maichel, Karol. *Guide to Russia reference books.* J. S. G. Simmons, editor. Stanford, The Hoover Institute on War, Revolution, and Peace, Stanford University, 1964.

1454. Miller, Wright W. *The U.S.S.R.* London, Oxford University Press, 1963.

1455. Mohrenschildt, Dimitri von. "Early American observers of the Russian Revolution, 1917–1921". *Russian Review,* III (November, 1943), 64–74.

1456. Mohrenschildt, Dimitri von. *Russia in the intellectual life of eighteenth century France.* New York, Columbia University Press, 1936.

1457. Murray, Hugh. *Historical account of discoveries and travels in Asia, from the earliest ages to the present time.* 3 vols. Edinburgh, Archibald Constable, 1820.

1458. Overseas Press Club of America, compiler. *As we see Russia.* New York, Dutton, 1948.

1459. Page, Stanley W., editor. *Russia in revolution. Selected readings in Russian domestic history since 1855.* Princeton, New Jersey, D. Van Nostrand, 1965.

1460. Phillips, (Sir) Richard, editor. *New voyages and travels consisting of originals and translations.* 9 vols. London, Phillips, 1819–23.

1461. Pinkerton, John, editor. *A general collection of the best and most interesting voyages and travels in all parts of the world; many of which are now first translated in English. Digested on a new plan.* 17 vols. London, Longmans, et al., 1808–1814.

1462. Purchas, Samuel, compiler. *Hakluytus posthumus, or Purchas his pilgrimes: contayning a history of the world in sea voyages and lande.* 20 vols. Glasgow, J. MacLehose, 1905–07.

1463. Putnam, Peter, editor. *Seven Britons in Imperial Russia, 1698–1812.* Princeton, Princeton University Press, 1952.

1464. Riha, Thomas, editor. *Readings in Russian civilization.* 3 vols. Chicago, University of Chicago Press, 1964.

1465. Schapiro, David, editor. *A select bibliography of works in English on Russian history, 1801–1917.* Oxford, Blackwell, 1962.

1466. Senn, Alfred Erich, editor. *Readings in Russian political and diplomatic history.* 2 vols. Homewood, Illinois, Dorsey Press, 1966.

1467. Spector, Ivar and Marion, editors. *Readings in Russian history and culture.* Boston, Allyn & Bacon, 1965.

1468. Stipp, John L., editor. *Soviet Russia today; patterns and prospects.* New York, Harper, 1956.

1469. Strakhovsky, Leonid I., editor. *A handbook of Slavic Studies.* Cambridge, Massachusetts, Harvard University Press, 1949.

1470. U.S. Department of State. Library division. *American correspondents and journalists in Moscow, 1917–1952: a bibliography of their books on the U.S.S.R.* Washington, U.S. Department of state, 1953.

1471. Walsh, Warren B., editor. *Readings in Russian history. From ancient times to the post-Stalin era.* 4th ed. 3 vols. Syracuse, Syracuse University Press, 1963.

1472. Walsh, Warren B., editor. *Russia under tsars and commissars. A reader's guide.* Syracuse, Syracuse University Press, 1946.

1473. Walsh, Warren B. and Roy A. Price. *Russia, a handbook.* Syracuse, Syracuse University Press, 1947.

INDEX

෯

Numbers below refer to entries in the bibliographies.

Meignan, Victor, 316

Melroy, Vivian; see Plievier, Hildegard Piscator

Melville, George W., 338

Melvin, Frank E.; see Walter, Jakob

Memoir of Col. Charles S. Todd, 222

Memoirs and recollections of Count Segur . . . , 111

Memoirs and travels of Mauritus Augustus Count de Benyowsky . . . , 97

Memoirs of John Quincy Adams . . . , 145

Memoirs of Benjamin, Lord Bloomfield, 180

Memoirs of Sergeant Bourgogne, . . . , 159

Memoirs of Peter Henry Bruce . . . , 76

Memoirs of Jacques Casanova de Seingalt . . . , The, 94

Memoirs of Jeremiah Curtin, 287

Memoirs of the Comte Roger de Damas, 119

Memoirs of Field Marshall Lord Grenfell, 424

Memoirs of Herbert Hoover . . . , The, 537

Memoirs of Howard . . . , 107

Memoirs of John Paul Jones . . . , 121

Memoirs of the Count de Rochechouart . . . , 136

Memoirs of Russia . . . , 79

Memoirs of Thomas Oliver Selfridge, Jr., . . . , 423

Memoirs of the Baron de Tott, . . . , 95

Memoirs of James Whishaw, 250

Memorials of John Venning, Esq., . . . , 241

Memorials of a short life, 363

Memories of many men in many lands, 460

Memories of travel, 581

Men and machines in Russia, 960

Men and things Russian, 330

Men, medicine and food in the U.S.S.R., 1066

Men on the horizon, 1004

Menon, Kumara Padmanabha Siva-Sankara, 1273, 1274

Merick, John, 38

Meriwether, Lee, 357

Merry, Walter Mansell, 596

Merv oasis, The, 336

Metaxas, Alexander, 1307

Mewes, George H.; see Washburn, Stanley

Meyendorff Stella Zoe (Whishaw), 615

Meyer, George von Lengerke; see Howe, M. A. DeWolfe

Michael, M. A.; see Waxell, Sven

Michie, Alexander, 284

Midnight sun, The, 353

Miège, Guy, 56

Mignan, Robert, 189

Mihajlov, Mihajlo, 1422

Miles, Frederic James, 1092

Miles, Nelson Appleton, 440, 488

Military attaché in Moscow, 1240

Military Europe, 440

Miller, Alvin J., 786

Miller, James G.; see Miller, Jessie L.

Miller, Jessie L., 1391

Miller, Maurice Solomon, 1294

Miller, Orie O., 770; see also Hiebert, Peter C.

Miller, Paul, 1405

Miller, Wright W., 1065, 1454

Milton, John, 17

Milton's literary craftsmanship, 17

Minney, Rubeigh James, 1308

Mirror to Russia, 1247

Mirrors of Moscow (Louise Bryant), 795

Mirrors of Moscow (Harry James Greenwall), 881

Mission to Moscow, 1103

Mission to Tashkent, 719

Mitchell, Elsie Reed; see Wilson, Helen Calista

Moats, Alice-Leone, 1142

Modern Russia as seen by an Englishwoman, 1033